MEASUREMENT FOR EDUCATIONAL EVALUATION

CLINTON I. CHASE
Indiana University

▲
▼▼
ADDISON-WESLEY PUBLISHING COMPANY
Reading, Massachusetts · Menlo Park, California · London · Don Mills, Ontario

To the women in my life: P.L.C. and A.J.C.

This book is in the
ADDISON-WESLEY SERIES IN EDUCATION

ISBN 0-201-00989-7
ABCDEFGHIJ-MA-79876543

PREFACE

Teachers and other school people are in the business of causing changes in student behavior. Whether intentionally or not, they will assess the magnitude of these changes. Some will use formal measuring tools; others will use subjective impressions developed through their daily encounters with students. In any case, educators are continually making assessments—and subsequent conclusions—about children's progress, about curricular programs, and about themselves. This book can provide the basic knowledge about formal procedures that will help educators do a better job of the evaluations they will be doing anyway.

The purpose of this book is to lay out a basic set of generalizations from which teachers can attack their own problems. General guidelines for building and evaluating tests are presented, but specific tests are not discussed in detail, except as an occasional example. Instead, the emphasis is on features to note in a class of tests. Although standardized test forms are revised and new editions are put on the market, the distinguishing character, the limitations, and the applications of a category of tests seem to persist. Equipped with a set of generalizations about tests, educators should be prepared to deal not only with instruments currently on the market, but also with those to appear, at least in the near future.

The basic concepts of reliability and validity pervade all uses of tests. Therefore, these concepts are first dealt with on a general level and then as they have been used with each type of test. The intent is to emphasize that validity and reliability are indeed functional ideas that must be understood if tests of any type are to be serviceable.

The structure and application of the teacher's own tests are of paramount importance in the classroom. The pace of instruction is gauged largely through these tools. A child's promotions are typically tied to his success with classroom tests. Grades are based heavily on classroom tests, and much of a child's attitude toward school may be associated with his experiences with teacher-made tests. The judgments a teacher makes about his students and about himself are often a function of how effectively he has dealt with classroom assessment. *It therefore seems reasonable to insist that teachers*

iii

be skilled test writers and users, and these skills are emphasized in the book.

In addition, educators should be able to exploit available standardized tools to much greater advantage than has typically been the case. The application of achievement-test results, as well as supporting contextual and process data, need to be mined more extensively in many school systems across the country. It is hoped that the skills this text is intended to promote will help educators expand their use of currently available data, hence getting all possible advantage from their test dollars.

In a testing situation the child is not alone with the stimuli presented in the test. A variety of other stimuli are also impinging on the examinee. In at least one chapter in the text, therefore, we try to see the relation of these conditions to test scores.

The intent in structuring this book was to provide in simple fashion the basic information educators will find most useful. Thus, although the material is based on theory, its focus and orientation are on practice in the classroom. Topics were selected for their usefulness for school people. Statistical and other mechanical operations have been held to that minimum which will allow explication of topics and utilization of materials. The text is for people in practice, and nonpractical excursions into the psychometric maze have been avoided.

To provide the practical application of material, exercises are interspersed within the chapters. These applications allow the student to immediately work with concepts in problem-solving, thus promoting both learning and retention of the material. Answers to the exercises are available within the text material immediately preceding the exercises. In the author's experience, students often turn to the ready answer instead of making a diligent effort to solve the problem. Therefore, answers are provided for computational problems only. The student is asked to consult the textual material for other answers.

A number of persons have played a role in putting together this book. A special note of appreciation is due to each of them. I especially want to mention Henry Dizney's detailed commentary on the manuscript; his advice was most helpful. Also, Robert Ebel, Daniel Mueller, and James Hamilton submitted a number of useful and encouraging comments. Valerie Smead and Judy Kaiser did an excellent job in assisting me with selected literature.

In a number of textbooks of this type, the authors have acknowledged their family's support and patience during the writing period. If this seems patronizing to the reader, it should not. Only after having completed such a writing project does one realize the number of family activities that have been postponed and the number of hours that the writer has been closeted away from his family. For this reason I wish to thank my family for their indulgence. My wife, Pat, not only tolerated my detour from normal family routines, but also aided and abetted me therein. She contributed many hours of clerical and professional assistance. Her aid has been invaluable and sincerely appreciated.

C.I.C.

Bloomington, Indiana
October 1973

CONTENTS

CHAPTER 1

MEASUREMENT:
IDEAS ABOUT APPLICATION

Educational testing is big business. Although no recent estimates have been published, at least 150 million commercially printed tests were sold to school systems in America in one year's count (Goslin 1963). Literally millions more teacher-made tests are applied annually, but go untabulated. From their first year in school, children are regularly exposed to tests. By the time they reach high school, children have labored through thousands of examinations—some well designed and purposefully utilized; some crudely constructed and awkwardly applied.

The widespread use of tests appears to indicate at least a moderate endorsement of measurements by the educational profession and by the society that supports it. However, popular critics of testing point to the limitations and misuses of examinations (Black 1963, Gross 1963, Hoffman 1962). Persons who use tests cannot dismiss these critical voices as irrelevant. Their charges must be answered. To provide the answers, test users must acquire a wider knowledge of test theory and its application. Without this knowledge we cannot avoid the pitfalls that critics exploit.

Although teachers generally support the application of psychological tests, they do not do so uncritically (Sharp 1966). Test specialists, also, have viewed with anguish the careless, devious, and often uninformed uses to which tests have been put (Mehrens and Lehmann 1967, Ebel 1964, Dyer 1962). However, the potential for social benefit through proper use of examinations must also be acknowledged. If tests are to create social good rather than ill, test users must sharpen their skills and expand their knowledge of test usage. Therefore, the purpose of the chapters ahead is: (1) to provide fundamental understanding of the theoretical foundation of test development, and (2) to use theory as a guideline for constructing, evaluating, and applying educational measurements so that more effective educational decisions can be made.

It is of utmost importance that test users know the characteristics of good tests and are able to develop these characteristics in their own examinations. But a second element also stands large in importance—the test

1

taker himself. Before we can use tests intelligently, we must recognize some of the conditions which bear upon the test taker as he reacts to a test. This topic, as part of the total testing situation, is explored in Chapter 12.

PURPOSES OF TESTING IN EDUCATION

Before we can appreciate how really important informed application of tests can be, we must first look briefly at the educational process. Teachers are in the business of changing their students' behavior in certain socially approved directions. Children who come to school in the first grade unable to read leave ten months later with a significant sight vocabulary. They leave grade school six years later with an extensive reading and speaking vocabulary, as well as skill in computing, writing, and manipulating scientific concepts. Also, for some children, old anxieties have subsided; for others, new and impelling anxieties have arisen; for all, attitudes about a thousand referents have changed.

Schools are designed to bring about changes. But typically, we want to promote changes in a given direction. How do we know we are doing it? If we think we are doing it, how well are we doing it? What are we doing to children that we did not intend to do? Before we can answer these questions, some kind of assessment must be made. A teacher's impression is an informal kind of measurement. She has collected some unsystematic observations and made a conclusion. How good are her observations? We all know how our moods, motivations, and past experiences act on our perceptions. Shall we rely solely on the teacher's quick and informal survey of a situation? Without better data, we may have to.

Clearly, some kind of observation of children's behaviors will go on in the school, whether or not we use tests, and conclusions will be made on the basis of these observations. Our need, therefore, is to make observations as accurately and as purposefully as possible. This means applying the systematic procedures prescribed by educational evaluation techniques.

Many questions arise daily in education which depend on some kind of assessment—formal or informal—for an answer. This point leads us to an essential characteristic of the educational role of measurement, i.e., we employ measurements in reference to an educational decision we must make. This means that values are involved. We use measurements to make data-based judgments about programs, etc., in relation to these values. This process of taking measurements so that we can make decisions about programs, policies, etc., in reference to objectives is often referred to as *evaluation*.

Educational programs are designed to change behavior in accordance with a particular value system. This means that we expect our students to reach certain objectives. Although many teachers do not specifically state these objectives, they are implicit in their act of teaching. A teacher performs a collection of acts because he believes his students will acquire behaviors they have not yet evidenced. The teacher has outcomes in mind when he plans the instructional unit; he believes that the children are capable of attaining the outcomes and that the instruction is adequate to lead the children to the objective.

Such an arrangement has a number of contingencies. The extent to which children can acquire a given skill depends on the complex of abilities and experiences they bring to the learning situation. The fact that an instructor attempts to teach something to his class carries with it the assumption that the children already have the necessary prerequisite skills to accomplish the learning task. That is, the instructor has made some assessments and has come to the conclusion that the class can indeed proceed to acquire the skill to be taught.

If we agree that before an instructional unit begins, the teacher has made some judgments about the nature of the children being taught, we can also agree that he has made some decisions about values. What is being taught apparently is important to learn, i.e., valuable to the learner for some reason. Whether or not a teacher has specifically stated his objectives, the fact that he has learner outcomes in mind indicates that his work is directed by objectives. It therefore seems reasonable to: (a) make objectives explicit, since they are implicit anyway; (b) make formal assessments to establish the status of children before instruction, to make periodic formal assessments during the course of instruction to see if the instruction is indeed leading toward the behavioral changes planned for, and if not, why not; and (c) make specific measurements of the extent to which the desired behaviors are evident at the end of instruction.

Since objectives are at least implicit in all instruction, we can build our measuring devices in such a way as to ask children to perform the behaviors we expect they will acquire, i.e., test content will be determined by objectives. But objectives must be clearly formulated if they are to regulate test content. If you have ever taken a class in which at test time you had no idea what the test was going to be like, you probably also had a very fuzzy idea of what objectives had been posed for the course. We really must do a better job of specifying objectives if we are going to do a better job of educational evaluation.

If we are going to write objectives so that their attainment can be observed systematically and objectively, the desired outcomes of instruction should be described in such a way that several people can independently agree that a given child has or has not achieved the desired outcome. This means that we must list the actual behaviors that characterize attainment of the objective. Statements like "respects the law," "works effectively with other people," and "reads effectively" do not provide a basis on which several observers could agree that a given student has indeed reached the objectives involved. Such statements simply do not point to the things children do after instruction that they did not do before instruction. They do not tell us what specific behaviors our tests should call for.

What, then, shall we do? The answer is that we must now translate these broad outcomes into a list of things children will do as evidence of having attained the objective. If we see the listed behaviors, we can then agree that the objective has been achieved. When the child does indeed perform an act, we can say, "See there! He can do it." We have seen the acts that we said are evidence that the objective has been reached. Our observational devices, including tests, can be built not only to call for these acts but also to record the frequency of occurrence of the desired behaviors. Following this procedure, we translate our broad, general objectives into statements that use what Bloom, Hastings, and Madaus (1971, Chapter 1) call "point-at-able" verbs, e.g., "to state . . .," "to distinguish correct from incorrect . . .," "to use adverbial forms . . .," "to list results or outcomes of . . .," "to answer questions on a topic after having read. . . ." These statements describe things a student does to show that he has reached a given objective. With a list of "point-at-able" behaviors, two or more observers could probably agree that the child has or has not done what the objective says he must do in order to have attained a given outcome.

In summary, then, we can say that some kind of assessment goes on in classrooms, whether or not it is formal; that these assessments are made before, during, and after instruction; and that assessments are made because the teacher must make decisions about the objectives she has in mind, whether or not her objectives have actually been stated. If all of these events are taking place implicitly, it seems reasonable to list objectives in terms of observable behaviors and to use systematic devices such as tests to make the observations. Therefore, in the chapters ahead when we talk about the teacher as an evaluator, we will encourage the use of objectives stated in terms of acts that can be seen and will emphasize the role of classroom tests as uniform procedures for making decisions about a child's attainment of objectives.

So far, we have been speaking largely to teacher uses of evaluation, but in education there are a variety of other applications for measurement, all tied to the common purpose of decision-making. A curriculum coordinator measures to decide whether one set of student experiences in a given context is superior to another set in reaching special objectives. He may also measure to see if one package of materials produces more efficient attainment of outcomes than does another. Administrators measure to provide evidence that the school is indeed accomplishing the variety of missions set up for it by the society that supports the educational institution.

All of these applications of measurement are predicated on the assumption that the school is designed to bring about behavioral changes. Of course, we can see many of these changes taking place without formal measurements of them. But without data, we can say very little that is definite about the range of progress among our students, about the potential for progress, or about choices of vehicles for instruction. Our assessments are too impressionistic and subjective and are colored by our personal biases for various children and by the particular behaviors we have chosen, often unconsciously, to observe for each child. For example, I like Susan very much. I quickly note the new words she has learned this week. But for Jinks, whom I do not like, I recall the errors she has made on her spelling test. This unsystematic assessment provides no common ground for making dependable decisions about either programs or children. My emotionally toned impressions have not given me a basis for comparing Susan and Jinks on their verbal skills and in fact have probably mitigated against my ability to make such a comparison.

Clearly, there is need for prescribed procedures providing common situations for all children in which behavior can be recorded and about which dependable conclusions can be made. Only systematic measurements can meet these requirements. We also see that if magnitude of change is to be established, it must be stated in relationship to some standard. Testing procedures allow us to compare our children's behaviors with the behaviors of a defined, carefully selected national sample of children of an age or school grade in common with our students. The informal impressions of teachers cannot provide us with this reference group.

With each addiitonal year in school, the student is given an increasing number of alternative routes in his pursuit of the academic program. Each year, he must make an ever-larger number of important decisions about himself. If these decisions are to be made effectively, they must be made by self-knowing individuals. Information that tests provide to a student about himself can show him how a given set of his behaviors compare with criteria of proficiency, or with the performance of his peers. This information allows him to make a more realistic decision about his status in the behavior domains from which the test situations are samples. Helping students define their skills, aptitudes, and temperaments is a primary use of tests in education.

There are clear and important roles for mental measurements in education. But tests should be asked to do only the job for which they were built, and they will do that job only to the extent that they are in the hands of skilled and intelligent users.

PROBLEMS*

1. I look at Ms. Davis' lesson plan for her fourth graders for today and see that she has allotted 45 minutes for a reading period. She has listed two stories to be read in a basic text by the entire class and has cited ten questions on story content to go with each story.

    a) What decisions has Ms. Davis made about her class before developing this assignment?

    b) What speculations can we make about Ms. Davis' objectives for this reading period?

    c) What decisions can we speculate that Ms. Davis could make from her test?

    d) Does Ms. Davis' procedure tell us something about her ideas about children and how they learn?

2. List several reasons for the differences between school administrators and classroom teachers in their use of tests. (Note: decisions each must make are related, but not identical.)

THE LOGIC OF BEHAVIORAL TRAITS

Before we build a measuring device, we should first have an idea of what it is we intend to measure. This means that the educator has to identify the mental trait to be assessed and delineate its characteristics before he is ready to develop a test.

Identifying mental traits, e.g., intelligence, neuroticism, etc., is much more complex and less an exact process than identifying physical traits. We cannot see the mind as such; we can only see behaviors that it produces. However, a highly related set of behaviors may appear to be explainable by hypothesizing a given mental characteristic or trait that regulates all behaviors in that set. We then label this set of behaviors with a trait name. For example, a child successfully completes several problems in numerical reasoning, in verbal reasoning, and in analogies. All of these behaviors are tied in with abstract thinking and problem-solving. We may therefore wish to conclude that there is a trait called abstract reasoning. A mental trait, then, is defined in terms of the observable behaviors that can be explained by reference to the trait. A test designed to measure a particular mental trait would pose a number of situations which elicit the appropriate behaviors, and we infer the child's status in this trait from how he responds to these situations. Mental measurements are therefore inferences. We see behaviors. From these behaviors we infer various mental characteristics.

---

* Problems and exercises appear throughout this text so that the reader can become involved in applying the materials just presented when the ideas are most fresh in his mind.

The procedure used by psychologists and educators to assess mental abilities is similar to the procedures used by other scientists in their work. A study of electricity is an example. When you look at a wire, you cannot see electricity in it. Although electricity has no form or substance, we can assess it by its manifestations. We study the electricity in a wire by putting the wire in various situations that will elicit reactions. From these reactions, we make inferences about the characteristics of electricity.

This is essentially what the behavioral scientist does in identifying and measuring mental traits. When he looks at a child, he cannot see intelligence because it has no form or substance. However, by putting the child in various situations and observing his reactions to them, the behavioral scientist (or the teacher) can identify various categories of behavior and make some conclusions about their nature.

Our ideas about mental traits depend on accurately observing a set of related behaviors and making inferences that explain the behaviors. This means that mental traits are hypothesized characteristics—characteristics that are believed to be reflected in the set of behaviors which can be observed through, and recorded in, the testing situation.

However, the identification of a mental trait and the construction of a test to assess it are far from simple tasks. The most highly developed tests begin with extensive building of a detailed theory of the trait and painstaking experimentation to verify the postulates of the theory. Not until the theory of the trait has been well established by empirical data are we ready to build a test that will elicit the behaviors the theory says are manifestations of the trait. The data collection that goes into test building is also extensive. In short, identifying a mental trait and constructing a test to measure it are enormous tasks.

PROBLEMS

1. Suppose I gave you a collection of different bits of metal, asked you to determine the characteristics of these metals by placing them in various chemicals, etc., and then told you to classify them into groups based on common reactions to the chemicals. How is this similar to the procedure used to identify mental traits?

2. Imagine that no intelligence tests are available and that you have been asked to construct a test that could be used to identify "genius." How would you locate tasks to include in the test?

3. Imagine that you are going to make up a classroom test for a unit of instruction in your major teaching area. Make a list of conclusions about the student this test allows you to make. Which of these conclusions are inferences and which are statements of fact?

CHARACTERISTICS OF MEASURING DEVICES IN GENERAL

A measuring device is generally thought of as a tool with a carefully calibrated scale beginning at zero and running in equal-sized units up to a large quantity of some specified amount. But many measuring tools do not have this level of sophistication. For example, when children run a race, we rank them first, second, third, etc., depending on their order in finishing the race. We do not suppose that the distance between the first and second child was the same as the distance between the second and third child. In other words, our units are not equal. But this process is a useful application of numbers to the identification of differences in the behavior of a group of children, and we do not worry about the fact that the units we used to identify position in the race are not equal.

S. S. Stevens (1951) has described four general types of scales. Each scaling type provides a procedure for identifying individuals by assigning numbers to them, but each successive level allows us to make a wider range of conclusions than does the previous level. We shall look at these different types of scales so that we can see where educational measurements rank among them and so that we can see what conclusions are appropriately made by the tests we will use.

The simplest level of scale types is called the *nominal scale*. Here, numbers are assigned to individuals in much the same way we use names. No magnitude of a trait is reflected by the number, which is only a label. Have you ever ordered an item from a mail-order catalog? Suppose I tell you that one pair of shoes has a serial number of 69178, whereas a second one has a serial number of 67539. Which pair of shoes is the better pair? We cannot tell from the serial numbers, since they are only "names" for the shoes. Now, let us imagine that we have randomly sorted 100 children into ten teams and numbered the teams 1 through 10. Since the children were randomly assigned, the numbers tell us nothing about the abilities of the teams; they merely separate teams from one another by giving each a "name." These applications of numbers to distinguish individuals or groups represent the nominal scale.

The second level is called *ordinal scaling*. Here, individuals are placed in order on the basis of magnitude of some trait and are given number names based on that order. For example, we might put ten children in order from tallest to shortest, calling the tallest number one, the next tallest, number two, etc. These numbers identify differences in height among individuals, but the height between each pair of adjacent numbers is very likely to be unequal. We are merely ranking the individuals by height. Ordinal scales are used to identify the outcomes of races, to pick a winner in a contest, to select beauty queens, and to place children in reading groups. Ordinal scaling allows us to arrange people in order from "most" to "least," but we cannot say much about how one person compares with another. These scales have some deficiencies in accuracy, but no one can deny that they are useful.

At the third level of scaling, *interval scaling*, there are equal units between adjacent numbers, but the zero point on the scale is arbitrary. On frosty mornings, we consult our thermometers and read 20°F. This gives us a meaningful message about the temperature outside. The thermometer is divided into equal units, but the Fahrenheit zero does not mean the absence of all heat. Rather, it is a level of temperature we arbitrarily agree to use as a starting point to apply our numbers.

Its use of equal-sized units gives the interval scale some advantages over the ordinal scale, but it also has some disadvantages. For example, we cannot say that 60°F is twice as warm as 30°. Similarly, we cannot say that a child with an IQ of 80 is only two-thirds as intelligent as one with an IQ of 120, or that a child who scores at the third-grade level in reading reads only half as well as one who scores at the sixth-grade level. In other words, we cannot talk about results of these tests in terms of ratios of one to the other. Rather, interval-scale numbers represent quantities of a given characteristic beginning at some arbitrary starting point.

This leads us to the most refined group of measuring devices, the *ratio scales*. With these we have not only equal-sized units along the scale, but also zero as the true absence of the characteristic. We measure the length of a sheet of paper and find it to be eleven inches; each inch on our ruler is the same length as every other inch; and zero really means no length at all. Four inches is half as long as eight inches, and we can state these two quantities in terms of the ratio of one to the other. We get maximum meaning out of the application of a ratio scale, since it alone has equal units along the scale and a true zero point.

Why have we looked at these different ways of applying scales in identifying individuals? There are essentially two reasons. First, when we mention measurements, most people think of ratio scales with equal-sized units and a true zero. In understanding mental measurements, a fixation on the ratio scale can be misleading, since many ways of observing differences among people simply do not fit the requirements of a ratio scale, and conclusions based on the assumption of a ratio scale may therefore be erroneous. Second, classifying scaling techniques into four groups allows us to place educational tests on a hierarchy of sophistication in measurement. In this way we can decide what decisions can be made with various tools and as a result, we can select the most appropriate testing devices for the purposes we have in mind.

This takes us to the classroom, where Ms. Ecks is marking a spelling test for her fourth grade class. John gets 12 words correct, Bill gets 13, whereas Joes gets 16 and Jack gets 17. Can Ms. Ecks say there is as much difference between John and Bill as between Joe and Jack? No, Ms. Ecks' test is merely a ranking device for her children. It is an ordinal scale, as are most classroom tests. Clearly, the words on the test are not on a scale of equal difficulty and therefore do not make equal units on the spelling scale. If we look into the cumulative records of Ms. Ecks' students, we find scores on standardized achievement and intelligent tests. If these devices are thought of as scales that identify changes in child development associated with given time intervals, e.g. age, we may wish to classify them a little higher than teacher-made tests, but at best they would be only interval scales. The reason for this may become evident in later chapters, when we deal at length with these tests.

What can we conclude from this brief study of types of scales? We must conclude that the measuring devices most widely used in schools are relatively gross and unsophisticated. The majority are simply ranking devices. The ranking of individuals is of considerable assistance to us in making a number of decisions; however, it does limit the conclusions that can be made from the data collected.

PROBLEMS

1. Classify each of the following as to its most sophisticated scale type, and tell which of the following purposes could be served from use of the device: (1) comparing one student's performance with another in terms of a ratio of their two scores; (2) noting scale differences between students, but not comparing scores as a ratio; (3) ranking students; (4) identifying students without regard to differences in behavior.

    a) The school nurse measures the weight of all children in Mr. Zee's fourth-grade class.

    b) Ms. Jones holds a spelling bee, using words children have found in the Sunday newspaper. Students are ranked on the number of words spelled correctly.

    c) A team of judges gives 1st, 2nd, 3rd, 4th, and 5th prizes to products built in last semester's shop class.

    d) Ms. Ecks gives a test of 50 multiplication facts to her fourth-grade class. A child's score is the number of correctly solved combinations.

2. Of these applications of measures to educational problems, how many of them are ratio or interval? Would you guess that this is about typical for most uses of measurement in education?

WHAT IS A TEST?

We are probably now ready to state what a test is. Since mental traits are varied in nature, the devices we use to assess them must also be varied. A definition that covers all of these will therefore be broad, but it must point to the salient common features among tests. *A test is a systematic procedure for comparing the performance of an individual with a designated standard of performance.*

Two parts of this definition are most important—"systematic procedure" and "comparing." If we are going to make an inference based on a class of behaviors, situations must be devised to elicit these behaviors and a plan arranged to observe the behaviors. Now, if I want to say something about how Mary's performance in these situations compares with Susan's, I must observe them in the same circumstances. This is what we have in mind by "systematic procedure." We have an *a priori* plan for presenting a common set of stimuli to all persons and for recording responses to these stimuli.

Further, a test score is meaningless unless it is compared to something. I receive a score of 74 on a test of verbal reasoning. What does this mean? Before I can say that it is a "high" score, or a "low" one, or one that shows "satisfactory" proficiency, I need something with which to compare it. Typically, we have two bases for comparison—the scores of peers and criteria of minimum proficiency.

Suppose this test of verbal reasoning was given to 500 students like me. Their average score was 60; the highest score was 81, the lowest, 26. I can immediately begin to get some meaning out of my score of 74. If I have a list of all scores from low to high, with the number of students who got each score, I can find out how many of the 500 people got scores lower than my 74. Suppose 477 students scored lower than my 74. Now we get even more meaning out of my score.

Comparing my score with those made by my peers provides us with an indicator of my relative status on the test (and presumably on the behavior domain involved), but it does not tell me how well I have mastered an essential skill. The second basis for comparison is therefore tied to a definition of minimum proficiency in the skill being assessed. Compared to the scores of my peers, my score of 74 looks good. But suppose we were fourth graders working the 100 basic multiplication facts, and my school says that at the close of the fourth grade, one should be able to complete these combinations with 99 percent accuracy. My score of 74 does not even come close to reaching this criterion of proficiency.

Let us look at another example of the proficiency criterion as a basis for score comparison. Suppose reading achievement at the end of first grade is defined as the child's being able to identify 48 words from a selected list. Further, he must read without error sentences made up of these words, each sentence not exceeding six words in length. In this manner we are not comparing John against a large mass of children at the end of grade one; instead, we are looking at John's performance by holding it up to a criterion of proficiency.

Essentially, then, we interpret test results from two frames of reference. In one case we compare a child's performance with the performance of his peers, whereas in the other case we compare his performance to a predetermined criterion of adequacy. The purpose of testing determines which basis of comparison we should use. We assume that in a large group of children, some will have less of a given trait, some will have moderate amounts, and some will have a considerable amount. If we want to make inferences about a child's status on this trait, we will use a peer-reference approach. But if we want to know how capably children deal with specific tasks, a proficiency criterion is called for.

We have defined a test in order to direct our attention to certain characteristics of the tools we shall examine in later chapters. In looking at tests, we shall want to note how carefully the procedure is controlled and how detailed a base is provided against which we may compare scores of individuals who have gone through the prescribed procedure. The chapters ahead are designed to help you become more skilled in establishing both the adequacy of procedures and the utility of the basis provided for making judgments about the behaviors of children in educational settings.

PROBLEMS

1. For each of the following, decide if the tasks as described are a test as defined above:

    a) I am observing the physical skill of two boys. I ask the first boy to jump a set of three 30-inch hurdles laid out over a 50-yard course (he must do this in 11 seconds to get credit for the task); to throw an 8-lb shot (he must have an average of 35 feet for two throws to get credit); and to long-jump from a standing position (average distance of two jumps must be 5 feet for credit).
        I ask the second boy to do the hurdles as above, the shot put as above, and to high-jump over a bar that is 4' 6". When the boys have completed these tasks, I will compare them on the number of successfully completed tasks.

    b) I prepared 15 essay questions for my physics class. Each question is worth ten points. I ask the students to select any five on which to write. For each student I will total the points he gets on his five questions. I will then compare each student against the range of scores for the whole class to show his position in the group.

PROTECTING TEST TAKERS

Mental tests, including teacher-made tests, can be a source of great and unnecessary pain to students if they are not capably built and intelligently applied. Most tests probe private information that deserves to remain private. In a democracy, one's right to beliefs are inviolate, yet we inventory beliefs with psychological tests and retain the answer sheet for reference. When we use a tool such as a personality inventory, we do not read a client's responses, item by item, to pick up his feelings about politics, religion, etc., but tests do not destroy themselves after they are scored, and files are not safe from possible intruders. Test takers need a better guarantee of protection than they often get.

Teacher-made tests also pose important problems of security. Teachers are often very careless about exposing a child's performance to other children, with little regard for the emotional impact this has on the child who is exposed. How many of us have sat in classes where the teacher has tabulated the score distribution on a test by a show of hands? How many times have we had tests "returned" to us by having them placed on a table where students thumb through the stack (reading the scores of their peers) to find their papers? In both of these situations, we are exposing to the class what ought to be a private matter for each child. No wonder students who are having difficulty in school lose their will to continue. We are singling them out from their peers as incompetents. Above all, teachers should be able to do a better job of protecting students, and students have a right to demand that a better job be done.

The use of mental tests must be accompanied by a guarantee to the test taker that his recorded behavior is to be private and that the utmost security will be maintained to guarantee this privacy. Tests are designed as an aid to the client. Every precaution must be taken to ensure that aid is the only outcome of testing. This means that materials, especially used materials, must be kept locked up. It also means that marked test booklets and answer sheets must be systematically destroyed as soon as the scores have been recorded.

SUMMARY

If educators are to apply tests within the limits of their intended use, they must be knowledgeable about basic test theory and application. Educators are in the business of changing behavior. The assessment of change and of the circumstances under which it occurs will be made whether or not tests are used. It seems reasonable, therefore, to employ the most accurate and objective means available to make these assessments. This means testing, and testing means that educators, to know their trade, must know basic test theory and its use in everyday evaluation.

Tests are samples of behavior intended to reflect the nature of behavioral traits. To this end we infer the quality of one's traits from his test performance. If we are to make consistent inferences from person to person, our test must provide the same set of stimuli, presented under the same conditions, for everyone. To make conclusions about the quality of the behaviors observed, we must have an *a priori* standard. Typical standards are collections of scores from identified groups of individuals who have previously taken the test, or criteria of minimal proficiency such as successful completion of 90 percent of the tasks presented.

Test performances are typically to be regarded as confidential. If test takers are to be guarded against possible adverse effects of testing, confidentiality must be given utmost attention. This is true of classroom tests as well as more sophisticated devices. The benefits educators and students can derive from proper use of mental measurements is extensive, but improper use can result in adverse social consequences and personal pain for test takers.

REFERENCES

Black, Hillel. *They Shall not Pass,* New York: Morrow, 1963.

Bloom, Benjamin S., J. Thomas Hastings, and George F. Madaus. *Handbook on Formative and Summative Evaluation of Student Learning,* New York: McGraw-Hill, 1971.

Dyer, Henry S. "Is Testing a Menace to Education?" *New York State Education,* **49** (1961): 16–19.

Ebel, Robert. "The Social Consequences of Educational Testing," *School and Society,* **92** (1964): 331–334.

Goslin, David A. *The Search for Ability: Standardized Testing in Social Perspective,* New York: Russell Sage Foundation, 1963, pp. 53–54.

Gross, Martin L. *The Brain Watchers,* New York: Random House, 1962.

Hoffman, Banesh. *The Tyranny of Testing,* New York: Crowell-Collier-Macmillan, 1962.

Mehren, William A. and Irvin J. Lehmann. *Standardized Tests in Education,* New York: Holt, Rinehart and Winston, 1969, p. 280.

Sharp, E. W. "How Teachers see Testing," *Educational Leadership,* **24** (1966): 141–143.

Stevens, S. S. "On the theory of scales of measurement," *Science,* **103** (1951): 670–680.

CHAPTER 2

HOW WE GOT WHERE WE ARE

INTRODUCTION

Mental measurements are not as precise as tools used in some other sciences. Why? Part of the answer to this question lies far back down the road that brought us to the present point in test development. But the road back is not really that long. Antecedents of mental measurement go back centuries, but the development of mental measurements, as we know them today, occurred primarily in the twentieth century.

Several rather early uses of tests served their purpose and then died away without contributing to basic test theory or leading to subsequent development of more advanced instruments, e.g., the civil-servant tests used in ancient China (DuBois 1965). In the days of the feudal lords in China, candidates for governmental jobs were periodically examined. Each successfully passed examination moved the candidate higher and higher among the ranks of contenders for appointment. Even though a candidate was not yet fully qualified for a position, he was given various distinctions for having passed tests at various levels. Although this early system of examination apparently produced a competent group of civil servants, the emphasis was on the pragmatic use of tests rather than on the development of psychometric theory.

Before scientific attacks could be made on the measurement of mental traits, the predominating philosophies that dealt with the nature of man had to describe the mind as something that could indeed be measured. Since early philosophers typically looked on the mind as intangible, if not entirely etheral, the consideration of devices to measure mental traits was quite inappropriate. This viewpoint found its most profound spokesman in Descartes (1650) whose pronouncement of the complete separation of mind and body removed mental traits from the realm of biological phonomena and placed them in a class of spiritual operations.

The pervasiveness of this idea of mind-body dualism deterred serious thinkers from considering the measurement of mental functions. However, a rather contrasting view of mental operations was presented by John Locke (1690) some forty years following Descartes. Locke described the mind as a

15

blank tablet upon which successive experiences were recorded. In the process of recall, one reproduced events just as they were "pressed" onto the mental record. Presumably, keen minds recorded events in more detail, but depended on sharp perceptual equipment to make the finer discriminations necessary for detailed recordings. Sharpness of perception appeared to be the prerequisite of expansive minds.

At last the door to mental measurements seemed to be opening. However, concerted efforts to enter this door had to wait for another two hundred years, when three separate but equally important developments emerged. First, in the late 1800s Charles Darwin noted conspicuous biological differences among members of any given species, differences that caused some to flourish whereas others failed to survive. Could these differences also be identified among the mental traits of human beings? Second, a group of British philosophers emphasized an empirical, or experiential approach to the study of man, capitalizing on, but pressing beyond, the ideas of Locke. Lastly, a group of German psychophysicists began to study human sensations and perceptions. Although these men regarded the differences they observed among people as "experimental error," the tools and techniques they had devised were fundamental to the procedures early test makers would employ.

Therefore, mental-test development appeared in the late 1800s because at this point in time biologists were showing how differences in traits among individuals explained differences in their ability to cope with the world; philosophers were emphasizing the empirical study of man; and the psychophysicists were providing the tools to quantify reactions to the environment. It was but a short step to combine these ideas and begin the study of mental measurements. If keener minds allow us to cope more successfully with the world and keen minds depend on sharp perceptual ability, an assessment of the acuity of one's perceptions should reflect the expansiveness of his mind. The job was, then, to find ways to assess one's ability to perceive the world around him. The psychophysicists were building the very tools needed to do this.

The work of Sir Francis Galton in England in the 1880s was the most prominent example of the emerging mental-measurements study. Galton's interests focused on the characteristics that made people great successes in life. In an attempt to identify these characteristics, he compiled a collection of devices that measured sensory acuity. Although Galton was disappointed in his efforts to find tests that distinguished successful individuals from less successful ones, several methodological developments did emerge from his work. Probably his most pervasive invention was a graphic procedure for illustrating the relationship between two variables, e.g., a person's height and his strength of grip. This procedure was later developed into a mathematical operation by a colleague, Karl Pearson. The procedure

FIG. 2.1 E. L. Thorndike. (Photograph courtesy Columbia University)

has since been widely used and is known as the Pearson product-moment correlation. It shows quantitatively the extent to which two variables are related. This statistical procedure has been fundamental to the development of present-day measurement tools. We shall deal much more with correlation coefficients in later chapters.

Although the foundation for modern testing procedures was laid by such men as Galton and Pearson, it was E. L. Thorndike who established the scientific practice of test development in America. Probably no individual in the history of testing has had a more pervasive influence than Thorndike (Fig. 2.1). In 1904, he published the first textbook in educational measurement, thereby making basic measurement theory and techniques available to a wide audience. He built several popular achievement and general abilities tests himself and pioneered the use of tests in college admissions. With Thorndike's work, the efforts and ideas of a number of pioneers in the field were integrated and broadly disseminated. The field of mental measurement was unified under a collection of basic procedures, and these were made available to all interested educators and psychologists.

The advent of World War I had a significant impact on test development in America. Faced with many personnel classification problems, the army pressed the construction of mental tests, with some obvious success. For the first time, objective tests were utilized to assess talent on a massive scale. The army's success led to a flurry of test publications in the decade following the war. By the end of the roaring '20s, more than 1300 tests were on the educational market (Cook 1952). Considering how recently basic test theory had been integrated and disseminated and noting the unavailability of rapid data-processing hardware, we must conclude that a tremendous effort had been made in the 25 years following the publication of Thorndike's book. Some rather well-made tests emerged, but among this flourish of test-making, a number of poorly designed and poorly developed instruments were also pressed onto the market.

It was exactly this appearance of gravely inadequate documents, exaggerated claims for, and erroneous interpretations of, tests that set the tone of the writings of test specialists in the 1930s and early 1940s. Skepticism and caution burst forth, and an appeal went out for greater care in the design and development of tests. In addition, a plea for recognizing the limitations of tests was being heard in gatherings of psychologists and educators. This, then, was the predominant atmosphere when World War II began to demand from the test industry new tools for the gigantic task of mobilizing millions of men in a few months' span.

World War II brought about two events of great significance: it unified research efforts in test development under several government agencies, and it produced the "battery" approach to assessment, i.e., using groups of tests to provide a broader picture of men's talents and achievements. Following the war, these procedures were continued by private organizations. Large test-developing companies, such as the Educational Testing Service, which was established in 1947 in Princeton, New Jersey, continued the unified research approach to advance and exploit measurement theory in building new assessment tools. The use of test batteries, widely employed during World War II, has continued to find much favor in educational institutions.

The advances in computer technology during and immediately after World War II also introduced a new dimension into educational measurement. Large volumes of tests could be processed, and many variables could be related statistically at a very rapid rate. This facility provided the setting for nation-wide assessment programs. Most notable among these was the longitudinal study begun in 1959 and known as Project TALENT, which was designed to assess and interrelate a variety of skills, interests, and personality traits in an effort to better adapt educational programs to the changing character of American youth. In more recent years the National

Assessment Program has developed a broad testing project to determine the educational progress of American children.

Another significant trend in testing in the decades following World War II was the strengthening of the humanist movement in America. Many people began to regard tests as insensitive to the often agonizing circumstances of people to whom the tests were applied. In the 1950s and 1960s, the great concern in psychological measurement came in reference to: (1) the extent to which tests were biased against, and hence imposed limitations on, subgroups of the population; and (2) the ethical questions involved in using tools that may tend to invade the individual's privacy. Although progress has been made, we are still wrestling with these questions.

PROBLEMS

1. If you were building an achievement test in the 1890s would you use a proficiency criterion or peer-reference criterion? Why? How would you establish your criterion in the context of that era?

2. Suppose you were a test publisher in the 1890s and wanted to build an arithmetic test for the commercial market.

   a) How would you collect the test content?

   b) How long do you suppose it would take you to develop this test with the tools available for reproducing the test, collecting data, scoring and calculating descriptive information (such as average performance) for each grade level? Does this tell you something about why standard tests emerged so slowly?

Throughout the history of mental measurement, three related, yet somewhat distinct, efforts have appeared. One thrust was in the direction of improving assessment of school learning, a second was in the development of tools to measure intelligence, and the third was an effort to assess characteristics of personality. We shall look at a few landmarks in each of these areas of work.

ACHIEVEMENT TESTS

By the time Galton's tests were reported, considerable work had already been done in America to improve the use of measurement in the schools. The oral examination had long been used as the primary vehicle for the assessment of learning. However, in 1845 Horace Mann led the attack on oral tests. Children must have been delighted to see this time-worn process indicted for its weaknesses.

But the real inventor of objective tests with standards against which a child could be compared was J. M. Rice (Ayres 1918). Rice, a physician by training, had studied pedagogy in Germany, and was intrigued by the possibilities of applying some of the psychophysicists' techniques to the study of educational assessment. His greatest achievement was the construction of spelling tests which he administered to almost 30,000 children. In the 1890s no equipment for automated data analysis was available, not even a desk calculator. The whole job had to be done by hand. Clearly, Rice accomplished a monumental task in building his spelling test. The enormity of the job appears even greater when we realize that almost half of Rice's data was collected under his personal direction.

The spelling lists themselves are not the most important feature of Rice's work. Rice developed the idea that the best way to establish a child's performance was by comparing it with the performance of other children who had taken the same examination under the same circumstances. This technique for interpreting test scores is basic to almost every standardized test on the market today.

After the appearance of Thorndike's milestone textbook in measurement, a number of achievement tests began to appear, e.g., Stone's arithmetic scale in 1908 and Ayre's handwriting scale in 1912. Also, at this time, studies of grading tests and assigning marks were beginning to cast doubt on the widely used informal and essay testing procedures (Meyer 1908). These studies, which continued to appear for the next two decades, produced some startling findings. For example, even in the seemingly objective field of mathematics, a student's mark was found to depend heavily on who read his paper rather than on what he had written on his test (Starch and Elliott 1913). Also, a given teacher on a second reading of a paper was likely to disagree noticeably with the mark he had given on the first reading (Starch 1913). Studies of this type clearly demonstrated a need for more objectivity in testing methods.

The 1920s saw widespread activity in test development, due partly to the success with which the army had built classification tests in World War I and partly to the emergence of scientific investigation as a basis for establishing teaching procedures. A landmark in objective testing in the schools was the appearance in 1923 of the *Stanford Achievement Test*. Here, for the first time, was a collection of tests in each of the basic academic subjects typically taught in the public school. In addition, the tests had been tried out on thousands of children who were used as a reference group for test interpretation. The basic procedures for test construction used with the Stanford achievement battery provided a blueprint for other test makers and are, in fact, in use today.

Two principal changes in achievement tests have occurred since World War II. A wider variety of skills has been assessed, and greater emphasis has been placed on the student's use of information rather than the mere reproduction of facts. New tests in such areas as study skills have appeared widely, and some batteries, notably the *Sequential Tests of Educational Progress*, emphasize the application of information in solving problems to the complete exclusion of factual, recall items. It should, however, be noted that much factual content remains in many achievement-test batteries.

INTELLIGENCE TESTING

From the springboard of ideas provided by the empirical school of philosophers, Galton had developed a number of tests of sensory discrimination. His intent was to identify fine sensory abilities which set notably successful men apart from less successful people. This approach to measuring intellectual ability was continued in America by James McKeen Cattell, who had studied in the experimental psychology laboratories in Germany. He brought back to the United States many of the techniques used by the psychophysicists in studying mental states. It was Cattell (1890) who coined the term "mental tests" in describing a series of instruments he was using in his studies. In spite of the care with which these tests had been developed, several studies showed a consistent lack of relationship between test scores and cognitive ability reflected in school achievement (Wissler 1901). Hence, the tests were abandoned as measures of intelligence.

A breakthrough in intelligence testing came with the work of Alfred Binet (Binet and Simon 1905). Commissioned in 1904 by the French Minister of Public Instruction to develop a procedure for identifying mentally retarded children, Binet developed a series of tasks that might classify children as having significant learning disability. These tasks, described in a publication in 1905, were arranged from easiest to most difficult, but beyond this had little standardization. Task difficulty was determined by trying out the tests with 50 children. By today's standards, this is a meager sample, but it represented an early attempt at standardization by providing a reference group as a basis for test interpretation. In 1908 Binet published a revision of the tests. This time, tasks were arranged not only in order of difficulty, but also according to the age at which a child was expected to pass any given item. The world had seen its first age scale, and the concept of "mental age" appeared. For example, a child who passed the items scaled at the six-year level had a "mental age" of six. Binet's tasks were brought to America by H. H. Goddard in 1910 and translated to English for use at the mental retardation center in Vineland, New Jersey.

Binet presented the third revision of his tests in 1911, the year of his death. This scale not only refined previous procedures, but also extended

FIG. 2.2 Lewis M. Terman. (Photograph courtesy Stanford University)

the ability range to include items of appropriate difficulty level for normal children as well as the mentally retarded.

The success of the Binet tests was based on his complete about-face from the atomistic work of people like Galton. Binet defined intelligence in terms of ability to comprehend, to make judgments, to maintain a mental set, and to perceive and correct errors. To Binet, intelligence was a broad, pervasive ability rather than a collection of discrete sensory acts as explored by earlier psychologists. The ability of his tests to show differences between capable and less capable pupils lent much credence to the labeling of the scale as a measure of intelligence.

When Goddard brought the Binet scales to the United States, he translated them directly from French into English. It was soon evident, however, that cultural differences between France and America made the tests somewhat inappropriate for general use in the United States. Therefore, in 1916 Lewis Terman (Fig. 2.2) published the *Stanford Revision of the Binet Scales*. Terman used many items from Binet's tests, but also devised many of his own. The test was applicable to people between the ages of 3 to 18, with three additional levels to assess adult intelligence. The individual tasks in the test were placed at various age levels in accordance with extensive trials with American children (largely in California). Terman also incorporated the idea of the IQ, a ratio of mental age (as shown by the test) and chronological age.*

The 1916 *Stanford Revision of the Binet Scales* was the principal individual intelligence test in America for 20 years. During this time Terman and his colleague Maude Merrill undertook research that led to a major revision of the 1916 scale. The 1916 scale was found to be highly verbal in content; it lacked sufficiently difficult items to assess accurately the upper levels of intelligence; and there was only one form of the test, which limited its use for retesting. Therefore, in 1937 Terman and Merrill produced the second Stanford revision of the Binet scales. This test had two forms (L and M), item content was updated, and the range was extended from 2½ years to adulthood. Like its predecessor, the 1937 revision was a leading scale for over 20 years. In 1960 the best items from the two forms, L and M, were combined into one test with readjustments of items to correspond with age levels appropriate to the changing abilities of children. The 1960 revision, like other "Stanford-Binets," has held high favor among individual intelligence-test users.

Now we must go back again to World War I to pick up more developments in the measurement of intelligence. The primary limitation of the Binet scales was that they were individual tests, i.e., they could be administered to only one person at a time. In 1917, when the United States entered World War I, the army was faced with tremendous classification and training problems. A group of leading psychologists was quickly called together to prepare a technique for assessing the abilities of large numbers of men as rapidly as possible. At this time Arthur Otis had been experimenting with a number of paper-and-pencil tasks which required a range of problem-solving skills. The army's psychologists exploited the experimental work of Arthur Otis in producing the first widely successful paper-and-pencil, group test of mental ability, the *Army Alpha*.

The *Army Alpha* proved to be not only a very serviceable tool for the armed forces, but also became the principal ability test used by psychologists across the nation in the 1920s. In addition, it was the prototype of a large number of group tests of intelligence to emerge in the two decades after the war. Notable among these were the Otis in 1920, the Kuhlmann-Anderson in 1927, the Henman-Nelson in 1931, and the *California Test of Mental Maturity* in 1936. Revisions of these original tests are still in use.

---

* The IQ, or intelligence quotient, was first presented by William Stern in 1912. IQ will be dealt with extensively in Chapter 7.

Although tests were widely used and many specialized tests were constructed during World War II, few unique or clearly innovative procedures appeared. However, the development of batteries of tests that assessed several components of ability was one significant outcome from the classification work done during the war. In a mechanized army many highly specific skills were required. In assigning men to specific tasks, broad, general estimates of ability often masked the presence or absence of special talents. Therefore, tests of rather specific abilities were clustered together into batteries, and men were classified on the basis of their best specific talents rather than on their general level of performance.

Since World War II significant developments in the measurement of intelligence have dealt largely with further defining intelligence and relating it to race and social-class differences in basic experience. This effort has led to greater sensitivity to the limitations of intelligence tests and to more specific interpretation of test results.

PROBLEMS

1. Contrast the methods of assessing ability used by Galton and by Binet. Which person appears to have been posing problems most like those found in school settings?

2. Suppose you were Alfred Binet and had been asked to make up a device to identify slow-learning children. Remember that laboratory-tested psychological theories of learning had not yet emerged, that mental functions were still widely left to philosophers to explain, and basic statistical procedures for analyzing data were very rudimentary and hand-calculated. What would have been your point of departure? What viewpoint (philosophical, etc.) current in the early 1900s could be a base for your point of departure?

3. After considering the problems in item 2, how would you characterize the work of Binet as to difficulty and time requirement?

4. Do you see the greatest difference in basic theoretical position between Galton and Binet, or between Binet and the makers of the *Army Alpha?*

PERSONALITY

The development of techniques for assessing personal characteristics occurred quite apart from intelligence and achievement testing. A considerable body of interest had built up in clinical psychology by the late 1800s, but treatment was on an individual basis, and assessment of personal characteristics was handled largely through the interview, a favored technique of many clinicians even today.

But as with mental ability, the army in World War I was faced with classifying large groups of men on personality characteristics. As a result, Woodworth's *Personal Data Sheet* was developed as a standard "interview" in which men could respond "yes" or "no" to 116 statements about behavior. Its purpose was to identify men who might have difficulty adjusting to the stress of military life. As gross a tool as this was, the inventory proved to be quite useful to the army in its preliminary screening of recruits.

But the results from Woodworth's inventory were far from diagnostic, and the scheme lacked a theoretical structure of behavior for either test content or interpretation. Items were selected merely because men who stood the rigors of military training typically answered them differently from men who broke down in military life. Clinicians quickly sought more sophisticated techniques. Probably the most widely accepted pencil-and-paper inventory to emerge in the post-World War I years was the *Bernreuter Personality Inventory.* This instrument provided scores on four descriptive characteristics of personality—neurotic tendencies, self-sufficiency, introversion, and dominance. Since many psychologists regarded personality as a combination of habit patterns, these categories of behavior seemed rather attractive. The Bernreuter received wide use for many years and is still used in some locations.

While many psychologists were busy working on group, paper-and-pencil inventories in the 1920s, Herman Rorschach was experimenting with a quite different technique. Pursuing the idea that differences in personality among people are tied to differences in how they perceive the world around them, Rorschach began experimenting with the abstract designs found in ink blots as stimuli for the perceptions of clients. He published his experimental work in 1921. Quite rapidly, his ink blots were taken up by other clinicians, and soon the blots were being used as standard tools for diagnosing personality problems. The Rorschach ink blots, which are still used in clinical work, gave rise to a variety of other tools that asked the client to interpret nondescript stimuli. These tools are known as projective techniques because it is assumed that the client casts his own personality characteristics into the organization of the pictorial stimuli presented to him.

Production of personality inventories, like the production of ability tests, expanded rapidly after World War I, but fell under severe scrutiny in the late 1930s and 1940s. Even now, tools for assessing personality are accepted with considerable caution by many psychologists and educators. Further, test users in the public sector have become increasingly aware of the fact that personality inventories may be used more than any other type of test as a vehicle for invading the privacy of test takers. A renewed interest in the ethics of test use emerged to protect the individual from the unscrupulous divulgence of his private attitudes and beliefs expressed in a test situation. As a result, a vigorous interest in ethical questions emerged.

SUMMARY

Sophistication of any tool depends on the time and effort invested in it. Mental-measurement tools are only moderately sophisticated, because the history of mental measurement, as shown in Fig. 2.3, is a short one. Tests could not emerge until philosophers had viewed the mind as measurable, psychophysicists had built the tools, and biologists had seen differences among individuals as a key to evolutionary survival. In America, the greatest single impetus to the development of testing tools came with World War I. The instruments produced by government research teams were not only transferred directly into nonmilitary uses, but also served as models for the development of a vast number of tools for a wide range of consumer requirements. By the 1930s test specialists were becoming increasingly sensitive to the lack of sophistication among many test makers and users and to the limitations inherent in most kinds of testing procedures. A period of cautious reappraisal began in the late 1930s and lasted into the 1940s.

The use of a test-battery approach to appraising human talent emerged with World War II. Following the war, several widely used classification batteries appeared. The current trend is one of redefining traits, e.g., intelligence, and reconstructing instruments that more precisely measure the redefined trait. Complementing this effort is an increasing appreciation for the integrity of the person being tested and sensitivity to such factors as invasion of privacy and possible affront to human sensibility. Test builders are attempting to be more definite about what they are measuring and are attending more to the impact of testing on the test taker than ever before.

We can hardly leave an historical overview without noting the impact of electronic data processing on test development. In 1935 the IBM 805 scoring machine opened the door to mechanical processing of test data. In recent years extremely rapid machine scoring of answer sheets and computer analysis of test data have vastly accelerated the rate at which tests can be developed, revised, and utilized. Without these machines the extensive experimental work that goes into building a test would be conspicuously delayed, and much of the convenience in using tests would be eliminated.

In summary, tests have become useful tools as aids to decision making. Although much progress in test development and application has been made, much work remains to be done. The development of substantial theories that can explain mental processes and that could serve as springboards for test development has been slow, and the short history of testing has not provided time for the accumulation of the necessary research and

WORLD EVENTS   MEASUREMENT EVENTS

Plymouth colony established

1650   Descartes' dualism

Leeuwenhoek's microscope
Wm. Penn colony chartered
                                                John Locke's "blank tablet"
1700

1750   Antecedents to mental measurement

Watt's steam engine

American Revolution
Whitney's cotton gin
1800   Fulton's steamboat

                                                Horace Mann attacked oral examinations

1850   Pasteurization discovered
        Civil War

                                                J. M. Rice's spelling test

                                                Galton's sensory tests

1900   Binet's intelligence scales
        Wright brothers' flight   Thorndike's textbook in statistics and measurement
        World War I   Modern test period Stone's arithmetic test, Stanford-Binet scales,
                                                Army Alpha, and Woodworth Personal Data Sheet
                                                Stanford Achievement tests, Rorschach ink blots
        World War II   IBM 805

1950   Educational Testing Service

                                                Project TALENT

FIG. 2.3 Historical events in educational measurement.

technical sophistication. Of these problems, the first—lack of substantial theories—is probably the most important in promoting conspicuous advancements in the measurement of mental traits.

REFERENCES

Ayres, L. P. "History and present status of educational measurements," *Seventeenth Yearbook of the National Society for the Study of Education, Part II.* Bloomington, Indiana: Public School Publishing Company, 1918.

Binet, Alfred and Theodore Simon. "Methods nouvelles pour le diagnostic du neveau intellectuel des anormaux," *Année Psycholgique* **11** (1905): 191–244.

Cattell, James McKeen. "Mental tests and measurements," *Mind,* **15** (1890): 373–381.

Cook, W. W. "Achievement Tests," *Encyclopedia of Educational Research,* rev. ed., New York: MacMillan, 1952, p. 1461.

Descartes, René. "Passions of the Soul 1650," cited in Gardner Murphy, *Historical Introduction to Modern Psychology,* rev. ed. New York: Harcourt Brace, 1949, Chapter 2.

Dubois, Philip. "A test-dominated society: China 1115 B.C.-1905 A.D., in *Proceedings of the 1964 Invitational Conference on Testing Problems,* Princeton, N.J.: Educational Testing Service, 1965, pp. 3–11.

Goddard, H. H. "A measuring scale for intelligence," *Training School,* **6** (1910): 146–154.

Locke, John. *Essay Concerning Human Understanding* (1690 ed.), London: E. Campbell Fraser, 1894.

Meyer, M. "The grading of students," *Science,* **27** (1908): 243–250.

Starch, Daniel. "Reliability and distribution of grades," *Science,* **38** (1913): 630-636.

Starch, Daniel and Edward C. Elliott. "Reliability of grading work in mathematics," *School Review,* **21** (1913): 254–259.

Wissler, Carl. "The correlation of mental and physical traits," *Psychological Review Monograph Supplement* **3, 6** (1901): 1–62.

CHAPTER 3

TEST SCORES
AND THEIR INTERPRETATION

INTRODUCTION

Every examination has a prescribed procedure for summarizing the test-taker's work. Typically, we count the number of right answers chosen by the student, e.g., counting the number of correctly solved problems in an arithmetic test. In this way, the score assigned to the test taker indicates how often the student made a desired response on the test.

But a score by itself has almost no meaning. However, if we can compare a given person's score with the range of scores assigned to other persons like him, the number begins to tell something about the test-taker's status among his peers in the behavior being observed. For example, if we know that John got 18 spelling words correct, we can say very little about his spelling ability. But if we know that among 100 children like John, the average number of words spelled correctly from this list was 12 and that only ten percent of the group got 18 or more, John's score of 18 begins to have meaning. Since a few arithmetical computations will help us get this type of meaning from test scores, we should look at several procedures that show us how a given person stands in relation to his peers.

At this point it is important to recall that tests are not ratio scales; therefore, test scores do not indicate magnitude (measuring from zero) of the trait. But we do have a point from which we can begin measuring, i.e., the average score for a large group of people like those to whom we want to apply our test. How much a given score deviates above or below this mean helps us decide how "good" a score is. We shall need to know, then: (a) some ways to find averages, and (b) some ways to show how far above or below average a given score deviates.

We shall generally ask four questions about scores. First, what was the pattern of scoring? Are the scores spread quite evenly along the possible score range, or are there points along the range at which many scores "pile up"? Second, what is the typical, or average, score on the test? This is the value we often use as our point of departure in determining a given person's status. Is John's score greater or lesser than the typical score for his group?

We can also use the average to compare our group with some other group, e.g., comparing a fourth-grade class in Greeley, Colorado, with a "national sample" of fourth graders.

Third, how spread out, or widely dispersed, are the score values above and below the average? Does everyone have about the same score, or do people differ widely in the scores they achieve? Suppose the five men on basketball team A made the following points per game last season: 15, 16, 15, 14, 15; the men on team B scored: 5, 7, 15, 20, 28. The averages for these two teams are the same, but the individual scoring abilities of players on one team are clearly different from the abilities of the men on the other team. The same can be true of test performance. The average does not reflect the range of differences in performance among the members of the group. Therefore, if we are going to describe a group and determine a given person's status in a group, we need not only an average, but also an indicator of how spread out the scores are.

The procedures applied to such analyses help reveal the status of a given person on the test. They do not, in themselves, identify portions of a group who are expected to be above or below a given score. Therefore, our fourth set of procedures will be those that specifically answer the question: How does a given person rank in relation to his peers on this test?

It is not the purpose of this chapter to present a short course in statistical analysis. That job is best done by textbooks devoted entirely to the topic.* However, certain procedures, are essential to our dealings with test scores. We shall explore these procedures, but only at a definitional and introductory computational level.

SCORE DISTRIBUTIONS: PUTTING SCORES IN ORDER

Let us suppose that we have given an arithmetic test composed of 35 problems to a class of fourth-grade children. The scores (number of correct answers) are given in Table 3.1. A visual scan of these scores shows us very little, even after some effort. If these test scores could be arranged from low to high with an indication of how many of our students achieved each score, a visual scan of the test results would quickly provide more information. This arrangement is given in Table 3.2. In Table 3.2(a) we can quickly see that the highest score was 34; the lowest, 5. A score of 16 occurred more frequently than did any other score, and almost half of the class scored between 15 and 19. This arrangement of scores from high to

---

* For a simple presentation of statistical analysis of test results, see Lyman (1971) or Chase (1967). A more detailed presentation may be found in Ferguson (1971) or Guilford (1965). A programed, self-instructional presentation is found in Stanley and Hopkins (1972), Ch. 2.

TABLE 3.1 Scores achieved by 30 fourth-grade children on an arithmetic test

Name	Score	Name	Score
Ann	12	Pete	24
Bill	18	Quent	12
Carl	19	Roger	34
Dick	18	Steve	10
Ellen	15	Tom	17
Frank	21	Ulla	7
George	16	Vera	31
Harry	15	Wes	15
Inger	24	Xavier	22
Jack	14	Yollanda	9
Kitty	17	Zeke	8
Lane	28	Albert	21
Mel	16	Bob	16
Neal	27	Cathy	17
Opal	19	Don	16

low, with the number of individuals who achieved each score (the score frequency), is called a *frequency distribution*.

The distribution of scores in Table 3.2(a) is not extremely spread out, so it shows fairly well the central area around which most scores are clustered. However, it is sufficiently spread out to produce a number of score values not achieved by anyone, i.e., scores with zero frequency. If the distribution of scores is very widely dispersed and the number of students involved is small, we will find many score values that have a zero frequency. These widely dispersed distributions typically fail to show a central clustering of scores because only one or two persons will achieve any given score value. If this is the case, we often *group* several adjacent score values into what is called a "class interval," or "step interval," and record the total number of occurrences, or frequency, for the interval, i.e., the total number of people who had scores within the step interval. For example, in Table 3.2(a) we could combine the lowest three scores into the interval 5 to 7. One person scored in this range. The next step interval would be 8 to 10, with three persons scoring in this range. The complete procedure for the entire distribution of scores is given in Table 3.2(b). Note that each step interval has the same range of score values, in this example, three score values.

The grouped data frequency distribution has eliminated the zeros from the frequency column; it shows more clearly the clustering of the scores near a central point. These characteristics are more evident than before the

TABLE 3.2 Data from Table 3.1 arranged into a frequency distribution

(a)		(b)	
Score	Number of children at score (frequency)	Score interval	Number of children in interval (frequency)
34	1		
33	0	32–34	1
32	0		
31	1		
30	0	29–31	1
29	0		
28	1		
27	1	26–28	2
26	0		
25	0		
24	2	23–25	2
23	0		
22	1		
21	2	20–22	3
20	0		
19	2		
18	2	17–19	7
17	3		
16	4		
15	3	14–16	8
14	1		
13	0		
12	2	11–13	2
11	0		
10	1		
9	1	8–10	3
8	1		
7	0		
6	0	5–7	1
5	1		

scores were collapsed into intervals. However, we group data into step intervals only when we can construct at least ten intervals within the total range of scores, since having fewer intervals tends to obscure characteristics of the distribution. Also, we typically construct intervals so that they contain an odd number of score values. (For example, in Table 3.2(b) each interval comprises three adjacent score values.) The reason for this is that sometimes we let the midpoint of an interval stand for all score values in that interval. If there is an odd number of score values in an interval, the midpoint will be a whole number, which simplifies computations. Although in Table 3.2(b) we used intervals of three score values, any odd number of scores will do, so long as it allows us to have at least ten intervals.

Average—the "typical" score value

There are several indicators of the typical, or average, score values for a group of individuals such as those in Table 3.1. Two of the most common of these indicators are the *median* and the *mean*.

The median is that score point on a distribution that cuts off half of the individuals below it and half above it. It is found by simply counting from the bottom of the frequency distribution to the score value below which exactly 50 percent of the individuals in the distribution fall. In Table 3.2(a) there are scores for 30 pupils, so to find the median we count up until we have passed the scores made by 15 individuals. Counting up from the bottom, we find that 14 people have been accounted for up through a score of 16. We need one more person to make up half of our group. But there are three people at the next score value, 17. We need one of the three to complete our 50 percent, i.e., we are moving into this group one-third of the way. But where does the score of 17 begin? It begins half way between 16 and 17, or 16.5, and runs up to half way between 17 and 18, or 17.5. This is a score range of 1.0 point, a third of which is .33. Therefore, if we move a third (.33) into the score range, beginning at its lower limit of 16.5, we move up to 16.83, i.e., 16.5 + .33. The median is 16.83.

A graphic description of this problem is given in Fig. 3.1. In Table 3.2(a) we had 14 cases below the score of 17. In order to get the 15 cases

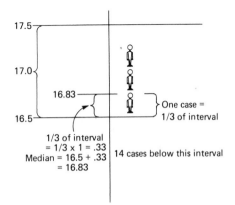

FIG. 3.1 Dividing a score interval in finding the median.

we need to make up half the group, we need one case from the score interval of 17. Now where does the score interval of 16 stop and 17 begin?
Actually, the score interval of 17 runs from 16.5 to 17.5. There are three
cases within this score interval (Fig. 3.1). We have 14 cases up to 16.5; we
need one more case to make up 15 people. Therefore, we move into the
interval 16.5 to 17.5 for one of the three cases, or a third of the way through
the people who fell into that score interval. If we take a third of the *people*,
we also move a third of the way into the *score range* of the interval, or one-
third of the way from 16.5 to 17.5. This is a score range of 1.0 point, a third
of which is .33 of the score interval. This value added to the lower limit of
the range (16.5 + .33) gives us the median score value of 16.83.

What is 16.83? It is the point on the total score range below which half
the cases fell and above which half the cases fell. This value is the median
for the distribution.

The median of the grouped data distribution in Table 3.2(b) can be
found in a similar manner. We count up to the bottom of the interval which
contains the fifteenth individual, i.e., 17–19. We have 14 people below that
point; we need one more person to locate the score value below which half
of the group falls. Therefore, we need one of the eight people in the interval.
Since we are taking one-eighth of the people in the interval, we move one-
eighth of the way into the score value of the interval (Fig. 3.2).

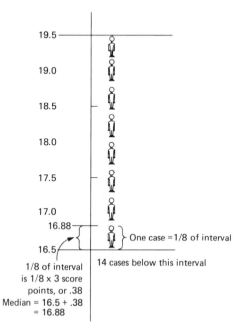

FIG. 3.2 Finding the median with grouped data.

But in Table 3.2(b), there are three scores in each interval, not just one as in Table 3.2(a). So when we move into the interval by one-eighth of the score range, we are actually moving in one-eighth of three units ($\frac{1}{8} \times 3$), or .38 score points into the interval, as shown in Fig. 3.2. The interval begins at 16.5, so 16.5 plus one-eighth of the interval (.38) is 16.88. This is our calculated median for the grouped data in Table 3.2(b).

The median for Table 3.2(b) is very close to, but not identical with, the median for Table 3.2(a). The difference arises from the assumption that the individuals in a given interval are spread equally across all scores in that interval. On the average of many intervals, this is a valid assumption, but for any one interval it is unlikely to be true. In any case, it typically does not markedly affect our computed median score value.

PROBLEMS

1. I have administered a test of 42 arithmetic problems to my middle school class of 30 students. The following scores were taken from the 30 tests.

39	35	25	28	30
33	31	17	30	18
36	31	29	10	14
28	26	27	24	28
23	18	15	22	20
24	21	26	23	27

    a) Construct a frequency distribution with intervals of one score unit, beginning

    12
    11
    10

    b) Construct a frequency distribution with intervals of three scores units, beginning

    13–15
    10–12

    c) Compare the two distributions for: (1) ease of identifying a central point among the student's scores, and (2) lack of zero-frequency intervals.

2. Using the data above compute the median for the frequency distribution in a) and again for the frequency distribution in b).

    ans: (a) 26.0 (b) 25.7

A second indicator of "typical" performance is the *mean*. What most people call an arithmetic average, test builders call the mean. To find it, we

TABLE 3.3   The mean computed from the grouped data in Table 3.2(b)

Score interval	Frequency	Interval midpoint	Frequency times midpoint
32–34	1	33	33
29–31	1	30	30
26–28	2	27	54
23–25	2	24	48
20–22	3	21	63
17–19	7	18	126
14–16	8	15	120
11–13	2	12	24
8–10	3	9	27
5–7	1	6	6
	30		531

$$\text{Mean} = \frac{531}{30} = 17.7$$

add up all scores and divide by the number of scores. If on a spelling test John got 5 right, Ann got 7, Mary 6, and Bill 2, we would find the mean by

$$\frac{5 + 7 + 6 + 2}{4} = \frac{20}{4} = 5.$$

When scores are in a grouped-data frequency distribution, this process does not directly apply, because we do not know which score in an interval goes with which person. For example, in Table 3.2(b), the interval 20–22 contains three people. Did one person get 20, one 21, and the third 22? Or did all of them get 21? Or did one get 21 and two get 22? Since we cannot be sure, we assume that the people are equally distributed across all score values in the interval. In that case the middle score is most representative of all the scores in the interval. Therefore, we multiply the midpoint of an interval by the frequency of the interval, and this produces a reasonable estimate of the sum of all the scores in the interval. Applying this idea to the data in Table 3.2(b) we arrive at the figures in Table 3.3. We then add all these midpoint-times-interval-frequency values and divide by the total number of individuals in the distribution to get the mean.

If scores on one end of a distribution do not deviate more widely from the central pile-up of data than do scores on the other end, the value of the mean and the median will be quite nearly the same. However, if scores do deviate markedly in the direction of one end of the distribution, the mean and the median will be quite different from each other. For example, suppose we have two groups of five people. Those in Group A had scores on an arithmetic test of 5, 4, 4, 3, 3, 2; those in Group B had scores of 13, 4, 4, 3, 3, 2. The median for each group is 3.5. The mean for Group A is also 3.5, but for Group B it is 4.8. This value for Group B is clearly higher than most of the scores on the test and consequently is not "typical" for most of the group. These figures illustrate that the mean is pulled in the direction of widely deviating scores, but the median is not influenced by these values. In deciding which "average" we will use, we must first decide which will best represent the data we have collected on our test. If possible, we select the mean, but if a few widely deviating scores at one end of the distribution pull the mean away from the central pile-up of scores, we may wish to use the median rather than the mean as our indicator of typical performance.

PROBLEMS

1. I have given the Handy Tool Skill Test to ten boys in my auto-mechanics class. Their scores (number correct) are as follows:

George	12	Roosevelt	13
Henry	9	Hickman	12
Willy	14	Jim	11
Jack	3	Phil	10
Bill	11	Henry	2

Construct a frequency distribution and:

a) Compute the mean.   (ans: 9.7)
b) Find the median.   (ans: 11.0)
c) Which value (mean or median) best represents the central grouping of scores on this test?

2. I have grouped my data on an achievement test into the distribution below. Find the mean by using the interval midpoint procedure.

Scores	Frequency	Interval midpoint	Frequency times midpoint
29–31	1		
26–28	1		
23–25	2		
20–22	3		
17–19	4		
14–16	3		
11–13	2	12	
8–10	2	9	18
5–7	1	6	6
2–4	1	3	3
	20		

(ans: 16.8)

INDICATORS OF DISPERSION

In describing a set of scores, we need more than just an indicator of "typical" performance. We also need a figure to show the spread of the scores. The following example illustrates this point. Suppose that we have two groups of five children each, and each child has attempted to spell a list of 20 words. The number of words correctly spelled by the children in the two groups is as follows:

Group A	16	12	9	6	2
Group B	10	9	9	9	8

The means of the two groups are identical, but we certainly could not say that the performance of these two groups is identical. The range of skill of the students in Group A is markedly greater than in Group B. Therefore, in describing the performance of these two groups, we need more than an average for each one; we also need an indicator of the spread, or dispersion, of scores.

A quick indicator of dispersion of scores is found by subtracting the lowest score from the highest one, and adding 1. This gives us the total inclusive range of scores in the distribution. But this method has one big problem. Its value depends on only two people in the group—the highest and lowest scorers. If the performance of either of these people differs markedly from that of the group, the range can be a misleading indicator of dispersion for the group. The range is useful as a quick indicator of dispersion of scores, but for many purposes a more precise indicator of spread is required.

Since we do not use ratio scales in psychological measurement, we decided that the mean could be our point of departure and that we could look at scores in terms of their position above or below the mean. We might, therefore, try to show how widely spread the scores are by computing an average of their differences from the mean. More widely dispersed distributions would have larger average deviations from the mean than would less widely dispersed distributions. We could subtract the mean from each score, add up these differences, and divide by the number of individuals. This way we would get an average deviation of scores from the mean. But Table 3.4 illustrates why this procedure is not used. The sum of all deviations around the mean is zero. If this is divided by seven, it does not help us very much in deciding how widely dispersed the scores are around the mean. But deviations of scores above and below the mean are still useful in getting an indicator of dispersion.

There is also another method for finding an indicator of dispersion that starts by computing deviations from the mean. However, once we have the deviations, we then square each of them, add up the squared deviations, and divide by the number of scores in our distribution. This gives us the average of the squared deviations. Now we "unsquare" this value to get our indica-

TABLE 3.4 Computing an indicator of dispersion—the average deviation

Score	—	the mean	=	deviation
18	—	13	=	5
16	—	13	=	3
15	—	13	=	2
12	—	13	=	−1
11	—	13	=	−2
10	—	13	=	−3
9	—	13	=	−4
$\frac{91}{7}$				0

tor of dispersion, which is called the *standard deviation*, often abbreviated with the Greek letter sigma, σ. For the data in Table 3.4 we would begin by squaring each deviation value, i.e.,

$$5 \times 5 = 25, \quad 3 \times 3 = 9, \quad 2 \times 2 = 4, \quad -1 \times -1 = 1, \quad \ldots$$
$$-4 \times -4 = 16.$$

We then add these squared deviations, getting 68. This value divided by 7 (we had seven scores in our distribution) equals 9.71. Next, we take the square root of this value,

$$\sqrt{9.71} = 3.12.$$

The result is that indicator of dispersion of scores above and below the mean, which we call the standard deviation.

TABLE 3.5 Computation of a standard deviation

Score	—	the mean	=	deviation	Deviation squared
21	—	13	=	8	64
17	—	13	=	4	16
15	—	13	=	2	4
12	—	13	=	−1	1
11	—	13	=	−2	4
8	—	13	=	−5	25
7	—	13	=	−6	36
					150

$$\sigma = \sqrt{\frac{150}{7}}$$
$$= \sqrt{21.42}$$
$$= 4.6$$

Now suppose we take the distribution of scores in Table 3.4 and spread them out to look like the scores in Table 3.5. The mean is again 13, but the standard deviation has become larger.

The procedure for computing the standard deviation as described above is especially arduous when the mean contains a fraction such as 12.76 or 117.81 and when there are scores from many individuals in the distribution. A shorter, but slightly less precise procedure has been suggested by Lathrop (1961). If the frequency distribution is reasonably symmetrical, i.e., scores on one side of the mean are distributed in roughly a mirror image of scores on the other side of the mean, Lathrop's procedure is useful. We first add together the scores of the people in the highest 1/6 of the distribution. From this amount we subtract the sum of the scores of the lowest 1/6 of the people in the distribution. We then divide this difference by half of the number of individuals in the total distribution. An example is given in Table 3.6.

TABLE 3.6   Computation of the standard deviation by the short-cut method

Scores	Frequency	Computations
21	1	1/6 of 44 = 7.33
20	0	top
19	2	7.33
18	2	scores
17	4	Top 7.33 scores Bottom 7.33 scores
16	5	21 4†
15	7	19 12
14	8	19 top 7 12
13	7	18 scores 12 bottom
12	4	18 11 7 scores
11	2	bottom 17 11
10	1	7.33 17 10
9	1	scores 5.7* 9
	44	134.7 81

$$\sigma = \frac{(\text{sum of top } 1/6 \text{ of scores}) - (\text{sum of bottom } 1/6 \text{ of scores})}{\text{half the total number of individuals}}$$

$$= \frac{134.7 - 81}{22}$$

$$= \frac{53.7}{22}$$

$$= 2.44$$

* .33 of 17 = 5.7.
† .33 of 12 = 4.

In Table 3.6 we have found 1/6 of 44 individuals to be 7.33. Starting at the top of the distribution, we add the scores of the seven highest individuals. Beyond that, we need .33 of the next individual's score, or .33 of 17, which is 5.7. The total of the top 7.33 scores is 134.7. Similarly, we begin at the bottom of the distribution and start adding the lowest seven scores, plus .33 of the next one (or .33 of 12). This sum is 81. These figures are then put into the formula, and an estimate of the standard deviation is computed.

Mason and Odeh (1968) have shown that this procedure is a good approximation of the standard deviation with as few as 24 individuals in a distribution of scores, and becomes quite close to σ when there are 36 or more cases. Sabers and Klausmeier (1971) found considerable accuracy with as few as 25 cases. It is therefore suggested that for convenience, this procedure be used in hand-computing the standard deviation when the distribution is approximately symmetrical and when there are at least 25 individuals represented in a distribution. It is, however, important to remember that the standard deviation is an indicator of dispersion of scores from the mean, not from the extremes of the distribution. Starting at the mean, we shall apply the standard deviation as a "yardstick" for determining the position of a score above or below the mean of the group.

PROBLEMS

1. I have given the Distraction Tolerance Test to ten third-grade children with the following results. Compute the standard deviation, beginning by getting the squared deviations from the mean.

Scores (X)	f	$X-\overline{X}$ = Deviation	Dev^2
20	1	$20-17 = 3$	9
19	1	$19-17 = 2$	4
18	2	$18-17 = 1$	
		$18-17 = 1$	
17	3	$17-17 = 0$	
		$17-17 = 0$	
		$17-17 =$	
16	1	$16-17 =$	
15	1	$15-$	
14	0	$14-$	
13	1	13	Sum of
Mean $(\overline{X}) = $ 17.0			squared dev =

$$\sigma = \sqrt{\frac{\text{Sum of sq. dev.}}{\text{No. of scores}}} =$$

(ans: $\sigma = 1.9$)

2. A group of 33 children take the Digit Dexterity Test. The distribution of their scores is shown below. Compute the standard deviation by the method used in Table 3.6.

Scores	f
40	1
39	1
38	2
37	2
36	3
35	6
34	4
33	3
32	2
31	2
30	1
29	3
28	2
27	1

(ans: 3.33)

THE NORMAL DISTRIBUTION

Earlier, we said that one of the functions of a standard deviation, beyond showing dispersion of scores, is to reveal the status of a given score in relation to others in a distribution. We shall look at that procedure now.

For years, mathematicians have utilized a particular bell-shaped curve in solving such questions as: How likely is it that a given event will occur? This curve, known as *the normal curve,* is especially useful in test-score analysis because the results of so many tests come close to fitting the normal curve. The normal curve is shown in Fig. 3.3.

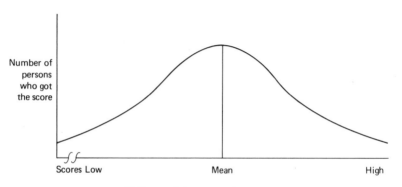

FIG. 3.3 The normal curve.

Remember that since tests are not ratio scales, we do not know where to locate true zero. Instead, we use the mean as a point of departure in determining how high or low a given score is. But before we can decide how that score ranks, we need a unit of measurement. For example, suppose we have a centigrade thermometer on which only zero is marked. The mercury in the glass tube is above the zero mark, but how high above zero must it go before the temperature reaches boiling? We need a unit to mark off degrees above and below our point of departure. With test scores, we also have a point of departure, but before we can decide how "hot" a score is, we need a unit of measurement above and below that point. The unit used is the standard deviation.

Before we see how the standard deviation can be used to show how far above or below the mean a given score ranges, let us look at this situation. Suppose you are standing at the 50-yard line on a football field. Five players are spaced between the 50- and 40-yard lines in each direction, four more players are between the 40- and 30-yard lines, three are between the 30- and 20-yard lines, two are between the 20 and 10, and one is between the 10-yard line and the goal line. This situation is depicted in Fig. 3.4. For this example let us use a "measuring stick" of ten yards. If we measure in either direction from the 50-yard line, how many players are between the 50- and 30-yard lines? If we know how many players stand in each ten-yard area, we can figure this out. We know that five men are between the 50- and the 40-yard line and four more are between the 40- and 30-yard line; therefore, there are nine players between the 50- and 30-yard lines.

Suppose all the players are facing Goal 2. John Smith is at the 20-yard line nearest Goal 2. How many men stand behind John Smith? Again, if we know how many players are standing in each ten-yard interval, we can determine how many men are behind Smith. It is $3 + 4 + 5 + 5 + 4 + 3 + 2 + 1$, or 27 men.

Now let us "stand" at the mean (the 50-yard line) of a normal distribution of scores and measure off segments of the base line of that curve with standard deviation units (similar to the ten-yard measuring sticks). Just as we knew how many men were to be found within each ten-yard segment of the football field, so, too, we know what percent of the people are expected to fall within the area cut off by each successive standard deviation unit in a normally distributed population. Therefore, we can locate a person's ex-

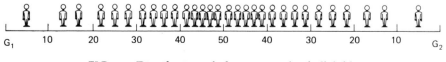
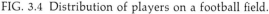

FIG. 3.4 Distribution of players on a football field.

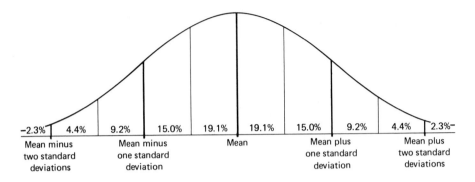

−2.3%	4.4%	9.2%	15.0%	19.1%	19.1%	15.0%	9.2%	4.4%	2.3%−

Mean minus two standard deviations   Mean minus one standard deviation   Mean   Mean plus one standard deviation   Mean plus two standard deviations

FIG. 3.5 Areas of the normal curve divided by units of one-half a standard deviation (percentages rounded to one decimal place).

pected rank in a group if we know how many standard deviations his score is above or below the mean. First, we find how many standard deviations from the mean the score is; second, we find how much of the area under the normal curve falls below that point. The area of the curve below the score is assumed to be proportional to the number of scores falling below that point. The normal curve, divided by units of half a standard deviation, is shown in Fig. 3.5. We shall now use this figure to solve the problem: How high is a given score?

Suppose I have a set of scores with a mean of 50 and a standard deviation of 10. The score on Bill Zee's test is 60. How high is Bill's score? We quickly see that this score is one standard deviation above the mean (50 + 10 = 60). If we now add all portions of the normal curve below this point, we can decide what percent of people who took the test can be expected to rank below Bill. The mean to plus one standard deviation gives us 19.1 + 15.0, and the area below the mean is 50 percent, i.e., 19.1 + 15.0 + 9.2 + 4.4 + 2.3. Thus, we find that 84.1 percent of the people taking the test had scores lower than Bill's. How does Mary Ecks' score of 45 on this test rank? Did you find 30.6 percent of the group below her? Since 45 is a half a standard deviation below the mean, adding the areas of the curve below that point gives us 30.6 percent.

We can now see how the standard deviation and the normal curve can be used to establish the relative position of a given score among a group of scores. But what if a score is not evenly divided by half a standard deviation unit? For example, suppose Bill Zee's score had been 63 rather than 60? Books on statistical procedures provide tables that can answer this question precisely. However, test users can often operate effectively with only general indications of a given person's status in the group. Figure 3.5 provides these general indications of status and is quite serviceable for much test-score interpretation.

When we began talking about computing a standard deviation by the short method, we noted the need for a reasonably symmetrical distribution of scores. It should now be noted that a symmetrical distribution is not necessarily a normal (or bell-shaped) curve and that to use the standard deviation in dividing up the area under the curve as we did in Fig. 3.5, we need a normal distribution. Symmetry alone will not suffice in this task. However, if the distribution of scores is reasonably bell-shaped, we can use this procedure to make a satisfactory estimate of a person's position in the group.

PROBLEMS

1. Backtown Middle School gave the Trickiletter Spelling Test to all eighth-grade students. The mean was 24; the standard deviation was 6. The distribution looks quite bell-shaped.
   a) John got a score of 30. What percent of the group will probably be below John on the spelling test?   (ans: 84.1)
   b) Mary got a score of 21. What percent of the group can be expected to be below Mary?   (ans: 30.9)
   c) What percent of the group can be expected to fall between John and Mary on the spelling test?   (ans: 53.2)

Percentile ranks

We have just seen how to identify the rank of a given score in a group by finding out what percent of the group has scores lower than the one being considered. We can go one step further by converting a given person's score to the percent of people who had lower scores and using this percentage as his score. Since tests are ranking devices, the actual score is not as important as is the position of the score in the group. In fact, we sometimes use a figure showing a person's rank rather than his actual score. When we identify a given score by the percent of people who had lower scores, this percent figure is called a *percentile rank*.

Although percentile ranks can be estimated from the normal curve, they become increasingly inaccurate as the distribution begins to depart noticeably from the bell shape. However, a procedure that is not tied to the bell-shaped curve is available for computing percentile ranks. Table 3.7 shows how this procedure is applied.

We shall begin with the lowest score in the distribution. The score of 52 is the midpoint of the interval 51.5 to 52.5. If we want the frequency of scores below the score 52, we begin at the midpoint of the interval, i.e., 52, and add all scores from that point down. We assume that scores in a given interval are equally spread throughout the interval, so the frequency of 1 in

TABLE 3.7 The procedure for computing percentile ranks

Scores	Frequency	Frequency— midpoint to midpoint	Cumulative frequency to midpoint	Percentile ranks
61	0			
60	2		29.0	97
59	3	2.5	26.5	88
58	5	4.0	22.5	75
57	2	3.5	19.0	63
56	10	6.0	13.0	43
55	4	7.0	6.0	20
54	2	3.0	3.0	10
53	1	1.5	1.5	5
52	1	1.0	.5	2
51	0	.5		
	30			

the interval 51.5 to 52.5 is split—half going in the lower half of the interval (51.5 to 52) and half going in the upper portion of the interval (52 to 52.5). Hence, the frequency below the score 52 is .5. Similarly, we divide the frequency in the next interval, 52.5 to 53.5. Half of its frequency (.5) is below 53; half above. The *cumulative* frequency below 53 is therefore 1.5, or half of the frequency in the interval 52.5 to 53.5, plus all frequencies below 52.5. If the data were grouped by the real limits of the intervals rather than by the scores, they would appear as in Table 3.8.

Once we have obtained the cumulative frequencies to the interval midpoints, we divide each of these cumulations by the total number of scores (in Table 3.7, it is 30) to give us a percentage of scores below each interval midpoint. This value is rounded to the nearest whole number and is called the *percentile rank*. In Table 3.7 the percentile rank for a score of 58 is 75, i.e., 75 percent of the group had scores lower than 58. For a score of 55 the percentile rank is 20; 20 percent of the group fell below 55.

You may have noticed that the highest score obtained by anyone, 62, has a percentile rank of 97, not 100. If percentile ranks are defined as the percent of people below a given score, the highest ranking person cannot be below himself; therefore, a percentile rank of 100 is impossible.

A percentile rank indicates status among the group of people who took the test, but it tells us nothing about quality of performance. A student with an arithmetic test percentile rank of 50 among a group of accelerated fifth graders is not to be compared with another student who had a percentile rank of 50 among a group of retarded youngsters. In interpreting a percen-

TABLE 3.8   The procedure for computing cumulative frequency

Scores	Frequency	Real limits and midpoints	Frequency above, below midpoint	Frequency from midpoint to midpoint	Cumulative frequencies
		54.5	1		
54	2	54.0			
		53.5	1 .5 }	1.5	3.0
53	1	53.0			
		52.5	.5 .5 }	1.0	1.5
52	1	52.0			
		51.5	.5 .0 }	.5	.5
51	0				

tile rank, therefore, it is very important to note the nature of the group from which the rank was determined.

Further, percentile ranks should not be confused with the percent of test questions answered correctly. If the highest ranking person in the group gets only 25 of 50 items correct, he will still receive a high percentile rank, probably in the 90s. Even though he got only half of the items correct, he still ranks above all other test takers. Percentile rank indicates status among people who have taken the test; it tells us nothing about proficiency.

Here is a word of caution about the use of percentile ranks: The addition or subtraction of percentile ranks may produce grossly misleading results, because percentile ranks do not represent equal units at all points along the scale. Ten percentile-rank units contain ten percent of the group tested. But, as Fig. 3.6 shows, ten percent at either end of the curve covers much more distance along the base line of the normal curve than it does at the center of the curve. We have as many percentile ranks between points A and B in Fig. 3.6 as we do between points C and D. It is clear that the ten ranks between A and B must have smaller units along the base line of the curve than do the ten ranks between C and D. Since percentile ranks are

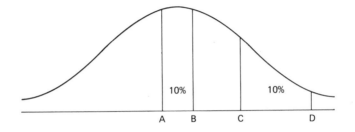

FIG. 3.6 Unequal base-line units for portions of area under the curve.

not equal units along the baseline of the distribution, they cannot be manipulated arithmetically.

For example, suppose we take the raw scores of three people from Table 3.7: 53, 54, and 58. To find the average score, we add the scores and divide by three. This average (55) converts to a percentile rank of 20. Now, if these raw scores had first been converted to percentile ranks (from Table 3.7) they would be 5, 10, and 75, and the sum divided by three would be 30. The percentile rank for the average of the three raw scores (20) is markedly different from the one we found by averaging the percentile ranks for the three scores (30). How, then, shall we deal arithmetically with percentile ranks? A safe procedure is to first convert the percentile ranks back to raw scores, where we may assume reasonable equality of units, do our arithmetic, and then convert the answer back to percentile ranks.

PROBLEMS

1.   I have given the Zyppidigit Arithmetic Test and have put the scores into the following distribution.

   a) Find the percentile rank for a score of 17.   (ans: 11th percentile rank)
   b) Find the percentile rank for a score of 22.   (ans: 61st percentile rank)

Score	Frequency	Frequency—midpoint to midpoint	Cumulative frequency to midpoint	Percentile rank (rounded)
28	1			
27	0			
26	1			
25	3			
24	3			
23	6			
22	3			
21	7			
20	5			
19	3			
18	2			
17	3			
16	1	1.0	2.5	
15	1	1.0	1.5	4
14	1	.5	.5	1
	40			

Standard scores*

When we applied the standard deviation to the normal curve, we first found out how many standard deviations a given score was above or below the mean. In effect, we were converting the raw score into units of the standard deviation. Since a score directly at the mean of the distribution does not vary from the mean any portion of a standard deviation, it has a converted value of zero; it is right at the starting point, namely, the mean. A score one standard deviation above the mean converts to +1 in units of the standard deviation; a score one standard deviation below the mean has a converted score of −1, etc. Scores converted to standard deviation units are often called z- scores.

But an origin of zero and the use of pluses and minuses are awkward for many people to manipulate. Therefore, many test makers use a score conversion that makes the test mean equal to a converted score of 50 and the standard deviation equal to 10. In this scale, known as the T-scale, the mean of the raw score is given a value of 50; a score one standard deviation above the mean has a T-score value of 60; a score one-half standard deviation below the mean has a T-score value of 45 (half of 10, or 5, below 50).

For example, suppose we gave a test of 30 spelling words. The highest score was 27 words correct; the lowest, 8 words correct. The mean was 18; the standard deviation, 4. Mary Wye got 22 words correct. She is one standard deviation above the mean. Her T-scale score would be 60, i.e., 50 plus a standard deviation of 10 points. If we are dealing with a normal distribution of scores, that one standard deviation above the mean leaves about 84 percent of the group below that point. What percent of the spellers had scores below a T-score of 60? You should have said 84 percent, since a T-score of 60 has a percentile rank of 84. (We probably should note here, however, that we need not have a normal curve to compute T-scores. But if we want to find percentages of the group below a given T-value, we must assume a normal distribution.)

Bill Zee got only 12 words correct on the test above. What is his T-score? His raw score is one and a half standard deviations below the mean, which on the T-scale converts to 10 plus 5 points below the mean of 50. Bill's T-score is therefore 35. Again, if we are working with normally distributed data, we know that one and a half standard deviations below the mean leaves only 6.7 percent of the group below that point. This puts a T-score of 35 at about the 7th percentile rank.

---

* Scoring procedures associated with a given type of test—e.g., IQ with general-aptitude tests, grade norms with achievement tests—will be discussed when the appropriate tests are presented.

Actually, we can set our test mean and standard deviation equal to any values we want to and convert our test scores to a scale based on these values. For example, the College Entrance Examination Board set the mean at 500 and the standard deviation at 100 for the subtests in the early form of the *Scholastic Aptitude Tests.* Figure 3.7 shows the normal curve with standard deviation units, percentile ranks, and *T*-scores so that equivalent values may be noted and so that converted scores may be evaluated in terms of what they tell us about status in the group.

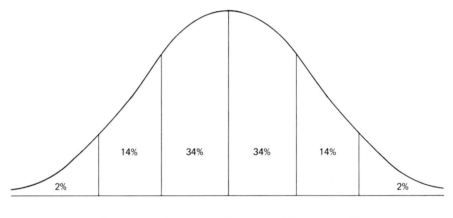

FIG. 3.7 Conversion of scores from one standard-score system to another.

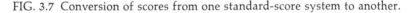

PROBLEMS

1. I have computed a mean of 25 for my test and a standard deviation of 4.

   a) What is the *T*-score equivalent of a score of 33?   (ans: 70)
   b) What is the *T*-score equivalent of a score of 19?   (ans: 35)

2. My *T*-score for an aptitude test was 40. Assuming that the scores were distributed normally, what percent of the group should score lower than me? (Hint: How many standard deviations below the *T*-score mean is a *T*-score of 40? Then consult Fig. 3.5.)   (ans: 15.9)

Stanines

An increasingly popular method of reporting scores is the use of stanine* units. Here, the base line of a distribution of scores is divided into nine units labelled one through nine. By moving one-fourth of a standard deviation above and below the mean, we cut off the middle, or fifth, stanine. The remaining stanines follow in one-half standard deviation units above and below this central location, as shown in Fig. 3.8.

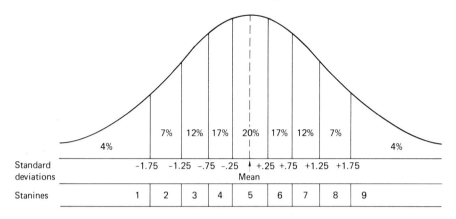

FIG. 3.8 Deriving stanines from standard deviation units.

A criticism of the use of stanines is that if the range of scores is greater than nine (it typically is), several scores go into each stanine band. The finer discriminations that could be made between individuals may therefore be masked by grouping people under one stanine when in fact they do not all have identical scores on the test. For example, on an intelligence test we would expect the fifth stanine to include the IQ scores 96 through 104. Any score in this range would receive a stanine of 5. If a score of 96 reflects even a slightly different quality of mental performance from a score of 104, this may be useful in making decisions about people with those scores. However, if we assign the stanine 5 to everyone in this range, we deprive ourselves of the use of this difference in judging quality of performance.

However, this criticism of stanines is often unimportant; in many situations the slight differences between people with adjacent scores on an intelligence test—98, 99, 100—are of no consequence in making decisions about a given task we want the individuals to perform. Here, stanines are quite useful in spite of the fact that they obscure minor differences among children in test performance. For example, we cannot say that a child with an IQ of 100 will learn to read at a slower rate than will a child with an IQ of

---

* Pronounced STAY-nine.

104, and we therefore use the same teaching approach with both children. Similarly, giving both children a stanine score of 5 does not lead us to change our approach to the teaching of reading to these two children any more than it would if we knew that one child had an IQ of 100 and the other, 104.

A convenience of stanines is that a small, one-digit number is easy to record and relatively simple to interpret. Also, it is often easier for persons unfamiliar with statistical procedures to perceive the relative position of a student on a nine-point scale than on a more complex scale such as the T-scale. In addition, stanines can be used in arithmetical manipulations without first converting them to raw data.

COMPARING SCORES

If the same group of students has taken several tests, we often wish to compare a given student's performance on Tests A, B, and C. Raw scores are not satisfactory for achieving this comparison. For example, how does Bill Aye's score of 12 correct spelling words compare with his 18 correct arithmetic problems? Before we can make this comparison, we need to know what the average performance for the group is and how widely spread out the scores are for each test. Only then can we say something about how 12 ranks among the spelling scores and how 18 ranks among the arithmetic scores. Then we can compare ranks. If we convert scores from both of these tests to a standard score scheme, such as T-scales, or stanines, we would: (a) put the two test means at a common point (50 for the T-scale and 5 for stanines); and (b) compare the scores by the number of standard-deviation units above or below the mean they were. A convenient formula for applying the T-scale to this problem is

$$T = \left(\frac{X - \overline{X}}{\sigma}\right) 10 + 50. \qquad (3.1)$$

Here, X is the person's raw score on a given test, $\overline{X}$ is the mean in raw scores for that test, and σ is the standard deviation. Suppose we found that the mean on our spelling test was 15 and the standard deviation was 3. Applying Formula 3.1 to Bill Aye's spelling score of 12, we would have

$$T = \left(\frac{12 - 15}{3}\right) 10 + 50$$

$$= 40.$$

Now, suppose the arithmetic test had a mean of 21 and a standard deviation of 6. Bill Aye's score on this test was 18. By Formula 3.1, his T-

score would be

$$T = \left(\frac{18 - 21}{6}\right) 10 + 50$$

$$= \ 45.$$

We can already see that Bill's score of 18 in arithmetic ranks higher among the scores of the class than does his score of 12 on the spelling test. We were able to reach this conclusion by comparing his T-scores of 45 and 40.

If we can assume that our distributions are normal, we can carry our comparison of scores one step further. By referring to Fig. 3.5, we see that about 30 percent of the group rank below the arithmetic T-score of 45, compared to the 16 percent below the spelling T-score of 40. Now we can compare scores on the basis of their ranks within the group. Raw scores alone do not allow us to make this comparison, but standard scoring schemes do. We must note, however, that if we wish to compare two scores by converting them to standard scores, both tests must have been administered to the same group of students. In the example above, we can compare Bill's arithmetic and spelling scores only if the same group of children has taken both tests.

SUMMARY

A test score by itself really has little meaning. Therefore, we employ various statistical procedures to help us relate a given person's score to a collection of scores from many people. In this manner we can make a variety of statements about how one individual's behavior ranks in comparison with that of other individuals.

Typically, we are interested in an indicator of "average" and of the spread of scores. For the average, we generally use the mean or the median. The mean is the sum of the scores divided by the number of scores, whereas the median is the point above and below which half the scores lie. The standard deviation is the most common indicator of the spread, or dispersion, of scores. We use it as a "yardstick" to measure how far a given score lies above or below the mean for the group. In conjunction with knowledge about the normal curve, we can use the standard deviation to estimate what portion of the group will have scores below (or above) a given value.

We often use various score conversions in an attempt to make a raw score more meaningful. Three common converted scores are percentile ranks, T-scores, and stanines. A percentile rank converts the score to a value equal to the percentage of cases that fall below it. A T-score equates the mean of the group to 50 and the standard deviation to 10. A score that stands one standard deviation above the mean is 60 on the T-score scale (50 + 10); one standard deviation below the mean is 40, i.e., (50 − 10), etc.

Stanines divide the base line of the distribution into nine units. A stanine of 5 is in the center of the distribution. Stanines clump several adjacent score values together to make up a unit; this tends to reduce our ability to make fine discriminations, but usually this does not affect how we teach children in schools.

The statistical procedures presented here are the minimum for dealing with test scores. You should not proceed further until you have mastered these few statistical techniques. When scores such as IQ for intelligence tests and grade placements on achievement tests are discussed in the chapters ahead, the ideas presented here will be required if you are to get maximum information from your use of tests.

REFERENCES

Chase, Clinton I. *Elementary Statistical Procedures,* New York: McGraw-Hill, 1967, pp. 245.

Ferguson, Geor. A. *Statistical Analysis in Psychology and Education,* 3rd ed., New York: McGraw-Hill, 1971, Part 1.

Guilford, J. P. *Fundamental Statistics for Psychology and Education,* 4th ed., New York, McGraw-Hill, 1965.

Lathrop, R. L. "A quick but accurate approximation to the standard deviation of a distribution," *Journal of Experimental Education,* **29** (March 1961): 319–321.

Lyman, Howard B. *Test Scores and What They Mean,* 2nd ed., Englewood Cliffs, N.J.: Prentice-Hall, 1971, p. 200.

Mason, G. P. and R. E. Odeh. "A short-cut formula for standard deviation," *Journal of Educational Measurement,* **5** (Winter 1968): 319–320.

Sabers, Darrell L. and Richard Klausmeier. "Accuracy of short-cut estimates for standard deviations," *Journal of Educational Measurement,* **8** (1971): 335–339.

Stanley, Julian C. and Kenneth D. Hopkins. *Educational and Psychological Measurement and Evaluation,* Englewood Cliffs, N.J.: Prentice-Hall, 1972, p. 520, Ch. 2.

CHAPTER 4

CHARACTERISTICS
OF A GOOD TEST

Educational tests are instruments designed to provide data relevant to making practical decisions. Therefore, good tests should have the following characteristics: they should allow us to make useful decisions about a given question; the data produced should be consistent, i.e., stable, hence dependable; and the data should be easy to secure. An example will illustrate how the requirements of good tests are the same as those we impose on any data source in making real-life decisions.

Suppose you are standing on a Chicago street corner on a warm spring day. You are waiting for the traffic light to change to green so that you may cross the street. Mr. Ecks is also standing on the corner and is taking pictures of the city street scene with his movie camera. He has carefully noted the light intensity on his meter and has set the focus of his camera for maximum depth of field. Suddenly, a car (we'll call it car A) darts into the intersection through the red light and strikes a second car (car B) that was moving with the green light. You saw the accident, and Mr. Ecks recorded it in his camera.

A policeman is now at the scene and is questioning the witnesses. You report that you believe car A came through the red light and struck car B. You think car B had the right of way, but you are not absolutely certain. Mr. Ecks, who stood on the corner with you, has offered his film as evidence, but first it must be developed and projected. The policeman again asks you to tell what you saw. The driver of car A is now standing beside you. He is tall and muscular and looks very angry. This boggles your memory, and you finally report to the officer that you cannot say with any certainty what happened. At this point Mr. Ecks goes home to develop his film. Soon he is at the police station with the film. He runs it through the projector twice, each time showing that car A did indeed pass through the red light and that car B had the right of way.

How is all this tied to measurement theory? We often must make decisions, but impressions that are influenced by irrelevant variables cannot be relied upon as a basis for making good judgments. We need other data, but they must indeed represent the relevant variable and must do so consistently. Your testimony in Chicago was of little use in reporting the accident because you could not accurately represent the facts and your story changed with repetition. However, the film produced by Ecks showed the conditions of the event as they occurred (albeit from a single vantage point) and showed these conditions the same way each time it was projected.

These are the characteristics we want in a test. We want it to be an accurate representation of the variable (intelligence, interest, etc.) we are observing; we want the results of the test to be consistent on two or more applications; and we want to collect the data as conveniently as possible. These three characteristics of a good test are, respectively: validity, reliability, and employability.

VALIDITY

There are a number of definitions of validity, but most of these present essentially the same idea. A test is valid to the extent to which it provides truthful information about people in regard to a specified class of behaviors.* For example, an intelligence test is valid to the extent that it tells us the truth about an individual's capacity to perform intelligent acts. A mechanical-aptitude test is valid to the extent that it tells us about one's ability to acquire the manipulative skills we define as mechanical. Since we sort behavior into a variety of categories, a test is valid for measuring a given category of behavior to the extent that it truly describes one's capacity to perform in this category.

If children in a classroom have different general aptitudes, a valid test of intelligence will provide data that will help us assign each child to learning tasks appropriate to his ability to accomplish them. A valid test of general anxiety would probably present a second ranking of these children. This time the ranking of scores would help us to make effective judgments about the children's feelings of anxiety.

It should also be noted that tests are not simply valid or invalid. Validity is a matter of degree. For example, suppose we have two intelligence tests—A and B. We discover that Test A has often provided scores that

---

* For an enlightening discussion of definitions of validity, see Robert Ebel, "Must all tests be valid?" *American Psychologist*, **16** 1961: 640–647.

Also note: *Standards for educational and psychological tests,* Washington, D.C.; *American Psychological Association,* 1966, pp. 12–24, and Lee J. Cronback, "Validation of Educational Measurements," *Proceedings of the 1969 Invitation Conference on Testing Problems,* Princeton, N.J.: Educational Testing Service, pp. 35–52.

relate more closely to achievement in complex learning tasks than has Test B. Shall we say that Test A is valid and Test B is invalid? No, both have degrees of validity, but Test A is more valid than Test B.

To be valid, a test does not have to measure a trait directly. The rankings of people on the test only have to correspond with some useful ranking of people about whom a decision is to be made. For example, intelligence is often defined as the ability to learn, but few test items assess learning in progress. Instead, they rely heavily on the ability of people to recall what they have already learned. The reason for this is that a person's ranking on what he has already learned (relative to age) has been shown to correspond moderately well with ability to learn in the future. Thus, although the test does not measure directly what it purports to measure, it does provide useful data for ranking people on the trait about which we wish to make decisions.

Validity is sometimes defined as the extent to which a test measures what it is supposed to. Under this definition, a test is administered, and the results are compared to the person's actual performance of the trait being measured. This definition conveys the idea of validity, but operationally, it is not very helpful. It assumes that we have some means available of measuring exactly the trait the test is supposed to assess. This is likely not to be true. For example, against what data can I compare the results of an intelligence test to see how well they reflect the "supposed to" trait? School success is not merely a matter of intelligence, nor is success in an occupation. The available criteria against which we may compare our test are in no case complete measures of the trait, unadulterated by irrelevant variables. Therefore, we cannot know to what extent our test measures intelligence because no criterion against which we might compare the test results is exactly measuring intelligence. But if I want to predict how well John will learn to read, an intelligence test may help me make a reasonably good prediction of John's success. To this end the test is useful and has a degree of validity.

There are several ways to determine the validity of a test. The most commonly used procedures are: (1) criterion-related, (2) content, and (3) construct validation.

Criterion-related validity

Criterion-related validation, also called empirical validation, is the process of comparing peoples' test-score rankings with one based on actual performance on a criterion task. For example, Joe's Machine Shop wants to try out a test purported to show mechanical ability. Joe administers the test to job applicants, puts them on the job, and then compares the test scores with ratings given by the new employees' foreman. Miss Smith's Secretarial School wants to use a test to admit students to the typing program. A

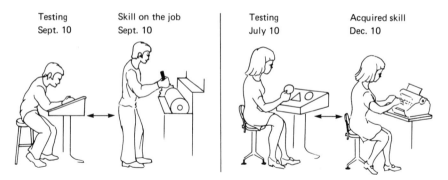

FIG. 4.1 Criterion-related validity.

finger-dexterity test is given to the applicants, and the students' rankings on the test are compared with their rankings in speed and accuracy on the typewriter six months later. To the extent that the tests are valid, Joe's employees will be ranked similarly by both the test and the foreman; Miss Smith's students will be placed in similar order by both the test and their six months' achievement. These two examples are illustrated in Fig. 4.1.

At this point we should note that questions for tests based on criterion-related validity are selected because the persons who rate high on the criterion, e.g., job performance, mark them differently from persons who rate low. The subject of the item is of little importance as long as high- and low-criterion people mark it differently. For example, suppose one item on a college-aptitude test is "Do you prefer blue to red?" If students who do well in college say "yes" and those who do poorly in college say "no," this is a good item for predicting college success, despite its seemingly irrelevant content. Some test critics do not understand this point.

Another very important consideration is that tests sometimes fail to correspond with a criterion because the tests have been poorly developed. But even good test rankings cannot be expected to show correspondence with the criterion ranking if the criterion ranking itself is inaccurate or invalid. If the foreman ranks his men carelessly and capriciously, even the best test cannot be expected to correspond with job rankings. If the teachers at Miss Smith's Secretarial School are careless graders who are influenced more by the personality of the student than by her achievement, no test will correlate with the school's achievement indicators. Therefore, before we conduct an empirical validation of a test, it is essential to have an exceedingly well-prepared procedure for assessing criterion performance.

Some tests are built to identify present abilities or other behaviors, whereas other tests attempt to predict what behavior will be like at some future time. Whichever objective we have in mind, the validation of our test should correspond with the way the test will be used. The comparison of test rankings with immediate criterion performance is often referred to as *concurrent validity*; the comparison of test rankings with some future criterion performance is called *predictive validity*. The procedures for these comparisons are essentially the same, but the testing objective is different. The objective of concurrent-validation testing is to rank people according to their present capability or mode of behavior. The objective of predictive validation, on the other hand, is to rank people in the same way they will be ranked by the criterion at some future date.

Joe's mechanical-ability test is an example of concurrent validation, since it was used to identify present proficiency. If we want to know what ability a person has on a particular date, we look for concurrent validity. Miss Smith's test is an example of predictive validity because a period of training was completed before the criterion ranking was established. A test that has concurrent validity will not necessarily have predictive validity and vice versa. In selecting a test, therefore, we must be careful to note whether the type of validity reported for the test (concurrent or predictive) corresponds with the objective we have in mind.

PROBLEMS

1. I have built a test that is supposed to rank young people on their ability to become good retail salesmen.
   a) Should this test be based on predictive or concurrent validation? Why?
   b) What criterion measure should I apply? When?
   c) What hazards may arise in attempting to establish a valid criterion measure? How might this affect my test's validity?
2. I want to build a test or tests that will help me select the "best" students to be admitted to a teacher-training program.
   a) How can I develop a test based on concurrent validity?
   b) How can I develop a test based on predictive validity?

CORRELATION AND CRITERION-RELATED VALIDITY

The statistical procedure for establishing the extent of relationship between a test and criterion rankings is known as correlation, and the resulting figure is a correlation coefficient (symbolized by r). The correlation procedure is used in many kinds of statistical problems. When we use it to show the relationship between test scores and criterion ranking, we call r a *coefficient of validity*. The relationship between the test and the criterion is indicated by a number somewhere in the range from -1.00 to $.00$ to $+1.00$. A positive

TABLE 4.1   Test rankings, job ratings, and correlation coefficients

| (a) | | | (b) | | | (c) | | | (d) | | |
Name	Test rank	Job rating	Name	Test rank	Job rating	Name	Test rank	Job rating	Name	Test rank	Job rating
Joe	1	1	Joy	1	2	Jim	1	5	Bud	1	4
Jim	2	2	Ben	2	1	Dan	2	4	Nan	2	5
Ann	3	3	Dee	3	5	Ann	3	3	Ben	3	2
Sue	4	4	Mac	4	3	Buzz	4	2	Al	4	3
Val	5	5	Flo	5	4	Nan	5	1	Joy	5	1
	$r = 1.00$			$r = .60$			$r = -1.00$			$r = -.80$	

coefficient means that people with higher test scores also tend to have higher criterion scores, whereas people with lower test scores tend to have lower criterion scores. A coefficient of +1.00 means that the test rankings are in the identical order of the criterion rankings, as shown in Table 4.1(a). These data have also been plotted in Fig. 4.2(a), where we find the test rank on the horizontal axis and the job rating on the vertical axis. The point of intersect is then plotted. In Fig. 4.2(a) the plots fall in a straight line, as is always true when $r = 1.00$.

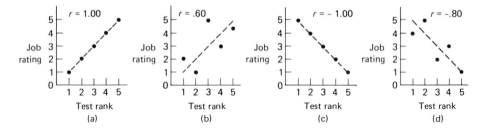

FIG. 4.2 Plotting the data that lead to correlation coefficients of various values.

But typically, we find validity coefficients somewhat smaller than +1.00, usually between .40 and .60. A figure in this general range means that as test scores increase, criterion rankings also tend to get larger, but the correspondence between test and criterion rankings is somewhat less than perfect, as shown in Table 4.1(b). These data are also plotted in Fig. 4.2(b). Here, we see the plots begin to deviate from the straight-line order of Fig. 4.2(a), but as test ranks get higher, job ratings tend to also, but the relationship is less than perfect. The closer r comes to .00, the more widely the plot deviates from a linear order.

A correlation coefficient of −1.00 means that as we find higher and higher test scores, we find lower and lower criterion scores and vice versa.

This is illustrated in Table 4.1(c) and Fig. 4.2(c). Typically, negative correlations are not a perfect −1.00, since this would mean that the test ranked the students in the exact reverse of the criterion rankings. Reverse rankings can be as useful as direct rankings, even though their coefficients of correlation are not likely to approach −1.00. Correlations in the midrange between .00 and −1.00 indicate a reverse relationship (though not completely so) between the test and criterion, as shown in Table 4.1(d) and Fig. 4.2(d).

As coefficients approach .00, the correspondence between test and criterion ranking becomes increasingly random. At exactly .00, knowledge of test scores tells us absolutely nothing about the criterion ranking. Therefore, a .00 validity coefficient, or one approaching zero from either the positive or negative side, indicates that our test is of no value in identifying the probable rank of test takers on the criterion.*

We can interpret the validity coefficient in several ways, but only one procedure will be noted here. Other ways will be applied later to specific tests.

A given person's test score is likely to deviate above or below the average. If two sets of scores (e.g., test and criterion) change together, we say that they have common variance. By common variance we mean that at least a portion of a test score's deviation from the test mean is reflected by a similar deviation in the person's criterion score from the criterion mean. For example, imagine that John Aye is one standard deviation above the mean on a given test and that the correlation between the test and criterion is moderately high, e.g., .80. With this correlation we expect that a portion of John's deviation above the mean on the test is matched by a similar deviation above the mean on the criterion ranking. In other words, if John's test score is one standard deviation above the mean, we expect that his job rating will also be in the vicinity of one standard deviation above the mean. The higher the correlation, the more nearly test-score deviation and criterion-rank deviation will be equal.

What constitutes an adequately large validity coefficient depends on our purpose for using the test. If we are trying to find the typical performance of a group, the students' scores that are overestimates of actual ability tend to average out with the scores that are underestimates. Therefore, we can tolerate lower validity coefficients (in the vicinity of, say, .45) for estimating *group* characteristics relevant to some criterion. However, if we are making judgments about individuals, we cannot depend on averages to compensate for errors. We have only one score; therefore, our test must rank that person on the criterion with considerable accuracy. Unless

---

* A simplified procedure for computing a correlation coefficient is given in Appendix A.

our tests have relatively large validity coefficients (i.e., above .70), we use them with added caution and look seriously for corroborating evidence in making decisions about single individuals.

Typical validity coefficients found in test manuals are likely to run somewhere between .35 and .80. Tests with low validity coefficients may be useful if we have no other information on which to base our judgments, but we must be aware that test scores and criterion rankings that correlate in the vicinity of .35 correspond with each other rather poorly. We will make many mistakes using these tests, but we will make better judgments than if we had no information at all. However, we can reduce the number of mistaken judgments noticeably if our test scores correlate with ranks on a relevant criterion at about .70 or higher.

PROBLEMS

1. I have a test on which the scores correlate .50 with freshman grades in college and −.60 with sales records of used-car salesmen after six months on the job.
    a) What does the minus sign in the coefficient mean for car salesmen?
    b) Will the test select potentially successful used-car salesmen more, or less, accurately than it selects successful college freshmen? Why do you say this?
2. For each situation below, decide whether the test is likely to be suitable for estimating average group performance only, or for either group or individual performance, and under what conditions.
    a) The correlation between an intelligence test and grades in a sewing class is .35.
    b) The validity coefficient for a college aptitude test, with freshman grades as a criterion, is .60.
    c) The validity coefficient for a personality test, with ratings of success in therapy is .76.

One tool through which we make use of criterion-related validity data is the expectancy table. Although there are a variety of procedures for laying out these tables (Schrader 1965), a typical one is a two-dimensional table with test scores on one axis and criterion scores on the other. In the body of the table, we record the percentage of people in a given test-score range who also fall within a given criterion-score range. A hypothetical example is given in Fig. 4.3. Here, IQ scores for high school freshmen are given on the horizontal axis, and grade-point averages for the end of the senior year are given on the vertical axis.

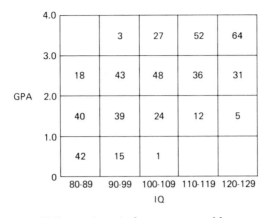

FIG. 4.3 A typical expectancy table.

Suppose we have a freshman whose IQ is 96. This falls in the range of 90 to 99. How will he turn out as a senior? The column of percentages cut off by IQs 90 to 99 tells us what portion of the freshmen in that IQ range in the past ended up with given grade-point averages (GPA). For example, 39 percent of freshmen with IQs between 90 and 99 had GPAs between 1.0 and 2.0; 43 percent had GPAs between 2.0 and 3.0, etc.

The expectancy table allows us to state (in terms of percentages) the likelihood of getting a particular GPA, given the student's IQ. These statements about students are based on the correspondence between test scores and criterion scores. If the validity coefficient is high, test scores plotted against a criterion score tend to fall in a narrow range around a straight line (see Fig. 4.2 again). Therefore, if test-criterion correlations are high, students in a given test-score category tend to bunch into one or two criterion categories on the expectancy table. These categories move to successively higher criterion levels as we move up on the test scale. Hence, the accuracy of our predictions based on the expectancy table will be greater than if we have lower validity coefficients.

It should be pointed out, however, that an expectancy table does not allow one to identify the performance of a particular individual. For example, if John Wye has an IQ of 102, will he be one of the 24 percent (in Fig. 4.3) who gets a GPA between 1.0 and 2.0? Or will he be one of the 27 percent above 3.0? I cannot say from the table. Almost half of the people with IQs similar to John's will fall between 2.0 and 3.0, and that is a favored betting range, but a few students will fall outside this most likely category. Will John? Our table does not tell us. It does, however, allow us to make useful predictions of student performance, especially in the absence of more precise means of prediction.

Content validity*

Imagine for a moment that you are looking at a map of California. You see that San Francisco is clearly represented in bold type, but Los Angeles is a mere dot identified by very small type. Death Valley is pictured as encompassing a large segment of the southern part of the state, but the Yosemite Valley is not even listed. Similarly, the Sierra Mountain Range is briefly sketched in and identified in small type, whereas the Sacramento Mountains appear huge and are conspicuously labeled.

A quick glance at this map would bring utterances of amazement from any school boy. The map simply is not an accurate representation of the terrain within the borders of California. It is not a useful, or valid, picture of the state because it has not sampled the geographic characteristics of the state relevant to their status in this commonwealth.

Keeping these details in mind, we now turn to Mr. Zee's American history class, which has just finished a unit on the role of the western frontier in the development of the United States. Mr. Zee now has prepared an essay test consisting of four questions to cover the unit: the first deals with Mormonism in Utah; the second, with Fremont's military activity in California; the third deals with ocean transportation around Cape Horn to the western states; and the last question has to do with the relationship between the demands of the Crimean War and the development of western agriculture.

The school boy takes Mr. Zee's test without the exclamation of incredulity he demonstrated when faced with our map of California. Yet Mr. Zee's test is as invalid a representation of the "academic terrain" of a unit on the role of the west in American history as was our map of California's "physical terrain."

This brings us to the concept of content validity. Content validity is reflected in the degree to which a test is a representative sampling of a segment of the behavioral domain we wish to assess. For example, the content of a classroom test should reflect the content of instruction. Significant objectives of instruction receive the greatest attention on the test; less significant outcomes appear less conspicuously on the test. Just as a valid map represents the characteristics of geography in relation to their stature on the terrain, so an achievement test with content validity represents the outcomes of instruction in terms of the relative emphasis they held in the teaching of the topic.

---

* For additional discussion of this topic, see Stanley, Julian C. and Kenneth D. Hopkins. *Educational and Psychological Measurement and Evaluation*, Englewood Cliffs, N.J.: Prentice-Hall, 1972, Chapter 4.

It is not a simple thing to map out a test for a given program of instruction. Several writers have provided a guide for classifying teaching outcomes. One popular guide was developed by Bloom *et al.* (1956) in the *Taxonomy of Educational Objectives*. This guide lays out a framework around which instruction can be built and test items can be devised to appropriately assess the outcomes of teaching. Bloom presents six classes of outcomes that are excellent guides for planning a course of study so that the test accurately reflects the objectives sought by the teacher. These six classes are as follows:

Class or category	*Related behaviors*
1. *Knowledge*—specifics, steps in dealing with specifics, stated principles and rules	Defines common terms, identifies objects, lists, gives sequence of acts, states rule to explain
2. *Comprehension*—translation from one symbol system to another, interpretation, extrapolation	States in own words, converts from words to a formula, infers, predicts, explains
3. *Application*—in problematic situations will draw upon the appropriate facts, principles, etc., for solutions	Explains relation of principles to practical situations, produces objects or procedures, solves problems, organizes for given purpose
4. *Analysis*—breakdown of objects and situations into their elements, showing basic relationships, seeing organizational principle	Differentiates, recognizes inferences and supporting facts, breaks down objects or ideas into components, identifies relevant and irrelevant components
5. *Synthesis*—putting together knowledge to produce unique communication, a new plan, or a new set of operations, or building a set of abstract relations	Develops a creative product, combines elements to produce plans or materials, restructures, reorders ideas or objects to produce unique product
6. *Evaluation*—judgments on the value of ideas, acts, solutions, materials, in reference to some objective or criterion	Judges adequacy of a plan of action, appraises product, critically evaluates, justifies organization of ideas or materials, supports a plan of action

Armed with these classes of educational outcomes, we are now ready to set up our technique for instructional mapping to produce a test that has maximum content validity. As we read through the taxonomy, we note that the typical classroom test deals heavily with the first two levels, whereas the demand of everyday life tends to require behavior at levels 3 through 6.

The basic procedure for applying the taxonomy to the planning of a course involves building a grid. The topics of instruction are listed on one axis of the grid; the levels of the taxonomy are listed on the other. Figure 4.4 shows a grid for a unit in basic fractions.

Within each cell of the grid, we can now list whatever instructional outcomes we expect. There are certain basic facts, sequential steps, etc., in each of the units we have taught. We can list them now. There are also certain translations and interpretations to be made for each topic. We can now list these. Following this procedure, we can complete the list of behaviors we expect the students to have acquired throughout all levels of the taxonomy and across all topics of instruction. These steps are only good teaching practice in planning a course of instruction and require no more than what a competent teacher typically puts into lesson-planning, i.e., they are a listing of the processes instruction is intended to promote. Without such a listing it is difficult to either speculate about the outcomes of our instructional effort or build tests that assess these outcomes.

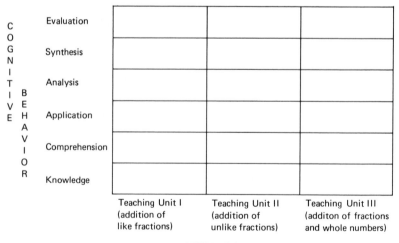

FIG. 4.4 Grid for applying taxonomy of objectives to planning a unit of instruction.

At this point we can count the number of topics in each row and column of our table in order to determine the proportion of test items for each topic and for each level on the taxonomy. Since we now have a view of the "academic terrain" of which our test is a "map," we are ready to begin constructing a test that will correspond with the terrain. The salient content will receive much attention on the test, the less important items will receive peripheral attention. To the extent that our test represents the outcomes of instruction in relation to their emphasis in the teaching process, our test, whether standardized or teacher-made, has content validity.

The procedures for establishing content validity are typically applied to achievement tests. Test makers go to some length to identify topics in their course content analysis. They survey the widely used textbooks in the field, they look at state and local study guides for appropriate courses, they collect opinions of teachers who teach these courses, and they note reports of professional study groups that have recently examined a given curriculum area. With this body of information on hand, they are ready to start mapping the content of instruction upon which the test will be built.

Typically, commercial test makers include material that is most common to the variety of sources they have surveyed, i.e., they use the most common components that have been found in study guides, textbooks, teachers' reports, etc. Less common topics may be sampled on many achievement tests, but such items are few in number. It should therefore be clear that typical achievement tests are based heavily on the central core of course content. Since a content-valid test should bear a high level of correspondence to teaching, it should also be clear that a given standardized achievement test is likely to have only a moderate level of content validity for a given school program. For this reason, standardized tests are neither extensive assessments of a given child's knowledge nor an accurate reflection of a given teacher's skill.

Some of the emerging instructional management procedures, e.g., the open classroom, place much emphasis on individualization of instruction. Here, traditional classroom tests are given only a minor role in assessing student progress. But children are learning; their ideas, attitudes, and values are changing. Teachers are continually assessing these changes in order to adapt materials to various skill levels observed in the class. As in the formal teaching methods, a systematized plan, modeled after the taxonomy of educational outcomes, can also improve the relatively informal inventorying of skills carried out by teachers using the less highly structured, individualized teaching methods. Student-teacher conferences provide most information when they are planned. The informal questioning that goes into these conferences should explore all levels of the child's achievement. Without a guide such as the taxonomy, teachers may inadvertently ignore some levels of the child's cognitive behavior.

So far, we have talked only about a *logical* approach to content validity, and our discussion has been limited to achievement testing. A second approach—used primarily in identifying the content of aptitude tests, personality, and interest inventories—is found in the *factor analysis* of the test.* Factor analysis is a statistical approach to the sorting of component abilities that go into a group of performances. In looking over a cake recipe, for example, we can probably sort out the components as liquids, leaveners, binders, and flavorings. Each of these components has a clear, unique characteristic that distinguishes it from the other components, but the items that constitute a given component all have the common trait of the component. Similarly, in analyzing the behaviors that are required by a test, we see that groups of behaviors can be classified according to some component operation. Thus, each factor that is sorted out by factor analysis represents a category of behaviors distinct from those that characterize other factors. Together, the factors are the component ingredients in the test performance. Factors, then, are categories of behavior that underlie test-sampled behavior. Factor analysis is a statistical procedure for identifying these categories. For example, in a test of arithmetic problems, we may discover by factor analysis that the behaviors assessed by this test could all be classified under three underlying categories—verbal ability, number ability, and reasoning. Such categories are called factors.

If a test item correlates with a factor, we say that the item "loads" on the factor; the correlation of the item with the factor is called the *factor loading*. Since more than one component of behavior may go into the solution of a given test item, a given item may load on more than one factor. For example, in doing an arithmetic problem, the student must have some verbal abilities as well as some number abilities. If these are two, distinct components of behavior, that arithmetic problem could correlate with, or load on, both a verbal and a number factor. It should be noted that the factor loadings reported in standardized test manuals are correlation coefficients and may be interpreted just as any other correlation coefficient.

There are three types of factors typically observed in factorial validity studies: the general factor, the group factor, and the specific factor. A general factor is one that pervades all items on the test, that is, all items correlate with this factor. It is represented in Fig. 4.5(a). Here, three separate test items all assess a common component of behavior. The group factor is characterized by having two or more (but not all) test items, loading on the factor, as shown in Fig. 4.5(b). Here, two items have a common component,

---

* Helmstadter (1964, Chapter 4) has described factor analysis as a content-validation procedure, and his reasoning is followed in this text. We shall cite factor analysis again in our discussion of construct validity.

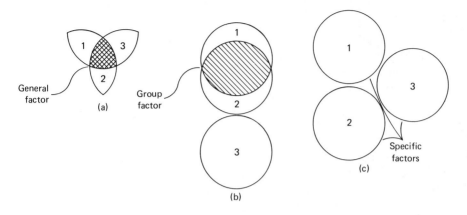

FIG. 4.5 Types of factors: (a) general; (b) group; (c) specific.

but the third item is independent. A specific factor is one in which a single item loads all by itself, as shown in Fig. 4.5(c), where each of the three items assesses behavior independently of the other two.

Actually, the three types of factors often appear together. For example, in a factor analysis we may identify a general factor and three group factors, as in Fig. 4.6(a), or only two group factors as in Fig. 4.6(b), or some similar combination of factor types.

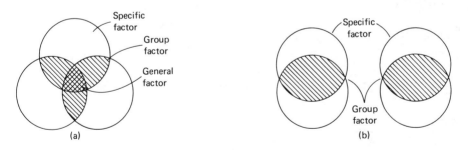

FIG. 4.6 Factor analysis: (a) general, group, and specific factors; (b) group and specific factors.

A completed factor analysis is given in Table 4.2. The test items are listed on the left. The correlations (loadings) of the items with the first factor (I) are in the first column of numbers, and the correlations with the second (II) and third (III) factors are in the next two columns, respectively.

TABLE 4.2   Results of a hypothetical factor analysis*

Test item	I	II	III
1. $4 + 5 =$	.32	.60	.07
2. $8 \times 1/3 =$	.40	.71	.10
3. Ubiquitous means ————.	.38	.06	.64
4. Hand is to glove as ———— is to shoe.	.30	.09	.50

* A factor analysis should include many more than four items.

This factor analysis shows all test items loading on (correlating with) the first factor; hence, it is a general factor. Only the first two items load well on the second factor, and only the last two items load nicely on the third factor. These are group factors.

Our next job is to decide what the factors are. This is a logical process. We begin by looking at which items load on which factors. We then try to decide what is common to the items that correlate well with a given factor. The first factor is a general factor, which we may wish to call general academic ability; if we want to be especially casual, we could call it general intelligence. Since the second factor is identified by the two arithmetic items, we can call it a number factor. The two items that identify the third factor are skills in the word knowledge area, so let's call this a verbal factor.

Since a factor analysis sorts the variety of skills that go into a test into several categories or factors, it tells us what factors a test is valid for measuring. In this manner we can define the test content in terms of categories of behavior.

A second way, then, of identifying the content of a test is by way of factor analysis. This procedure identifies the underlying components of behavior and tells us to what extent each item (or subtest in a battery) reflects each component. The procedure is typically used in identifying the content of aptitude tests, interest, and personality inventories.

PROBLEMS

1. Prepare a brief topical outline for teaching a unit in a subject area you are familiar with (mathematics, biology, home economics, etc.). Now build a grid similar to that in Fig. 4.4 for mapping out your content. Fill in the co-ordinate spaces in the grid with skills from each topic appropriate to each level of the taxonomy.

2. You are looking over a manual published to accompany a commercial test. You find the following factor analysis. What can you say about the content

of this test? What kinds of factors do we have here (general, group, specific)? What does the value .70 for item 1 under column I tell us?

Test items	I	II
1. Victory is a synonym for _____.	.70	.09
2. ⌐ is the same as a) b) c)	.05	.80
3. Truth is to lie, as hate is to _____.	.60	.05
4. ▷ is the same as a) b) c)	.04	.70

Construct validity*

In the study of behavior, we see certain groups of human operations that seem to be highly related. These operations suggest a basic trait as their organizer, source of energy, or control. However, because it is a mental operation we cannot actually locate this basic trait. Nevertheless, we act as though it exists because we can see its manifestations. Such characteristics are called *constructs*. Intelligence is an example. We cannot specifically point to a thing called intelligence, but we see children learning to read and to do number combinations, and we notice that some children acquire these skills more rapidly than others. A group of related behaviors—mode of attack, speed of change in behavior, etc.—can be observed. We have devised the construct of intelligence to explain these behaviors.

If we can identify a group of behaviors that characterize the construct, we can also rank people on the extent to which they demonstrate the behavior typical of the construct. The procedures for validating a test of this type will first of all depend heavily on how well we have described the construct. The first step, then, is to build and support with controlled observation a theory about the trait we wish to assess. This theory of the construct will allow us to make some predictions about what will happen when the various conditions that influence the construct are manipulated. This basic theory is called the *nomological net*.

* For a more detailed discussion of construct validity, see Cronbach, Lee J. *Essentials of Psychological Testing*, 3rd ed. New York: Harper & Row, 1970.

We are now ready to develop our test in light of what theory has established as characteristic of the construct. Evidence of construct validity comes from various sources (Cronbach and Meehl 1955). A well-validated test should provide evidence from each source. The important kinds of evidence for construct validity are as follows.

1.   If the test is a valid measure of the construct, persons who rank high on the construct will score very differently from persons who rank low. This procedure requires that we have an independent scheme for ranking the individual on the construct before we administer the test. An example of this technique might be a test of neuroticism. Psychiatrists, familiar with what is known as neurotic behavior, could identify a group of persons who rank high on the trait and a group of those who rank low. A test of neuroticism is valid to the extent that its scores show clear differences between these two groups. Items are selected for the test because the high neurotics answer them one way, whereas low neurotics answer them another way. It should be noted here that the content of the item is less important than the fact that the two groups respond differently from each other on the item.

A second example deals with intelligence. Our theory would support the hypothesis that students who rank high on intelligence should advance more rapidly in school than children who rank low. Hence, our test should show score differences between ten-year-olds who have been accelerated one grade in school and those who have been kept back one grade.

2.   If a test has validity for measuring the construct, conditions that our theory says will alter the construct should also affect how people score on the test. Again, let us look at the construct of neuroticism. Our theory says that certain procedures of psychotherapy should reduce one's neurotic behavior. Therefore, we give a group of classified neurotics our test. Half of these people are randomly selected for therapy. After therapy we again give our test to both the treated and the nontreated clients. If our test is valid, the change in scores for the treated group should be much greater than for the nontreated group. Our theory leads us to believe that with certain treatments, we can reduce neuroticism. We make these treatments. If our test is valid, it also will show an appropriate change in scores in the trait being observed.

3.   If a test is a valid assessment of a construct, it will correlate well with other assessments of that construct, *but* it will correlate less well with measures of other constructs. Again, let us look at intelligence. There are several tests recognized as fitting most of the requirements of a given theory of intelligence. If the test you have chosen is in fact a valid measure of intelligence as defined by the theory, scores on your test should correlate

well with scores on the other intelligence tests. However, we expect this examination to correlate less well with, say, a personality inventory. Test publishers frequently present as evidence of validity intercorrelations of their tests with other measures of the same trait, but we should note that this is only one source of validity among several available sources.

It should also be noted that tests are not the only way to assess a construct. Our test, if valid, should correlate with rankings on these other assessment devices. For example, if our theory says that more intelligent children learn novel tasks more readily than do less intelligent children, then the length of time or the number of trials it takes a child to learn a unique task could be used as a variable with which we could correlate our test scores. This is an important consideration, because correlation of scores on one paper-and-pencil test with scores on another could reflect a good deal of test-wiseness and motor skill, and little else.

In construct validation, correlational techniques may also be extended into factor analysis (Guilford 1948). Here, we wish to see if the underlying dimensions of behavior on the test are indeed those predicted by the theory. Factor analysis may also be used to "purify" a test, because it allows us to identify items that do not load well on the desired factors. We then eliminate these items from our test, retaining only items that have been shown to correlate with the appropriate factors.

4.   Additional evidence of construct validity can be found by analyzing the way a group of subjects responds to the separate items on our test. If our construct is indeed a unitary trait, the items on our test should all be samples of the same basic behavior system. Further, the items should be all assessing the behavior in about the same way. In other words, the proportion of people who get the first item "right" should equal the proportion of those who get the second item "right," and so on all the way through the test. This characteristic is known as *internal consistency* and can be statistically assessed, as we shall see when we look at test reliability.

We have looked at four ways to show evidence of construct validity. A test maker who is building a test to measure a construct should attempt to secure data from as many of these sources as possible, since each attacks the problem of validity from a slightly different angle. The more of these techniques that are used to support a claim for validity, the more confidence we can have in the results of the test when it is put to use. School testing committees should keep this fact clearly before them when reading the manuals on tests they are evaluating.

A final word needs to be repeated about validity. A test by itself is neither valid nor invalid. It always has validity in reference to: (a) some specific condition we are trying to observe, and (b) a defined group of people on which the test has been tried out. In either making statements about the validity of a test or reading about tests, we must always note the kinds of criteria for which the test is valid, i.e., we must note the purposes this test has been shown to serve and with whom. Evidence of substantial validity for a test for one purpose may have little to say about the validity for another, although seemingly related, purpose. Similarly, evidence of substantial validity for a test used with fourth graders in Brooklyn, New York, may have little correspondence with validity for third graders in Salmon, Idaho.

PROBLEMS

1. I wish to build an inventory to assess test anxiety (anxiety associated with taking a test).
   a) From the construct validity viewpoint, how will I go about this?
   b) What are some conditions I might use to identify the persons who have or who lack this trait?
   c) List four kinds of data you could collect to provide evidence of construct validity for this inventory.

RELIABILITY

In the story of the auto accident cited at the beginning of this chapter, your report of the event to the policeman was not the same on the two repetitions. Your story was inconsistent, or unreliable. By contrast, the movie film provided by Mr. Ecks showed the events occurring the same way each time it was run. The film was consistent, or reliable, in its report.

A test is reliable to the extent that it is consistent with itself, that is, ranks the individual in essentially the same position on successive applications. For example, if I measure the length of a room with a yardstick, I should get about the same result today as I did yesterday. My measuring procedure is reliable. But suppose I have an elastic measuring tape a yard long. Some days I tend to pull it too taut and get more than three feet in each unit. On those days I underestimate the length of the room. Other days, I do not pull it taut enough, and I overestimate the length of the room. My measuring device is inconsistent, or unreliable.

This example also illustrates the kinds of errors that usually plague mental measurements. If my tendency was to stretch the tape too tightly every day, each of my units would consistently be more than three feet long. This is an example of a *constant error*. Two applications of our tape would produce units of floor space that are very much alike, but each would be in error. Thus, although my measurement may be reliable, it may lack validity. But suppose that I sometimes stretched too hard and marked off more than three feet, whereas other times I did not stretch hard enough and marked off less than three feet. My yard rule is inconsistent, but on the *average*, my units may be very near the correct length of three feet, because my overestimates have equalized my underestimates. Inconsistent errors like these are typical in test results. We overestimate some children's characteristics and underestimate others. Across a group, these errors average out. Since neither the direction nor the magnitude of these errors can be predicted, we call them *random errors*. It is random errors that cause reliability problems.

If reliability is revealed by how well two applications of a test agree with each other, we have to measure a group of people twice and compare the results of the two measurements in order to determine reliability. If each person is placed in about the same order among his peers on both testings, the test is fairly reliable. If the ranking of persons on the first test tells us little about where the people will rank on the second testing, our technique is unreliable. The job in determining test reliability, then, is to get two assessments on all individuals in a sample from the population and to correlate these two assessments.

There are four standard methods of determining test reliability. Three of these involve getting two measures on one group of people, whereas the fourth method is a variation of this idea of repeated measurements. The four methods are: (a) give the same test to the same people on two occasions; (b) build two equivalent forms of the test and give each form to all persons; (c) give the test to all persons, get the first score on one-half of the test and the other score on the other half of the test; and (d) estimate the extent to which all items are assessing a common variable. Let us look at these procedures in greater detail.

Test-retest

The most obvious way to get two measurements on a group of people to see how consistent the first set of data is with the second set is to measure everyone twice with the same test. For example, we give my Test of Intellectual Temperament (a fictitious test) to a group of 100 high school students on January 10th and again on January 20th. We then correlate the two sets of scores, using standard correlational procedures. The result is a reliability coefficient such as .76, .91, or some similar value. The procedure is illustrated in Fig. 4.7.

January 10   January 20

FIG. 4.7 Test-retest.

There are some precautions to note in using test-retest procedures. Students may behave differently on the first and second tests simply because they learned something from taking the test the first time. For example, a student may gain in hand-eye coordination simply by taking a mechanical test. On the next testing, he will begin with a higher-level skill than he had on the original test. If practice effect is equal over all students, it will not affect reliability. However, if practice will affect some students quite differently from others, the retest method of assessing reliability may not be appropriate.

There is another problem with the test-retest method of estimating reliability. On the second testing, students may recall how they responded to many items on the first test. If answers to questions on our test are very likely to be recalled, the nature of the test has changed from one session to the next. What was originally a reasoning test has become in the second session largely a test of memory, i.e., if the student can recall how he solved a given problem, no reasoning is involved on his second encounter with the item. We can reduce this difficulty by allowing more time to elapse between the first test and the retest.

However, we must again note that during the time lapse, people are changing—children mature, students learn, neurotics gain stability (or lose it), old people become forgetful. If the time lapse between the two testings is too great, the two sets of scores may indeed fail to correspond, not because of lack of test accuracy, but rather because actual changes have taken place in the trait being observed by the test. Hence, in doing a test-retest reliability analysis, we must carefully establish the necessary time lapse between the two testing sessions so as to minimize the likelihood that memory is a factor in the second test scores. At the same time, however, we must take into account the likelihood that the trait being measured is itself changing.

Equivalent forms

If two forms of a test are equivalent, the distributions of their scores will look very much alike, but no question on one form appears again on the second form. Both tests are designed to be samples of the same behavior domain, but they do not overlap in specific content. Using these two tests, we get one measurement of our people with the first form and repeat the measurement with the second form (see Fig. 4.8). We then correlate the two sets of data to see how closely the two measurements correspond with each other. Once more, we have a reliability coefficient that reflects the degree of consistency between the two assessments.

FIG. 4.8 Equivalent forms.

Since the items of the first form are different from those of the second, memory of answers from one test to another is not a problem. We should, however, investigate to see that practice on the first form has not provided the student with a test-taking habit that will influence his performance on the second form. Has he learned a mode of attack on problems? Has he acquired a disposition toward the subject matter of the test? Test-taking habits that students acquire on one test can alter their performance on successive tests, in spite of the fact that no item on the first test form appears again on the second.

Split half

Suppose I have a test of 100 items, all of which presumably sample the same behavior domain, e.g., intelligence. How can I get two scores on everyone to compare for consistency without measuring everyone twice? I can do it as follows.

I give the test to a group of people. Then I treat the test as though it were two 50-item tests, getting one score from one set of 50 items and the second score from the remaining 50. But deciding which 50 items go into making up which half of the test is an important consideration. If we take the first 50 items, practice effects from that group would unfairly influence scores on the second 50 items. We cannot rule out practice effects, but we can try to distribute them equally across both halves of the test.

Two ways of splitting a test have been widely promoted. One method is to randomly assign items to the two halves of the test; the other is to count the odd-numbered items as one test and the even-numbered items as the other test. With each of these procedures, the items that make up either half-test should come from all sections of the test—some from the initial items, some from those centrally located in the test, and some from near the end. In this manner, practice acquired at different stages of the test-taking process should affect one-half of the test about the same as it does the other. An example of odd-even scoring is given in Fig. 4.9.

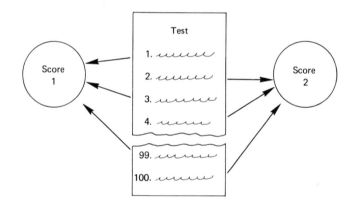

FIG. 4.9 Split-half procedure—odd-even scoring.

But let us digress for a moment. Suppose we have a tank full of water. We take a cubic centimeter out of the tank and test its bacteria count. We repeat the procedure and compare our results with our first test to establish the consistency of our estimates. Again, we take five samples from the tank and find the total bacteria count, then repeat this with five other samples. Which set of tests is likely to be the most consistent, the time we compared a single sample with another single sample or the time we compared five samples with five samples? Chances are that the larger number of samples will give us a more precise picture than will single samples of the bacteria count in the water.

Now let us go back to the test that we split into two parts. The 50-item tests are only half as long as the original 100-item test and are likely to be less adequate as a sample of the behavior domain than is the long test. That is, the correlation between two sets of scores, each based on 50 items, is likely to be lower than the correlation between two equally well-constructed measurements using 100 items.

Luckily, we can still split our test into two scores, correlate them, and come out with the reliability coefficient for the 100-item test. This is done by using the Spearman-Brown prophecy formula

$$r_t = \frac{2r_h}{1 + r_h} \tag{4.1}$$

where r_t is the reliability coefficient for the total, unsplit test and r_h is the correlation between the two sets of scores, each based on half of the test.

For an example of the split-half technique, let us suppose that a test publisher has an 80-item test. He administers it to a college freshman class in psychology. He then scores the odd-numbered items to get one score on everyone in the class, the even-numbered items to get the second score on everyone. Next, he correlates these two sets of scores, which produces a coefficient of .60. Putting this figure into the Spearman-Brown formula, we get

$$r_t = \frac{2(.60)}{1 + .60}$$
$$= \frac{1.20}{1.60}$$
$$= .75.$$

The prophesied reliability for the total 80-item test is .75.

(In looking at test manuals and reading reviews of tests, you may also run into Rulon's split-half procedure, as well as Guttman's and Flanagan's techniques. Given certain limitations, these three procedures provide results equivalent to the Spearman-Brown formula. If you see these approaches mentioned as you read, you can recognize the test reliability as having been established on a split-half procedure.)

The use of one or another of the techniques for determining test reliability is not an arbitrary matter. The three procedures each give us a slightly different picture of what the test can be expected to do. The test-retest procedure looks at *stability* of scores over a period of time. If you are going to use a test to predict future performance or if a score will be referred to a number of times for decisions over a period of months, stability with time is an important feature.

The other two reliability methods, split-half and alternate forms, tell us to what extent two present measurements of the trait are *equivalent* to each other. Stability over the time is not reflected here. Although tests that have fair reliability based on equivalency probably will continue to produce stable scores for short periods of time, we have no reason to believe that a reliability coefficient based on equivalence will indeed be stable over longer time segments. Therefore, tests using equivalency procedures to demonstrate reliability should be used as near as possible to the time when decisions are to be made. We can, however, apply the alternate-forms method with a time lapse between the administration of the two forms of the test. The correlation between the two sets of scores indicates the extent to which the test has *stable equivalence.*

Noting the different kinds of information we get from different reliability procedures, we should, in evaluating a test, always keep in mind the use to which we will put the tool. If we are assessing present status of a behavioral condition, equivalency procedures will do the job for us. But if we expect the test score to represent a person's status on a given variable at successive points in time, stability procedures are most appropriate.

Internal consistency

We have just seen that scores from one-half of the test should correspond with scores made on the other half if the test is reliable. Let us now imagine that we have divided the test into even smaller parts, so small that only a single item is left to make up each of the parts. Should scores on every one of these small "tests" correspond with scores on all the other small "tests"? If each of these is a measure of the same trait, the "tests" should produce scores that look alike. This type of correspondence among test items is referred to as internal consistency. Several procedures for computing a coefficient of internal consistency have been prepared by Kuder and Richardson (1939). Two of their approaches are most widely used; one makes no assumption about the difficulty level of the test items (Formula KR 20), whereas the other assumes that all items are equally difficult (KR 21).

PROBLEMS

1. I have a 50-item test of hand-eye coordination and only one form of the test. Describe three methods I might use to determine the test's reliability. What characteristic of reliability (stability, etc.) would each method represent?

2. I have an intelligence test which I will give in grade 3. I will not give another until grade 6, so the grade 3 score will also be used in grades 4 and 5. The

test manual reports split-half reliability coefficients. Is this satisfactory? Why?

3.   The manual for a test of clerical aptitude says that "the internal consistency estimate of reliability was .78." How do you suppose reliability was determined? What does such a reliability coefficient tell us?

The standard error of measurement

Earlier, we noticed that random errors of measurement are the problems that are reflected in low reliability coefficients. The nearer the coefficient is to zero, the more the scores are made up of error. A score may be thought of as having two parts. One part represents the actual trait being measured, and this part is called the true-score component. The other part is made up of errors in measurement. Sometimes errors add to our true-score component; sometimes they subtract from it. For example, I might guess at a question and get it right, adding to my score even though I did not know the correct answer. Other times I know the correct answer but accidently blacken in the wrong space on my answer sheet, thereby reducing my score from what it should be if it actually reflected my knowledge.

We noticed in Chapter 3 that a person's status on a test can be shown by the deviation of his score from the mean of the group. We now see that this deviation can be made up of two components—a true-score segment and an error segment. Since the standard deviation reflects the extent of the deviations of scores around the mean, it must also be influenced by both the true and error components of scores. In fact, the standard deviation squared (sometimes called the *variance*) for the total test is indeed composed of the standard deviation squared for the true-score components of scores plus the standard deviation squared for the error components. That is,

$$\sigma_t^2 = \sigma_\infty^2 + \sigma_e^2, \tag{4.2}$$

where σ_t^2 is the variance for the total distribution of scores, σ_∞^2 is the variance for the true-score component, and σ_e^2 is the variance of the error component.*

A test is reliable to the extent that the error component of scores is kept at a minimum. Statistically, we can define reliability (r_{11}) in terms of the portion of total variance of a distribution of test scores (σ_t^2) which is *not* error variance (σ_e^2). That is,

$$r_{11} = \frac{\sigma_t^2 - \sigma_e^2}{\sigma_t^2}. \tag{4.3}$$

* There is a reason for using the variances (the squared standard deviations), but this reason requires a statistical demonstration peripheral to our present interest.

From Formula 4.3 we can see that large error variances (σ_e^2) produce small reliability coefficients. In other words, as the portion of people's scores that is made up of errors of measurement becomes larger, the reliability (r_{11}) becomes smaller.

Since

$$\sigma_t^2 = \sigma_\infty^2 + \sigma_e^2,$$

and

$$\sigma_\infty^2 = \sigma_t^2 - \sigma_e^2,$$

true-score variance is equal to the difference between the total test variance and the error variance. Substituting this value in the numerator of Formula 4.3 for the reliability coefficient, we have

$$r_{11} = \frac{\sigma_\infty^2}{\sigma_e^2}. \tag{4.4}$$

Formula 4.4 says that the reliability coefficient is the proportion of total-score variance that is true-score variance. In other words, reliability tells us to what extent differences among peoples' scores reflect real (true score) differences; if reliability is low, observed score differences tell us little about real differences among people. Ideally, we would like to have all of the test variance be true-score variance, but this is not possible. We strive, however, to get as large a component of true score as possible into every observed test score.

As shown in Formula 4.4 reliability coefficients are proportions, and proportions multiplied by 100 are percentages. Therefore, the reliability coefficient can be interpreted directly as a percent, but a percent of what? The reliability coefficient, multiplied by 100, is the percent of the variance of the distribution of actual scores on the test, which is true-score variance. For example, suppose I have used two equivalent forms of a test, correlated the results, and found my coefficient to be .70. This means that 70 percent of the total test variance is true-score variance, and conversely, that 30 percent of the total test variance is error of measurement. Keep in mind that variances are squared standard deviations, and standard deviations are reflections of score deviations above and below the mean. The greater the percentage of test variance that is true variance, the more certain we can be that a person's position above or below the mean is based on true score and will not vary from test to retest.

We are now ready to say something about how large a test reliability needs to be. The necessary size of a reliability coefficient depends on how much error we can tolerate in our measurement. If 30 percent of test variance is too much error, then a reliability of .70 is not high enough. Of course, we must first consider how much error we were making in assessing our people without the test. Even a small gain in accuracy may be valuable, in spite of the fact that we still have a conspicuous error component in our test variance.

Typically, when we apply tests to making decisions about *groups* of people, we can tolerate lower reliabilities because our errors of measurement, being random errors, equalize themselves out across the members of the group. That is, for one person who is underestimated, another is overestimated, so the group average is a fair estimate of the characteristic for all its members. However, when we are dealing with *individuals*, we cannot average out our errors of measurement. If we underestimate a person, he goes underestimated. And we cannot tell if a given single score for a person is likely to be an underestimate or an overestimate. Therefore, when applying test results to making decisions about individuals, we must have high reliabilities; .85 or higher is desirable. Luckily, many published intelligence and achievement tests have reliabilities this high and higher. We often fail to reach this criterion with personality inventories, however.

It would be convenient if we could establish how much of a given score was due to errors of measurement. But errors are random, and we cannot even tell if errors have fortuitously increased or decreased a test score. If for every score we could calculate the error component, label it plus if it adds to the true score or minus if it takes away from the true score, we could construct a frequency distribution of error scores with zero as its central point. Even though we cannot actually build this distribution of error scores, we can calculate its standard deviation by the formula

$$\sigma_e = \sigma_t \sqrt{1 - r_{11}} \qquad (4.5)$$

where σ_e is the standard deviation of error scores (usually called the *standard error of measurement*), σ_t is the standard deviation of the distribution of actual scores from the total test, and r_{11} is the reliability coefficient for the test.

How shall we use the standard error of measurement? In Chapter 3 we saw that the area of the normal curve between -1 standard deviation and $+1$ standard deviation includes the central 68 percent of the scores. The standard error of measurement is also a standard deviation. If we add and subtract one standard error of measurement from a given person's test score, we will have the approximate range within which his *true* score actually lies.

For example, suppose we have an intelligence test with a standard deviation of 15 IQ points and a reliability of .91. Jane has a score of 110. What is the range within which Jane's true score is likely to lie? Well, we know that Jane's score of 110 contains a true-score component, plus (or minus) an error component. The standard error of measurement should give us a ruler to decide the likely range of that error component and hence give us the limits within which the true score is likely (at a probability of .68) to lie. First, we need the standard error of measurement.

$$\sigma_e = 15 \sqrt{1 - .91}$$
$$= 15 \times .3$$
$$= 4.5.$$

The standard deviation of the error scores is 4.5 IQ points. Jane's score, plus and minus one standard error, is (110 + 4.5), or 114.5 and (110 − 4.5) or 105.5. The probability is .68 out of 1.00 that Jane's true score lies between 105.5 and 114.5, i.e., 110 ± 4.5.

Now let us back up a bit to see what this means. First, we have Jane's test score. We realize that a portion of it is error; another portion, true score. We would like to know about the true-score portion. But has the error portion inflated Jane's score or deflated it? We cannot tell. But we can identify a range within which Jane's true score is likely to lie. We found that range to be between 105.5 and 114.5. We expect Jane's true score to be somewhere within that range; we expect it at the probability of approximately .68. What does this mean? If we could assemble a large number of girls with raw scores of 110 like Jane's and make a distribution of their true scores, 68 out of 100 of these true scores would fall in the range 105.5 to 114.5. Chances are good that Jane's true score is also in that range.

We are interested in the standard error of measurement because it helps us interpret test scores. When we see a score, we realize that what we see is not just the true-score component. We cannot identify the true score itself, but we can lay out a band within which we expect it will fall. We then temper our decisions by realizing that the student's true score could be as low as the lower end of the band or as high as the upper end.

PROBLEMS

1. A given intelligence test has a standard deviation of 15 IQ points and a reliability of .84.

   a) Compute the standard error of measurement. What does this figure tell me?   (ans: 6 IQ points)

   b) Mary has a score of 92. What is the range within which her true score is likely to be (.68 probability)?   (ans: 86 to 98)

   c) What is the standard deviation of true scores for this intelligence test? (Hint: Remember that a standard deviation is the square root of a variance.   (ans: 13.74)

2.   An achievement test in reading comprehension has a mean of 25 items correct, a standard deviation of 10 items, and a reliability coefficient of .91.

   a) Compute the standard error of measurement.   (ans: 3 score points)

   b) My score is 27. What is the range within which my true score is likely to be (.68 probability)?   (ans: 24 to 30)

We have already seen that the length of a test influences its reliability. The Spearman-Brown formula deals with this topic. Another variable must also be dealt with when we are computing reliabilities or interpreting computed reliabilities reported in test manuals. That variable is the time limit students have for taking the test.

Tests that are highly speeded, i.e., have short working-time limits, tend to produce higher reliability coefficients than do the same tests given under generous timing. A pure speed test is one in which a student gets right every item he has time to try. If this is the case, let us look at what will happen to a split-half reliability coefficient. If the student completes an even number of items, his two half scores will be equal; if he completes an odd number of items, his odd score will be one more than his even score. The greatest possible difference between the two half scores, then, will be one point. Therefore, we will have great correspondence between the score on odd items compared to the score on the even items. This will look like great consistency of measurement by the two half-tests, and the reliability coefficient will be high where speed, and only speed, is reflected in the scores.

Many tests have short time limits on them, and to the extent that speed is a large factor in getting through the items, reliability coefficients will be overestimated. When reading test manuals, therefore, we must be careful to note under what speed conditions the data were collected for computing reliability coefficients. We will discover that some attractively large reliability coefficients reported in test manuals are spurious and misleading because the data were obtained under highly speeded conditions.

Another condition that affects the size of the reliability coefficient is the heterogeneity of the group on whom we collect reliability data. Coefficients based on scores from eight-year-olds will likely be smaller than those based on a similar sized group containing seven, eight, and nine-year-olds. In a single age level, we find that children will be more alike on trait X than if the children were in three successive age groups. How this works is illustrated by Formula 4.3, where

$$r_{11} = \frac{\sigma_t^2 - \sigma_e^2}{\sigma_t^2}.$$

Heterogeneity will not influence the error component represented by σ_e^2 (why?), but the more heterogeneous a group is, the larger the total test variance, σ_t^2, will become, and consequently r_{11} will also become larger.

Again, when you read test manuals and other test information, note the heterogeneity of the sample on which reliability was computed. If I am going to use a test to discriminate between children at a single age level, but the reported reliability is based on a combination of four age levels, the test may not do a sufficiently accurate job for my purposes.

EMPLOYABILITY

The third characteristic of a good test is employability. This includes a variety of practical, common-sense considerations for making it easy to apply the test and interpret the results. Tests are used because they provide information in a relatively short time, are economical sources of data, and are relevant to some objective we have in mind. Thus, the easier the test is to administer and to interpret, the more employable it is.

A test is easy to administer to the extent that it does not have complex instructions for either the administrator or the persons taking the test, can be given in a relatively short period of time, and does not require highly trained persons to administer it.

A test is easy to interpret to the extent that scores can be made available quickly and in a useful form. This usually means, too, that the test maker provides sufficient data collected on students like ours so that we may refer the scores of our people to the "population" to see how our scores rank. Such tables of data collected on large samples of students are called *norms*.

And lastly, tests are employable to the extent that the whole operation is economical. The information obtained from tests must be worth the expense of acquiring it, or the process collapses.

For example, some intelligence tests that can be administered in about half an hour have sufficiently simple instructions so that any reasonably alert person can administer them, and even persons with moderately low levels of intelligence can understand them. These tests can be scored almost immediately and scores reported in any of several forms, depending on the type of scores the test user finds best suited to his purpose. In groups, the tests cost only a few cents per person to administer and score, and a variety of norms is available. These tests are employable.

On the other hand, some intelligence tests require graduate-level training to administer with accuracy, can be administered to only one person at a time, are difficult and time-consuming to score, and are too expensive for wide use in schools. Such tests have low employability, although their scores are typically believed to be more complete estimates of intelligence than are the more employable tests.

When decisions are to be based on only the most accurate information, we often must turn to less employable tools. However, many purposes for tests are quite well served by the more employable ones. This point helps us put employability into perspective. The first question must always be, "What must a test do to serve my purpose adequately?" Once we have answered this question, we can look for the most employable tool that meets our criterion of service.

PROBLEMS

1. Is an essay test or an objective test more employable in a classroom situation? Why? What must be considered in deciding the employability of these tests?

2. I have two tests, X and Y, about equal in all characteristics except that: (a) for scoring, test X must be returned to the company that sells the test, whereas test Y may be quickly hand-scored locally, and (b) test X gives me slightly more reliable scores than does test Y. Which test is more employable? What must be the guiding consideration in deciding which test to select?

SUMMARY

Good test data, like other sources of information, have three characteristics: they are valid, reliable, and employable. A test is valid to the extent that it provides truthful information about a person's performance in a specified category of behavior. There are several ways for establishing a test's validity. In empirical validity we relate scores to an independent assessment of the trait we wish to assess. In content validity we systematically sample the area of knowledge. Construct validity requires us to build a theory of behavior and then requires our test to produce results that reflect the predictions from the theory.

Reliability deals with consistency of test results. We can see how consistent a measurement is by comparing two applications. If the results of the first application agree with the second, the measure is consistent. Test-reliability techniques get two scores on people in a group by: (a) the test-retest method, in which we administer the test twice to the same students; (b) by using two comparable forms of a test, and (c) by using one test and scoring half for one measurement and half for the other measurement. Another procedure for determining test reliability looks at the extent to which performance of a group of students is consistent across all items.

Test scores are made up of true-score and error-score components. We are interested in the true-score component, but cannot determine it directly from a raw score on a test. Instead, we use the standard error of measurement to establish the approximate range within which we expect the true score to fall.

To be of service, tests must have the characteristic of employability. This means that they must be easy to administer, economical, and provide adequate aids for interpreting scores.

REFERENCES

American Educational Research Association, National Council on Measurement in Education. *Standards for educational and psychological tests and manuals,* Washington, D. C.: American Psychological Association, 1966, pp. 12–24.

Bloom, Benjamin, *et al. Taxonomy of Educational Objectives, Handbook I: Cognitive Domain,* New York: David McKay, 1956, 208pp.

Cronbach, Lee J. and Paul Meehl. "Construct validity in psychological tests," *Psychological Bulletin,* **52** (1955): 281–302.

Cronbach, Lee J. "Validation of educational measures," *Proceedings of the 1969 Invitational Conference on Testing Problems,* Princeton, N.J.: Educational Testing Service, pp. 35–52.

Cronbach, Lee J. *Essentials of Psychological Testing,* 3rd ed., New York: Harper and Row, 1970.

Ebel, Robert. "Obtaining and reporting evidence of content validity," *Educational and Psychological Measurement,* **16** (1956): 269–282.

Ebel, Robert. "Must all tests be valid?" *American Psychologist,* **16** (1961): 640–647.

Guilford, J. P. "Factor analysis in a test development program," *Psychological Review,* **55** (1948): 79–84.

Helmstadter, G. C. *Principles of Psychological Measurement,* New York: Appleton-Century-Crofts, 1964, Chapters 4 and 5.

Richardson, M. W. and G. Frederick Kuder. "The calculation of test reliability coefficients based upon the method of rational equivalence," *Journal of Educational Psychology,* **30** (1939): 681–687.

Schrader, W. B. "A taxonomy of expectancy tables," *Journal of Educational Measurement,* **2** (1965): 29–35.

Stanley, Julian C. and Kenneth D. Hopkins. *Educational and Psychological Measurement and Evaluation,* Englewood Cliffs, N.J.: Prentice-Hall, 1972, Chapters 4 and 5.

CHAPTER 5

TEACHER-MADE TESTS: PRELIMINARY CONSIDERATIONS

Among the many things that teachers do daily, one of the most important is their assessment of student achievement. Formally or informally, instructors make daily estimates of the status of their students in reference to a number of criteria. How does Jay rank among the students in this class in reference to a given knowledge area? Is John ready to take on task X at this point? Has Mary successfully managed Y? Is the class at point Z in a series of steps toward a given goal? What portion of the class is ready to be introduced to the materials in the green box of the Speed Spelling Kit?

Assessments like these are going on in all kinds of school programs. They are fundamental to good teaching. But if teachers are to evaluate changes in basic skills, they should do so as accurately as possible. Chapter 6 presents the basic information necessary for constructing adequate test items for classroom use. But several steps must be taken before we begin to write test questions, and in this chapter we discuss basic considerations necessary for competent test planning.

PLANNING A TEST

In preparing a framework for a test, we have two principal objectives:

1. We wish to assure ourselves that

    a) we are assessing all essential objectives of our instruction, and

    b) the test content appropriately reflects the relative emphasis given various topics in the course.

2. We want to build the test under procedures that will allow us to apply the test results in making appropriate decisions.

We shall first look at ways to plan test content. Then, we shall see how purposes for testing determine the method of test construction. Finally, we shall consider some general rules to apply in building a good test.

Since classroom tests are tied to content validity, they are adequate to the extent that they faithfully represent the body of content presented in the unit of instruction. To this end, classroom tests are samples of the domain of behaviors that reflect achievement in the subject-matter unit. Typically, units of instruction, even short ones, have complex objectives. We want students to acquire more than a list of facts. We want them to be able to apply their knowledge in solving problems, to analyze situations, and to make reasoned judgments about the quality of things, events, and procedures. If these objectives are important in the instructional process, they must also be assessed by the test we use to determine student status in regard to the subject matter.

But tests are not always this broadly designed. Frequently, little beyond basic facts gets into a teacher-made test, largely because the teacher has not laid out a plan for building his test. Mr. Jones, who teaches health, has just finished a unit on respiration and believes that this is an appropriate time for a formal assessment of his students' achievement. On Monday, Mr. Jones announces a test for Wednesday. After school that afternoon, he sits at his desk, textbook and notebook open before him. As bits of information appear to him on the pages of these references, he writes a test item. Forty minutes and 20 textbook pages later, he comes to the end of the chapter. Forty-two test items have been written. But a nice, even number like 40 would look better, so Mr. Jones scans his questions once more, finds two items that seem too obvious, and eliminates them. He sits back with a feeling of relief that his test-writing job is done. His class can be tested as scheduled on Wednesday.

Does this procedure sound familiar? Is anything wrong with it? Tests constructed in this manner typically reproduce the factual content of the textbook, whereas instructional objectives include much more than the knowledge level of Bloom's *Taxonomy of Educational Objectives* noted in the last chapter. In short, the test was not constructed according to a plan that reflected teaching objectives.

Good test construction is based on a table of specifications, or test plan. Such a table of specifications provides a basic outline for test development. It has essentially two purposes: (1) to establish the topical content for the test, and (2) to appropriately balance test items among the various instructional objectives. The teacher therefore begins by listing content topics for the unit on which the test is being built. This is best done when the unit is being planned, but may also be done during the course of the presentation, or in a careful overview of instruction after it is complete if students have been allowed to develop objectives as the unit progresses. To the right of this list of topics, we shall place tabulations to indicate which level of the taxonomy of educational objectives we will assess in regard to that topic. An example of a simplified test plan is given in Table 5.1.

TABLE 5.1 An example of a test plan for a short unit on addition of fractions

Topic	Know-ledge	Compre-hension	Applica-tion	Anal-ysis	Syn-thesis	Evalu-ation	Sum-mary
Like simple fractions	卄	//	//				9
Like complex fractions	////	/	//		/		8
Unlike simple fractions	///	/	//		/		7
Unlike complex fractions	///	/	//	/	/	/	9
Totals	15	5	8	1	3	1	33

Much more detailed and elaborate test plans are available, but the fact is that busy teachers simply do not have time to construct them and hence end up without any formal plan at all. Even with this simplified plan for constructing test items, we must write nine items on simple like-fractions. Five are knowledge items; two are interpretation; and two are application. Other content topics are managed in the same manner. Following a simple outline, our test will not include knowledge-level items alone, but will correspond to the objectives we had in teaching. Topics of central importance will have larger numbers of items devoted to them than will topics of less importance.

In neglecting to construct a table of specifications for building a test, we often end up by doing the easy thing, namely, loading our tests with factual content and neglecting higher mental processes. But teachers make decisions about student performance at many cognitive levels. Therefore, we need data at all levels. Wide use of carefully constructed test plans could go far in making teacher-made tests much more relevant to decisions teachers must make every day about their students.

The taxonomy applied in Table 5.1 is useful in directing our attention to assessing types of outcomes of instruction other than those at the knowledge level. How rigidly shall we conform to the outline of the taxonomy? Krathwohl and Payne (1971) surveyed the available research on the taxonomy of objectives and decided that the rationale of the first three categories—knowledge, interpretation, and application—was probably sound. However, they believed that the evidence did not support the three higher-level categories. These findings may reflect the fact that it is often very difficult to decide whether a test item fits the application category or one of the higher-level categories. For example, if in my physics class I ask how a given machine could be used in attacking a given job, am I asking an application question, or must the student first break down (analyze) the job into its components and see how the machine relates to each component? Indeed, a number of writers (McGuire 1963, Poole 1967, Stanley and Bolton 1957) have pointed out that test users are likely to disagree among themselves as to the taxonomy level represented by many items above the knowledge level.

What, then, shall we do with the taxonomy applied in Table 5.1? Its principal use should be in: (a) directing our attention to building test items that sample higher cognitive processes, and (b) pointing to the variety of higher-level cognitive acts that are represented in competent performance. Critics of testing have often made much of the emphasis that test writers place on the rote learning, knowledge-level items that make up many objective tests. Attention to the taxonomy may well help us to effectively break away from this appropriate criticism of many tests used in the classroom. However, in breaking away from the factual content format of tests, we should not be distressed if we are not certain our items fit perfectly a given higher-level category.

Hunkins (1969) has pointed to another value in building tests around higher levels of the taxonomy. His final unit test included both knowledge-level and higher-level items. Students who had previous experience in dealing with tests loaded with higher-level items during the course of instruction did just as well as other students on the knowledge items and did better than other students on the higher-level items. It appears that regular use of tests that contain items representing the higher levels of cognitive function may indeed have an instructional, as well as evaluation, role.

PROBLEMS

1. Look over the content of Chapter 4 in this book. Imagine that you are the instructor for the class and will soon give a test on the chapter. Build a table of specifications—a test plan—for Chapter 4.

2. Now imagine that you are teaching a class in your major subject-matter area. Choose a topic you might teach and draw up a table of specifications for building a test.

Once we have built our table of specifications, the next problem is to decide how we are going to observe the behaviors that tell us whether Jim and Mary have indeed accomplished the objectives laid out at each level. This means, of course, that each objective must be translated into lists of behaviors that we can see and count and that are indeed relevant to the objective, the achievement of which we are going to assess.

This leads us to another choice-point in test-writing. Do we want our test to rank our students according to their broad accomplishment in the unit of instruction, or do we wish to sort students into two groups—those who have and those who have not met minimum achievement standards? These two applications of tests obviously reflect different purposes. As a result, the way we develop test content for one purpose will be a little different from the way we proceed for the other purpose. This, then, leads us to our second objective in test-planning, namely, to build the test according to procedures that will allow us to apply the results in making the decisions we wish to make.

CRITERION-REFERENCED VERSUS NORM-REFERENCED TESTS

Much of our discussion in previous chapters has dealt with building tests so that we can compare the performance of one child with his peers. We ask, "How is Jack doing as compared with the other members of his class?" However, our definition of a test in Chapter 1 was broader than this. We can compare Jack with his peers, but we can also compare Jack's performance against a predetermined list of behaviors judged to be evidence of his ability in a given skill area. When we use test results to compare Jack with his peers, we refer to this as *norm-referenced testing*. The distribution of scores made by the group gives us a yardstick against which we can assess a given child's performance. Jack ranks above 16 percent of the class; Mary ranks above 80 percent. This procedure is often useful because it gives us a kind of developmental scale with which we can appraise the status of each member of the group. If the average for the group is "normal," how does Jack rank in development of the skill involved in our test? Norm-referenced tests help us answer this question.

But teachers often need more information than this. A child's status in the group tells us little about the specific tasks he can perform. Willie gets the best score on an arithmetic problems test in a group of 50 fifth-grade students. What does this tell us about his specific arithmetic and problem-analysis skills? Even after we make a careful, laborious study of the test content and Willie's work on the test, we can say only a little about specific kinds of tasks he can or cannot accomplish accurately.

But educators are in the business of developing a wide variety of skills. We should be able to assess how well we are doing it. Very often, attainment of skill B depends on the child's ability to perform skill A. Before we present B, we first must believe that the child can perform A. This means that we must develop tests that inventory at a minimum level of proficiency the skills we are trying to promote. Such tests are built of items that are all aimed at the level of lowest acceptable performance in the specific skills to be acquired by the learner and are not designed to show maximum differences among learners. Tests that assess a skill area by posing a series of hurdles that represent minimum levels of acceptable performance are called *criterion-referenced* tests. The meaningfulness of the score on these instruments comes *not* from comparing Donna's score with that of her peers, but rather from comparing the number of tasks she completes successfully with a number of tasks previously agreed upon as evidence of competence in the skill being observed. She is not competing with her peers for status in the group, but is instead pitting her skill against a skill-based criterion of success.

Criterion-referenced tests have been used for years, but typically in limited skill areas. Students in typewriting classes have been asked to type a given number of words per minute before being granted a passing grade. Physical-fitness courses have required students to perform a set number of each of several exercises to obtain a given level of award. The early practice of grading students on percentage of test items correct was tied to the criterion-referenced approach, but it typically failed to relate to behaviors *a priori* listed as criterion performances. Criterion-referenced testing is not new, but only in recent times have educators turned their attention to developing procedures for building these tests and expanding their application to a wide variety of curriculum areas.

Building criterion-referenced tests

How do we construct a criterion-referenced test? The job has basically four steps (Airasian and Madaus 1972):

1. Competencies to be demonstrated must be stated explicitly, i.e., in terms of behaviors that can be seen and counted. I want my science students to "think logically" in their attack on scientific questions. I believe Pete does this and that Kay does not. How did I get this impression? I must have seen each of them do something that led me to this conclusion. If so, why not systematically list the things that my students must do to evidence a "logical" mode of attack on a scientific question? When I do this, I have a list of behaviors we can agree are evidence of having achieved our objective.

2. Criteria that identify successful accomplishment of the competencies must be set. Now that we have a list of behaviors we accept as evidence that the student has met the relevant objective, what standard shall we set for each behavior and all behaviors together before we say the student has "mastered" the competency involved? How many times must a student

accurately perform X before we wish to say he has succeeded? Out of a given number of situations—test items, projects, etc.—how many of the desired behaviors must be evidenced before we agree a student has met our objective? No clear answer to these questions is available in test research, and indeed this is one of the great problems in the use of criterion-referenced tests. Block (1972) suggested that standards set in the range of 80 to 90 percent proficiency are probably realistic; however, further work on criteria levels is clearly needed. Since data in the area of standards are still somewhat tentative, the teacher must exercise his own judgment about the students' adequacy of performance.

Standards are of many types. They may be stated in terms of words per minute, a given error rate in spelling, or a list of qualities associated with a given product. Standards could also be stated in terms of accomplish-

TABLE 5.2 Check list for rating a report on a science investigation

1. Statement of the problem

4	3	2	1	0
problem clearly stated, necessary terms defined		problem stated in general or undefined terms		statement unclear, incomplete, or missing

2. Statement of hypotheses being tested

all hypotheses to be tested listed, include independent and dependent variables, and connection with problem noted		list of hypotheses incomplete or not tied to problem		hypotheses not given, or clearly inadequate

3. Description of the design of the investigation

variables involved are listed, operationally defined, controls cited, and values of manipulated variable noted		not all relevant variables noted or not operationally defined, controls and manipulated variables not described		definitions of variables absent or inaccurate, controls and manipulated variables not cited

4. Report of conduct of investigation

sequence of activities cited, data tabulated or graphically illustrated		sequence of activities not clear, or data not presented in effective manner		all activities not reported, data not reported

5. Conclusions

a clear statement of relation of variables given, findings compared with original hypotheses		conclusion does not indicate relation of variables or does not compare findings with hypotheses		conclusion missing or not supported by findings, or unrelated to hypotheses

ment of steps in a procedure or in listing a minimum number of viable alternative attacks on a problem. In any case, it is essential that both students and teacher have in mind what standards are to be applied.

3. Situations calling for the student to demonstrate his competencies must be devised. We may have to write test items that pose situations in which criterion-related performances can be counted. It may also mean that the student produces a product—a theme, a model, a report on an observation. When products are involved, they must be evaluated against criteria of proficiency. Here, check lists, or rating devices, should be used to count the relevant accomplishments. A sample of such a device is given in Table 5.2. Since projects will vary from class to class, teachers must construct their own rating devices and set their own criteria of proficiency.

4. A student's success in learning is judged according to predefined competencies. Once we have a record of student performances, we can count the events (test items, etc.) on which the student has performed successfully. Then, we can compare the number of successes with the minimum number required as evidence of achievement of the particular objective. For example, suppose our objective is to teach children to add two two-digit numbers. We must first decide what behaviors are evidence of this ability and how often the behaviors should occur in appropriate situations before we will agree that the child has acquired the specified skill. We decide that actually adding pairs of two-digit numbers is the behavior we want to observe and that our criterion of success will be nine out of ten problems solved correctly. Next, we must construct situations—test problems—for which such additions are appropriate procedures. Next, for any given child, we count the number of successful occurrences of the desired event. This count is then compared with our criterion of successes to see if the child has met the minimum requirements.

It should now be clear that criterion-referenced testing rests heavily on objectives that are stated in terms of observable behaviors. In this way it becomes possible to talk about the outcomes of instruction in terms of events that can be counted. If, for example, we want people to be able to use a map to find various points, we can state the behaviors we expect to see as evidence of the ability to locate geographical sites—can point to various lines of longitude and latitude, can recognize symbols for towns, mountains, etc. Then, we can build test items that call for minimum proficiencies and count the number of successes.

At this point, we should recognize the difference between objectives stated as abstractions and objectives described as performances. Typically, we state objectives as abstractions. We say that we want children to apply the scientific method in solving problems, we want them to read the newspaper critically, to appreciate music, etc. Clearly, these are valued objectives, but how do I know when my students have reached them? I must now translate these abstractions into the component performances that define the objective. We can then say, "When I say that a student reads the newspaper critically, I mean that he performs the following behaviors. . . ." Next, we can devise ways to call for the behaviors, count the number of times he performs them, and compare this number with our criterion of success. In this manner everyone knows how we have defined our objective, and everyone can see when a child has achieved the desired outcome.

Criterion-referenced tests, in spite of their recent popularity, have clear limitations (Ebel 1971). They do not tell us everything we need to know about achievement. They will tell us if a child has reached proficiency in a task area, but they do not show how good or how poor the child's level of ability is. This is a relative matter based on what other children can do. Is John's mastery of the multiplication tables "good?" At this point we need to know how other children of John's age do. This is a norm-referenced question.

Criterion-referenced tests also have general validity problems. The criteria and the tasks presented on criterion-referenced tests may be highly influenced by a given teacher's interests or biases. This means that the test could have very little general validity for the skill area. For example, suppose Ms. Rough believes that phonics is the heart of reading. Her criterion-referenced test for basic reading would look quite different from Ms. Broad's, who regards several word-attack skills as fundamental. Ms. Rough's test would probably have little general validity for labeling a child as a proficient reader. And certainly neither teacher's test would identify for us the really excellent readers in a group. This requires us to match behavior against a reference group, e.g., children who are of a given age. Norm-referenced tests are needed here.

Another validity question centers on the extent to which criterion-referenced tests can represent the multiplicity of objectives a given teacher has. In only a few areas can we readily list specific behavioral objectives around which criterion-referenced tests can be built. Ebel (1971) pointed out that being limited to these objectives may well be a constricting condition for teachers.

Lastly, Ebel argued that criterion-referenced tests are necessary for only a small fraction of important educational achievements. It is in fact the diversity in skills that helps us accomplish the wide variety of jobs in our society. And the promotion and assessment of diversity is an important function of the school. This requires norm-referenced testing.

Clearly, criterion-referenced testing has a role in education. It is important, however, to view this procedure in the total context of the educational endeavor.

PROBLEMS

1. Mager (1972) has called the abstract, generalized statements of objectives "fuzzies." From the list of objectives below, check the "fuzzies," the ones that do not readily indicate the performances to be counted.

   a) to add correctly any combination of two one-digit numbers

   b) to show good citizenship

   c) to give three examples of arachnids

   d) to appreciate good literature

   e) to understand the laws of magnetism.

2. Write an objective of instruction in your preferred curriculum area, first as a generalization, then "define" it with the observable behaviors that characterize the attainment of the objective.

Results of criterion-referenced tests are designed to provide us with a yes-no answer about a child's ability to perform in a given skill area. He either does or does not meet the criterion. But these tools can be even more useful. Because the essential component behaviors have been specified and items built so that component behaviors can be counted, criterion-referenced tests can also be diagnostic. We can locate a child's problem area by noting his performances that fail to meet minimum proficiency levels. In the example of adding pairs of two-digit numbers, one component behavior is the ability to carry values from the ones' column to the tens' column. If a child successfully completes items where carrying is not involved, but fails on items where carrying is involved, we have a clue about the area of his difficulty. Here, criterion-referenced tests are diagnostic. It should be pointed out, however, that paper-and-pencil testing can at best only point to a child's problem area. It does not show us the errors in the child's mental process that have led him into his difficulty. But knowing the behavioral acts on which the child makes his errors is of real help to both the teacher and the child. We can at least now point to things the child can and cannot do and begin exploring the reasons. Norm-referenced tests do not readily provide this type of information.*

---

* For help in developing tools in specific curriculum areas, see Bloom, Hasting, and Madaus. *Handbook on Formative and Summative Evaluation of Student Learning*, New York: McGraw-Hill, 1971.

Statistical differences between criterion- and norm-referencing

There are several notable statistical differences between norm-referenced and criterion-referenced tests (Popham and Husek 1969). In this regard we shall look at three topics: (a) spread, or variability, of the score distribution; (b) reliability; and (c) test validity.

In a norm-referenced test, we try to build items so as to maximize the range of scores made by a given group of students. We want to show small gradations of differences among students. The wider the range of scores we can produce, the more these gradations in knowledge or skill can be seen, and the more evident a given student's position among his peers is. However, in a criterion-referenced test, we try to decide whether students have met the criterion. Items are therefore constructed to show behavior at the criterion level. As a result we typically have much less variability of scores in criterion-referenced tests than we have in norm-referenced tests. In fact, if the entire class meets the criterion perfectly, we will have no variability at all. Everyone will get the same score. This does not mean that the test is poor. It simply means that everyone performed at a minimum level of skill, i.e., everyone met the criterion.

In the norm-referenced test, a score derives meaning from its relative position among all other scores. We can best tell Bill's position among Mary, Peter, and Paul if there are conspicuous differences among their test scores, i.e., if the score range is spread out. However, in criterion-referenced tests, a score gets its meaning from a criterion of minimum proficiency for the tasks comprising the test. A score is "good" if it shows that the child has accurately performed enough tasks to meet the criterion of success in the skill area involved. Spreading scores out on a wide continuum is not the intent here.

This fundamental difference in the purpose of criterion-referenced and norm-referenced tests carries over to how we prepare tasks to include on the test. The job of the test writer in both cases is to sample a domain of performances. But in the criterion-referenced case, we are sampling from the domain of acts that illustrate minimum levels of skill relevant to an objective; in the norm-referenced case, we are sampling the entire domain of skills, knowledge, etc., that defines the instructional unit. This could include performances clearly beyond, as well as below, a level we may wish to set as a minimum level of proficiency.

As with the use of any measurement, we expect criterion-referenced tests to be reliable. Here, we are concerned primarily with internal consistency. If all items require criterion-based performances, all items should be sampling a common pool of behaviors. But the method by which we can illustrate this internal consistency has not yet been agreed upon (Ebel 1971; Livingston 1971; Shavelson, Block, Ravitch 1972; Livingston 1972;

Harris 1972). Traditional procedures for computing reliability, described in Chapter 4, depend on variability of scores as shown by total test score and item variances (the square of the standard deviation). But criterion-referenced tests have little or no variability. In fact, with criterion-referenced tests, we hope that all children will get perfect scores; hence, no range of scores will appear at all. In this case, the usual internal-consistency procedures would produce a zero reliability coefficient, even though the test may be very adequate for our purpose. Because they depend on obvious variability, or spread, of scores, standard procedures for assessing reliability should not be applied to criterion-referenced tests.

Criterion-referenced measures are based primarily on content validity. The items are selected because they call for behaviors, the performance of which demonstrates achievement of the objective involved. Carefully made judgments that a test item does indeed call for relevant behavior is the foundation on which criterion-referenced tests are validated. Again, objectives stated in behavioral terms are salient in this process. As noted earlier, we must first translate our instructional objectives into the acts children can perform to show that they have indeed reached these objectives. We can then build criterion-referenced tests through which the desired behaviors can be observed.

One additional point should be considered here. Teachers often think of assessment as being applied only after a unit of instruction has been completed. However, measurements are also very useful during the course of instruction. How well are the students grasping a given fundamental concept? Do they have the steps in a fundamental procedure in hand? These kinds of questions are often important in our regulating the pace of instruction, in determining to what extent supplementary materials are needed, and in identifying points on which instruction should be repeated. In these developmental stages of instruction, criterion-referenced tests are especially useful. Some writers refer to these assessments made during the course of a unit of instruction as *formative evaluation*. In contrast, assessments made at the close of an instructional unit are called *summative evaluations*.

SOME GENERAL RULES FOR TEST CONSTRUCTION

Once we have laid out our table of specifications and have chosen a criterion- or norm-referenced procedure, we are ready to begin thinking about writing the actual test items. Regardless of the type of test items we choose to write, there are some general ideas about writing tests that are applicable to all types of items. (In the next chapter we shall look at specific rules for writing various kinds of items, e.g., true-false or multiple-choice types.)

1. We wish to determine how successfully students deal with a given body of knowledge. Can they interpret it, apply it, evaluate it? Memorizing and repeating special passages from the textbook do not show the abilities we typically wish to assess. Therefore, our first general rule is: *Avoid replication of the textbook in writing test items*. We could write a page of nonsense syllables, and students could memorize segments of the page. If our test items replicate the textbook, students could get the items correct. But what kind of understanding does the student have of the material? Some teacher-made tests are not unlike this example. We have all been subjected to them and therefore want to spare our students from this particularly poor pedagogy.

2. Our next rule: *The test item should be aimed at a specific objective and should therefore not be complicated by high demand on a variety of skills other than the one being assessed*. For example, if I wish to assess a student's ability to apply a concept in arithmetic, the problems I present should not be unduly demanding in reading level. My objective is to assess the student's ability in arithmetic, not his reading skill. If I have a problem that is hard to read and Janice misses it, did she not know the arithmetic principle, or did she not read the problem well? Similarly, if I wish to get at a concept in physics, the problems I present should not involve unnecessarily complicated algebra. I am assessing the student's ability to apply the physical concept, not his skill in mathematics. We make better judgments about a child when our assessment of his attainment of an objective is not unnecessarily confounded with demands that are peripheral to the objective.

3. Tests written at the last minute before they are to be used typically are not carefully worded and are not balanced among the objectives we wish to assess. Therefore, our third general rule is: *Begin writing items well ahead of the time when they will be used, and allow time for test revision*. A good time to write items is at the time a given topic is being taught. At the very least give yourself a week to develop a plan, write the items, and review and revise them. No test is complete until these three jobs have been carefully attended to.

4. Our next rule: *Consideration must be given to the difficulty level of the item in relation to the purpose of testing*. If we are using a norm-referenced approach for judging performance of our children, we want our tests to show differences in scores among the class members to the extent that differences in achievement exist. We have the potential for getting a maximum range of score difference when the items are of moderate difficulty. By this we mean that any given item should be sufficiently difficult that a portion of the class will miss it. In this way we will get a maximum

range of scores among class members, and consequently the differences in achievement among members will be most obvious.

Occasionally, we present material that we expect everyone to master, e.g., the multiplication combinations. In this case we would use a criterion-referenced test, and our rule of moderate difficulty would not apply. Here, we would use proficiency criteria as a basis for judgments, and we would expect students to cluster at the upper score levels on the test rather than to be broadly spread across the score range. Items in this case are written so that their level of difficulty represents a minimum proficiency in the skill being observed.

5. Almost everyone has taken a test in which he found a hint to the answer of one item unintentionally embedded in another item. In other tests, the correct solution of a given item was a prerequisite for attempting the next item. Interdependence between items, whether unintentional or intentional, is to be avoided. Our next rule, therefore, is: *Do not allow items to be interdependent.* Each item should be placed in a test because it assesses a unique element of knowledge or skill. If the answer to an otherwise "good" item is suggested by the content of another, the skill we are assessing is the ability to see the relationship between the two items. Conversely, if getting item 2 right depends on having chosen a correct answer to item 1, an error in item 1 really amounts to two errors, even though the student's answer for item 2 may be correct in reference to his answer to item 1.

EXAMPLE*

1. Which one of the following cities has the greatest average annual rainfall?

   a) Chicago, Illinois

   b) Denver, Colorado

   c) New York City, New York

   d) San Francisco, California

2. The average annual rainfall there is

   a) 15 inches

   b) 19 inches

   c) 33 inches

   d) 43 inches

---

* These data are taken from the *World Almanac,* New York: The New York World Telegraph and the Sun, 1965, pp. 896.

The answer to item 1 is (c) New York City; item 2, (d) 43 inches. But suppose I chose (a) for item 1 and (c) for item 2. My answer for item 2 is correct for the answer I gave to item 1, but because the items are interdependent, I get no credit for either item.

6. All students have taken tests in which the desired mode of attack was obscure. Students say "I didn't know what you wanted," and argue that a variety of rational alternatives be given credit. Typically, the problem can be solved by attending to some mechanics of test-building. Our next rule is: *Employ a test format that ensures that the student understands both what he is to do and how you will deal with the results of his job.* To do this, you must: be sure that the directions to the student are clear so that he knows exactly what he is to do; group together all test items of a given type, e.g., all true-false; advise the student how the answer is to be marked; avoid a pattern in correct responses, which a clever student may detect; and advise the student before he takes the test how the test score will be arrived at. Careful attention to these points will go far in directing class discussion after the test to the content of the unit of instruction rather than to the adequacy of the test.

7. And one last rule: *Avoid trick items and procedures.* The job at hand is the assessment of abilities, not the outwitting of students.

PROBLEMS

For each situation below, cite the general rule(s), the violation of which are evidenced.

1. Ms. Dubbelyu has built an arithmetic test. The first problem asks the child to find the area in acres of a given lot. The second problem says that if a farmer can raise 70 bushels of wheat per acre, how many bushels can be raised on the lot in problem 1?

2. In an experimental arithmetic program, the topic of fractions has been introduced and developed one year before most textbooks provide a systematic treatment of the topic. No standardized test of fractions was available with a controlled vocabulary at that grade level. Therefore, the problems from the test prepared for the next higher grade level were used.

3. On Friday, Mr. Em promised his students a vocabulary test in his physics class for next Wednesday. Today is Tuesday, and Mr. Em has not yet prepared his test, so after school he sits down with his textbook and begins writing items as he thumbs through the chapters.

SUMMARY

Several operations should be completed before we start to write specific test items. First, we should prepare a table of specifications for the topical areas to be covered by the test and note the levels of the taxonomy to be covered within each area.

Since we want the test to allow us to make a particular decision, the second step is to build the test so that its results will allow us to make that decision. If we want to show a child's rank among his peers, we should use a norm-referenced approach to test-building. Here, we sample the domain of content with moderately difficult items so as to show maximum differences among class members. But if we wish to see if our class members have achieved a set of skills, we will use a criterion-referenced test. Here, our test is composed of items at the level of acceptable performance in the skills, we set a minimum number of successful performances as evidence of adequate achievement, and compare each child's score against our performance criterion.

Third, we must consider the general rules that apply to building any good classroom test. These rules are designed to help us avoid fostering rote memorization of the textbook, to direct our attention more specifically to measuring the desired outcomes, to allow ourselves adequate preparation time, to avoid item interdependence, and to help us give better test-taking directions. Heeding these rules will go far in improving classroom tests.

REFERENCES

Airasian, Peter W. and George F. Madaus. "Criterion-referenced testing in the classroom," *National Council on Measurement in Education,* **3** (1972): 1–8.

Block, J. H. "Student Evaluation: Toward the Setting of Mastery Performance Standards," (Paper read at the annual meeting of the American Educational Research Association, Chicago, Illinois, April 1972.)

Bloom, B., T. Hastings, and G. Madaus. *Handbook of Formative and Summative Evaluation of Student Learning,* New York: McGraw-Hill, 1971.

Ebel, Robert L., "Criterion-referenced measurement: limitations," *School Review,* **79** (1971): 282–288.

Harris, Chester W. "An interpretation of Livingston's reliability coefficient for criterion-referenced tests," *Journal of Educational Measurement,* **9** (1972): 27–29.

Hunkins, F. P. "Effects of analysis and evaluation questions on various levels of achievement," *Journal of Experimental Education,* **38** (1969): 45–58.

Krathwohl, D. R. and D. Payne. "Defining and assessing educational objectives," in R. L. Thorndike, ed., *Educational Measurement,* 2nd ed., Washington, D. C.: American Council on Education, 1969, Chapter 2.

Livingston, Samuel A. "The reliability of criterion-referenced measures." (Paper presented at the annual meeting of the American Educational Research Association, New York: Feb. 1971.)

Livingston, Samuel A. "Criterion-referenced applications of classical test theory," *Journal of Educational Measurement,* **9** (1972): 13–26.

Livingston, Samuel A. "A reply to Harris' 'An interpretation of Livingston's reliability coefficient for criterion-referenced tests'," *Journal of Educational Measurement,* **9** (1972): 31.

Livingston, Samuel A. "Reply to Shavelson, Block and Ravitch's 'Criterion-referenced testing: comments on reliability'," *Journal of Educational Measurement,* **9** (1972): 139–140.

Mager, Robert F. *Goal Analysis,* Belmont, California: Fearon Publishers, 1972.

McGuire, C. "Research in the process approach to the construction and analysis of medical examinations," *Twentieth Yearbook of the National Council on Measurement in Education,* 1963: pp. 7–16.

Poole, R. L. "An examination of cognitive processes elicited by test items as a function of the taxonomy of educational objectives and selected cognitive factor abilities." (Paper read at the National Council on Measurement in Education, Los Angeles, February 1969.)

Popham, W. James and T. R. Husek. "Implications of criterion-referenced measurement," *Journal of Educational Measurement,* **6** (1969): 1–9.

Shavelson, Richard J., James H. Block, and Michael M. Ravitch." "Criterion-referenced testing: comments on reliability," *Journal of Educational Measurement,* **9** (1972): 133–137.

Stanley, J. C. and D. L. Bolton. "A review of Bloom's Taxonomy of Educational Objectives," *Educational and Psychological Measurement,* **17** (1957): 631–634.

CHAPTER 6

TEACHER-MADE TESTS: WRITING TEST ITEMS

Once we have made out a table of specifications and have considered the general rules for test construction cited in Chapter 5, we are ready to begin writing the actual test items. This chapter describes some ways you can improve your item-writing skills. We shall look only at the most commonly used types of items: true-false, multiple-choice, completion, and matching items. After that, a simple tabulation procedure will be presented through which we can identify "bad" items.

Essay tests have wide currency in education, and no text in the field would be complete without a discussion of the construction and use of these measuring devices. Therefore, the last section of this chapter is devoted to more effective uses of the essay test.

TRUE-FALSE TEST ITEMS

The true-false item is a declarative statement. The test taker must decide whether the statement is correct (true) or incorrect (false). This type of item has been widely used in classroom tests, largely because teachers can write mediocre items rapidly and can score these tests objectively with comparative ease.

However, the true-false test has been the object of much well-deserved criticism. It tends to emphasize basic facts and hence foster the memorization of a collection of unrelated details. It is very difficult to construct true-false items that adequately assess the upper levels of the taxonomy of educational objectives. Also, true-false tests involve a large element of guessing, and scoring formulas (e.g., score = number right − number wrong) do not solve this problem. All people are not equally bold guessers, and all people are not equally deterred from guessing by the presumed penalty imposed by scoring formulas. Nor are all people equally test-wise so that they may select "good guesses." To the extent that either of these elements—timidity or test-wiseness—enters into the score (and is not part of the skill our instruction was designed to promote), the test is departing from the assessment of the objectives of teaching.

Some critics of the true-false test charge that the negative-suggestion effect, i.e., the student reads a false item, marks it true, and leaves the test remembering the item as true, limits the use of this type of test. The validity of this criticism has little support in either the psychology of learning or the empirical literature of testing.

Despite criticism, it should be noted that true-false tests have some advantages. Although good items are not easy to write, items can be written faster than can quality items in several other types of tests. A wide variety of information can be sampled in a relatively short time—students can respond to three or four true-false items in the same time that they take to deal with one multiple-choice item. Achievement of topics in almost every subject taught in the public schools can be assessed by true-false tests. And, of course, these tests are easy to score.

Writing better true-false items

True-false items can be used effectively if a few common-sense rules are followed in writing test items. If you want to exploit the possibilities of true-false tests, here are some things to keep in mind when you write the items.

1. *Avoid use of "specific determiners,"* i.e., words that serve as special clues to the answer. For example, rarely do we find an event that "always" happens or "never" happens. Similarly, "all," "none," and "no" fall into this category. These are clues that the item is probably false. However, these terms may be used effectively in the limited number of cases for which there are in fact no exceptions to an event. In this way, we trip the student who depends on test-wiseness alone to make the correct response.

A second group of qualifying terms is equally to be avoided. Terms such as "sometimes," "typically," and "usually" suggest that the item may be true.

2. *Avoid the use of terms denoting indefinite degree or amount,* which make the item ambiguous. For example, such words or phrases as "often," "a long time," and "regularly" do not mean the same thing to any two

people or in reference to any two situations. A student who misses one class a month probably would not be classified as "regularly" absent, but a child who contracts pneumonia once a month might well be classified as "regularly" ill. What is "a long time ago" to a 10-year-old child may well seem like only yesterday to his 50-year-old teacher. If these words or phrases are to be used, defining limits should be included in parenthesis so that all persons can have a common reference. Note the following true-false items.

> *Poor:*   In his study of test-taking behavior, George Wye found a high correlation between reading speed and intelligence scores.
>
> *Better:* In his study of test-taking behavior, George Wye found a high correlation (.70 or greater) between reading speed and intelligence scores.

In the "better" item we have defined the indefinite term "high" correlation.

3. *True-false items should be positively stated declarative sentences, stated as simply as possible.* We are trying to assess the student's knowledge of the concept involved, not his skill in reading and interpretation. To this end, we should: use simple sentences whenever possible, avoid negative statements (especially double negatives), and include only a single idea in any one statement. Occasionally, however, we must use compound sentences because we wish to present a condition followed by an explanation, the explanation being either true or false. For example, we may wish to state, "Leaves of deciduous trees change color in the fall because the average temperature is lower than in summer." The initial clause in this type of item should be true; it presents the condition. The decision of truth or falsity is to be made about the second clause. It is ridiculous and ambiguous to present an explanation in a second clause for an initially stated condition that is itself false. Any procedure that detracts from the clarity of an item erodes the validity of true-false tests and reduces them to guessing games.

4. *For ease of administering and scoring true-false tests, the desired method of marking should be clearly explained before the student begins the test.* Do you want the students to mark plus for true and zero for false? If so, where should these marks be made? There are several methods of marking that are satisfactory, but one—plus and minus—is not satisfactory. Minuses are too easily changed to pluses after the test is returned, and students may then charge the teacher with misgrading.

A preferred marking procedure is one in which a short line is placed to the left of the item number, and students are requested to place their mark on the line. However, many teachers have devised their own mimeo-

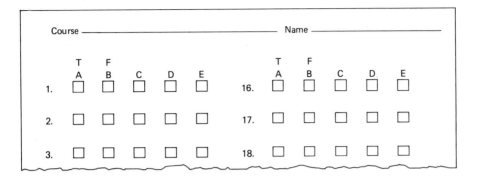

FIG. 6.1 An example of a teacher-made answer sheet.

graphed answer sheets with boxes to be crossed out for the correct answer, as shown in Fig. 6.1. This answer sheet may be used for true-false tests, multiple-choice examinations, or a combination of the two.

To facilitate scoring, templates with holes punched to expose the correct answer box can also be made. These templates are then laid over the student's answer sheet, making it easy to quickly count the number of correct answers. Of course, if electronic scoring equipment is available, it is to be preferred for speed and convenience. Gaffney and Maguire (1971) have shown that students in grades four and five can use mechanically scored answer sheets if adequate instruction and practice are provided. They found that above grade five, valid marks were produced by children with little instruction in answer-sheet use. However, answer sheets were ineffectively used by children below grade four. Supporting evidence for use of answer sheets by fourth graders was submitted by Solomon (1971), who used a "culturally disadvantaged" sample of children. However, since many schools do not have electronic scoring facilities, the teacher-made answer sheet is suggested as an alternative.

5. Another way to improve the true-false item deals not with its form, but with its application. *Do not limit the use of true-false tests to assessing knowledge of basic factual material.* They can also be used to assess higher levels of cognitive activity. For example, within the body of the test, write a paragraph describing a given practical situation. Then write several true-false items about that situation. Suppose the class has been studying Charles' and Boyles' laws of the effect of temperature and pressure on a volume of gas. We might proceed this way.

A child has been playing with a balloon, presumed to be perfectly air tight. At noon he laid it on the window sill. Now at 3 P.M. the sun has moved around to that side of the house and has been shining directly on the balloon for half an hour.

——1. The density of the air in the balloon is the same at 3 P.M. as when the boy put the balloon on the window sill.

——2. The total volume of the inflated balloon will be the same at noon as it is at 3 P.M.

In this manner we are employing true-false items to assess application. Similar examples could be devised to show how true-false items can be used to assess other objectives beyond the basic-knowledge level. We could show a diagram and require analysis of relationship of parts. Or, we could show parts of an object and require synthesis, etc. In any case, some imaginative writing will free the true-false item from its bonds with basic facts and will illustrate that it is really more versatile than some critics have supposed.

PROBLEMS

1. For each of the items below, note which of the rules for writing true-false items was violated.

    a) Thomas Jefferson was not the first Secretary of State for the United States.

    b) All insects have faceted eyes.

    c) Ancient man did not use tools made of iron.

    d) No president of the United States has really been financially poor.

2. Choose a topic in your teaching area and write two true-false items that assess the application level of the taxonomy of educational objectives.

MULTIPLE-CHOICE ITEMS

A multiple-choice item has two parts—a partial condition and several response alternatives, each of which appears to complete the condition. We shall refer to the statement that presents the condition as the "stem" and the alternatives for responding to the condition as the "options." The student's job is to select the option that correctly fulfills the condition stated in the stem. Sometimes, the condition is in the form of a question; sometimes, an incomplete statement.

In spite of the vigorous attack on the multiple-choice test in recent years, test makers still see it as the most versatile and most effective of the various types of objective-test items. As an example of its versatility,

(By permission of John Hart and Field Enterprises, Inc.)

Mosier, Myers, and Price (1945) listed 14 applications of the multiple-choice item, with an example of each. Their 14 applications are:

1. definition
2. purpose
3. cause
4. effect
5. association
6. recognition of error
7. identification of error
8. evaluation
9. difference
10. similarity
11. arrangement
12. incomplete arrangement
13. common principle
14. controversial subjects

This list of applications of multiple-choice items illustrates the extent to which all levels of the taxonomy of educational objectives can be assessed by this type of item. The examples presented by Mosier, *et al.*, are highly recommended as guides to anyone who wishes to introduce greater capacity into his test-writing skills.

Rules for writing multiple-choice items

Some textbooks provide long lists of rules for writing good multiple-choice items. Board and Whitney (1972) have shown that although violation of these rules may not appreciably affect test difficulty, it very well may reduce both reliability and validity. However, Dunn and Goldstein (1959) and McMorris, Brown, Snyder, and Pruzek (1972) have shown that some of these rules are not as important as originally believed. For this reason we shall try to keep our list of rules relatively short. Also, many rules deal with reasonable use of good grammar and syntax, which occasionally is a problem in multiple-choice items. We shall assume that you will attend to the grammatical requirements of writing declarative sentences so that our attention here can be focused on other rules for constructing better multiple-choice items. Yes, of course, every teacher has taken multiple-choice tests and has also written a few. But we can do a better job than we typically see being done, and here are some things to note in doing it.

1. *The stem should contain the central issue of the item, should be concise, and should be easy to read and comprehend.* At the outset of the item, we want the test-taker to know what we are getting at. The basic concept should therefore be laid out directly. Vocabulary and sentence structure should be only as complex as necessary to convey the idea with which we are dealing. Furthermore, we should not copy the textbook in getting the job of item-writing done. This only encourages students to do meaningless memorization of the text content; certainly, our teaching objectives are designed to achieve more than this.

2. *Arrange options in chronological order, in a series of magnitudes, alphabetically, etc.* Here are some examples.

Poor: In what year was the Declaration of Independence signed?
   a) 1784
   b) 1754
   c) 1776
   d) 1781

Better: In what year was the Declaration of Independence signed?
   a) 1754
   b) 1776
   c) 1781
   d) 1784

Poor: I have found a creature with three pairs of jointed legs. It is most like a member of which of the following?
   a) crustacea
   b) arachnida
   c) myriapoda
   d) insecta

Better: I have found a creature with three pairs of jointed legs. It is most like a member of which of the following?
   a) arachnida
   b) crustacea
   c) insecta
   d) myriapoda

In carrying out this ordering of options, we must be careful not to favor one option position over the others, e.g., making the (c) option correct more often than other positions. To avoid this, we may wish to consult a plan that provides randomized response positions. We can then place our correct answers in the location designated by such a randomized plan. Anderson (1953) has provided a guide which teachers may find useful for randomizing the position of correct answers.

3. It almost goes without saying that *all options should be plausible and attractive responses to the item*. If a teacher is writing four-option items and has three good options constructed, but cannot put together a good fourth option, he may choose a weak and implausible option to complete the four-option format. This practice is clearly to be avoided. If the option is a weak one—or a clearly unreasonable one—would you as a test taker select it? Of course not! Neither will your students. This option may as well not have been written. Indeed, it would be preferable to leave the item with the three good options than to add a poor one for the sake of retaining the four-option format.

4. *All options for a given item should be approximately homogeneous in content, form, and grammatical structure.* If one option is in the plural form, other options should also be in plural form. If one option is short, other options should be similarly short, etc. We often read that a conspicuously long option is more often selected as the correct answer when students are guessing. But one study (Chase 1964) showed that a long option must have at least four words for every one word in shorter options before it significantly catches the student's eye. It appears, therefore, that we have a fair amount of leeway in defining homogeneity of option lengths.

5. One advantage of the multiple-choice test over the true-false format is that the chance element of guessing the correct answer is reduced. If even three options per item are provided, random guessing should produce an average of 33 percent correct choices. If four options are provided, random guessing of correct answers is reduced to 25 percent. If the addition of one more option can cut down chance that much, why not write, as a rule, four good options per item? Five options reduce the chance factor to 20 percent; six, to 16.7 percent. At this point, diminishing returns set in pretty sharply. *A good rule, therefore, is to write at least four options per item or maybe five, but writing more than five is probably not worth the additional effort.*

6. *The use of such options as "none of these" or "all of these" may be useful, but they should be used only with care.* If we use "none of these" all options must be clearly wrong, or one must be indisputably correct. For example:

The ratio of the circumference of a circle to the diameter is:

a) 1.13
b) 2.16
c) 3.14
d) none of these

Now, sometimes *pi* is rounded to 3.14, but this ratio is not exactly 3.14. A student may therefore choose "none of these," even though he realizes that 3.14 is a "good" answer. On the other hand, a less precise student might settle for the rounded value of 3.14 and each student would have an argument to support his choice.

The use of alternatives like "all of these" reduces the student's discrimination task. For example, in a four-option item, only three options can provide data, since the fourth option is "all of these." The student must decide, not among four options, but among three. Therefore, rather than use an option like "all of these," it is often better to include a plausible fourth option, which will require the student to discriminate among four distinct topics in a four-option item rather than among just three.

Several research studies have investigated the effect of using "none of these" and combinations of options such as "Both (a) and (c) are correct," etc. Students often find that tests with these options are more difficult (Boynton 1950, Hughes and Trimble 1965). However, some writers (Wesman and Bennett 1946, Rimland 1960) claim that there is no advantage to the use of options like "right answer not given" or "none of these." It should be noted, however, that different types of subject matter were used by these investigators. It could well be that the effect of the combination of options was specific to the subject matter in which it was used. In any case, the advantage of using such options is far from evident. Therefore, the use of these options in multiple-choice items should be used with clear reservation.

7. To increase the difficulty of a multiple-choice test, increase the homogeneity of content among the options. For example, look at the following item.

Which of the following topics was dealt with at the Yalta Conference?

a) the rate of monetary exchange among nations
b) fishing rights in the North Atlantic Ocean
c) Russia's control of the Japanese Kurile Islands after World War II
d) the establishment of Israel as an independent state

One needs to know only that the conference had something to do with World War II in order to get this item correct. A more discriminating item on this topic might look like the following:

Which of the following topics was dealt with at the Yalta Conference?

a) joint Allied bombing of the Japanese-held South Pacific islands
b) implementation of a naval blockade of Japanese ports
c) Russia's control of the Japanese Kurile Islands after World War II
d) an Allied strategy for the postwar occupation of Formosa

One must know considerably more about the Yalta Conference in order to get the second example correct than is necessary to get the first item.

These items illustrate how the difficulty of multiple-choice items can be increased by making the topical content of the options more homogeneous. In this manner, tests do not have to deal with obscure information to be maximally discriminating.

Applications for multiple-choice items

One of the big advantages of the multiple-choice item is its great versatility. Most teachers have used multiple-choice items to assess basic content, but a sampling of classroom tests shows very little application to levels of the taxonomy of educational objectives beyond "knowledge." Here are some ways to get at the higher levels.

As with true-false items, one very productive approach is to write a short paragraph describing a practical situation. Then write items requesting application of principles to the solution of a problem in the situation. Or, we might request the student to make an evaluation of several alternatives, parts, or steps in a procedure described in the situation. In some content areas, a diagram of equipment may set the scene for requesting application, analysis, or evaluation. Or, we may wish to submit a quotation and ask for its interpretation, an analysis of its ideas, or an evaluation in terms of a given literary style.

Some alternative styles of writing multiple-choice items may also be found useful. For example, the options in a multiple-choice test can be listed at the top of the page; the items then become a series of statements, each of which fits one of the listed options best. For example:

a) mean
b) median
c) mode

——1. always divides the distribution into .5 n above and .5 n below it

——2. is most influenced by a few widely deviating scores on one end of the distribution

——3. is the arithmetic average

——4. is the most frequently occurring score

This technique can also be used to get at levels of the taxonomy beyond "knowledge." For example, in auto mechanics we could list three or four mechanical parts, e.g., fuel pump, distributor, followed by a list of operational symptoms related to each of these parts. The student would then have to diagnose the problem given by the statement and associate it with the faulty part. Similar situations could be devised for physics classes or for a chemistry experiment. Or, how about listing several fabrics in home economics? The items describe the demands of a given type of clothing, and students select the best fabric for the clothing. The range of applications is extensive. If test writers will avoid the temptation to load their multiple-choice tests with basic factual content and begin by devising practical settings calling for knowledge to solve a given problem, the quality of multiple-choice tests will rise significantly.

PROBLEMS

1. For each multiple-choice item below, decide what rule for writing items has been violated.

    a) The regulation distance between the bases on a baseball diamond is
        1) 45 feet
        2) 90 feet
        3) 65 feet
        4) 100 feet

    b) The cheetah is different from other "cats" in that it has
        1) retractile claws
        2) nonretractile claws
        3) no claws at all
        4) hooves

    c) In insects, we
        1) find only four or less legs
        2) see only a head and abdomen
        3) find only wingless creatures
        4) see a head, thorax, and abdomen

2. Select a topic in your teaching area and build two multiple-choice items at the application level and two at the evaluation level.

THE COMPLETION TEST

The typical completion item is a statement from which one or more key terms has been eliminated. It may also be a question, the answer to which is a single word or phrase. The student's job is to provide the terms that correctly complete the statement or answer the question. This type of item comes closer to assessing recall, as contrasted with recognition, than does any other type of objective test. In a completion test the student gets few cues and must largely construct his own response, whereas in other types of objective tests, he must only recognize the correct response among several alternatives. Since there is some evidence (Kintsch 1968) to suggest that retention as measured by recall methods shows a more rapid deterioration than when measured by recognition methods, there are situations in which each type of test has advantages.

However, the completion test has definite limitations. First, it is adaptable primarily to basic, factual material. It is very difficult to construct a completion test beyond the lower levels of the taxonomy of educational objectives. Also, the test is more difficult to score than are other types of objective tests, since typically, machine-scored answer sheets cannot be utilized. We shall see later, however, that scoring can be made easier than some critics of completion tests have admitted.

Rules for writing completion items

Anyone who has read over a collection of completion tests randomly picked up in public school classes must first acknowledge the fact that teachers like to use this type of test. But one must also concede that there is room for improvement in the quality of test items. Here are some ways we can improve that quality.

1. *If at all possible, items should require a single-word answer.* For example, this item

The purpose for a carburetor on a gasoline internal combustion engine is to ———.

could be improved to read

On a gasoline internal combustion engine the purpose of the ——— is to vaporize the gasoline.

The first question will require several words to complete, and different students will say it differently. This requires subjective judgment on the part of the teacher in scoring the item. It is this subjectivity that we are trying to avoid in the use of objective tests.

2. *Avoid lifting statements directly from the textbook.* This procedure for selecting items is sometimes seen as safe, i.e., in the face of student questions, the book can be directly quoted as the authoritative source. However, this method of promoting security for the instructor encourages rote memorization of selected content and teaches the student to neglect applying data to making generalizations and to the solution of problems.

3. Avoid statements so indefinite that they may be logically answered by several terms. For example,

Abraham Lincoln was born in ———.

Several answers could be submitted, all logical and correct. Lincoln was born in Kentucky, in a log cabin, in 1809, in February, and in poverty. Although the teacher undoubtedly had only one answer in mind, she would be hard pressed to explain why each of the other responses did not receive credit. Questions like this degenerate into guessing games. A clue to the presence of the game is when children state, "I didn't know what you wanted there." The item above could be improved by rewriting it to read:

Abraham Lincoln was born in the year ———.

or

Abraham Lincoln was born in the State of ———.

4. Delete only key words from statements. We are attempting to assess significant knowledge. Unimportant and peripheral details are therefore not legitimate subject matter for completion blanks.

5. Do not eliminate so many elements of a statement that the sense of the content is impaired. The objective of the item should be clearly evident to the reader. Eliminating too many terms in one statement makes it difficult to ascertain what that objective is. For example,

The ——— is the ——— divided by the ———.

What is the item getting at? Could it be "The quotient is the dividend divided by the divisor"? Or could it be "The diameter is the circumference divided by pi"? Or even, "The mean is the sum of scores divided by the number of scores"? The item is overmutilated, and we cannot decide what its objective is.

6. The blanks typically are better placed at the end of a statement rather than at the beginning. For example, this item

——— is the name given to picture writings made on stone walls by primitive people.

could be better written as

Picture writings made on stone walls by primitive people are called ———.

The reason for placing the blank near the end of the statement is that it allows us to present the proposition, topic, etc., before proposing the problem. This appears to be a more logical procedure than to pose the problem before we have advised the student of the topic about which the problem is concerned.

7. *Avoid giving clues to the correct answer in the structure of the item.* Clues might come in the use of the indefinite article placed before a blank. For example, if the children had read a story about Mary's visit to a farm in Michigan, and an item said that Mary went to the orchard and picked an ————, the student could quickly limit the possible answers to those that begin with a vowel, e.g., apple, orange, avocado, etc. But since Mary was in Michigan, a good guess would be "apple." We need not even read the story to come to this conclusion. If an indefinite article must be used, always write it "a(n)."

Another class of clues is the way in which blanks are constructed. Only one blank should be given for each completion task, and blanks should be of equal length from item to item. Do not give the students hints by writing short blanks for short answer words and long blanks for long answer words. Also, do not write two blanks if two words are needed. For example,

"The Empire State" is a name given to the state of <u>(New   York)</u>. Since we are measuring knowledge rather than skill at decoding clues, we should limit clues to the legitimate content of the topic being considered.

Application of completion items

The completion item does not have the flexibility of application that the multiple-choice item does, although some variety can be brought into its use. For example, we may present a complex graph and write items that require an analysis of the graph. We could do the same thing with diagrammatic pictures in which the parts of the object (machine, a biology specimen, a tool such as an art kiln) have been numbered. From there, we might begin to explore interrelationship of parts, e.g., when part 3 does X, Y is done by part ————.

Scoring is often a problem with completion tests. However, two suggestions may aid in attacking the scoring problem. First, we can number the blanks in the statements and place a column of numbered blank spaces along the right-hand side of the page. The student then writes the answer in the column space that corresponds with the numbered space in the statement. (An example is given in Fig. 6.2.) In this manner all answers are in a neat column at the side of the page. An answer key can be laid beside the student's paper and marking can be done quickly.

	Answers
Abraham Lincoln was born in the State of <u> 1 </u>	1. _____
and practiced law in the State of <u> 2 </u> . He	2. _____
became President in the year <u> 3 </u> .	3. _____

FIG. 6.2 A form for easier scoring of completion items.

A second procedure is to use a machine- or hand-scored answer sheet. For each item on the answer sheet, we have the full alphabet. We then write the statement, but instead of leaving a key word out, we substitute asterisks and a short blank. These symbols take the place of letters in the word that will correctly complete the statement, as follows:

1. Abraham Lincoln was born in the State of **___.

The two asterisks represent letters that precede the one to be recorded on the answer sheet. The blank space represents the letter that will be blackened in on the answer sheet. The asterisks and blanks do not typically, but may, correspond with the total letters in the word. Here is an example of how the item above would be marked.

1. a b c d e f g h i j k l m (n) o p q r s t u v

The "n" has been circled because the state is Kentucky. The two asterisks represent the first two letters in the word; the blank is the third letter, "n." For most scoring machines, answer sheets can be devised for this purpose. Also, hand-scored answer sheets can be mimeographed, and scoring templates with holes punched to expose the correct answers can be laid over the student's paper and the correct responses rapidly counted. At first, the procedure requires careful instructions, but older students will catch on to this procedure quite rapidly.

A word of caution is needed about the machine-scoring approach. It is entirely possible that a student could select the wrong word but get the item correct because his word and the correct one had a given letter in the same position in the word. For example, both "telephone" and "reaper" have "e" as the second letter, but Alexander Graham Bell did not invent them both. Therefore, in using this approach, we must give some attention to possible alternative responses that students might contrive. We must strive to avoid selecting a letter in the correct word that has the same position as that same letter in an alternative response that is likely to be given by the student. Also, the second letter is usually to be avoided, since so many words have vowels for their second letter. This reduces guessing to about five choices, considering the infrequency of some vowels.

PROBLEMS

For each item below, find the rule of writing good items that is violated:
1. The function of a carburetor is to ———.
2. The name of the city in which George Washington was inaugurated as president is ——— ——— ———.
3. The first president of the United States was ———.
4. ——— trees are all those that lose their leaves in the autumn.

THE MATCHING TEST

The matching test, a favorite for many years among primary school teachers, also has application at many upper levels. The matching test presents a column of items on the left-hand side of the page and a column of options on the right. For each item, the student's job is to select the option that is correctly associated with the item. Much learning involves this association act: names and dates, foreign words and their English translation, parts of a machine and their function, etc. The matching test is most applicable to assessing this type of learning.

However, the matching test has some limitations. It is not readily adaptable to the higher levels in the taxonomy of educational objectives. It is most commonly employed to assess knowledge, comprehension, and possibly some application. Although it is a relatively easy test to construct, students find it relatively time-consuming to take. In spite of these limitations, the matching test has a clear role in the measurement of instructional outcomes. Care must be used, however, in applying the matching test to the objectives which it best serves. This usually means using it in conjunction with another kind of test, e.g., multiple choice.

Guides to improving the matching test

If the matching test is to be retained among the teacher's assessment tools, we must do a much better job of constructing this test than is often done. Here are some ways we make the matching test a sharper instrument.

1. *The format that seems to facilitate taking the test calls for the stimulus items to be listed and numbered in a column on the left of the page, whereas the options to be associated with the items are listed and lettered in a column at the right.* Naturally, the list of options should contain more possible responses than required to complete the test. In this

way the last item is not answered by the student's simply having used all options except one.

2. Each matching exercise should contain only homogeneous material. In this way we increase the likelihood that all options appear plausible for all items. An example of the problem of not having homogeneous material might look like this.

1. Boston	a) the first capital city of the United States
2. Charles Pinckney	b) the place where tea was dumped into the ocean as a protest against taxation
⋮	⋮
5. Philadelphia	h) a signer of the US constitution
	i) one of the 13 original colonies

If Pinckney's name appears among a list of cities and other geographical sites, we can select (h) as the correct answer simply by elimination. It is the only item that could be matched logically with a person. If this exercise had contained only cities and towns, this test-taking skill would not have yielded that one point on the score in absence of the necessary historical knowledge.

3. Ease of taking the matching test is facilitated if the items and options are arranged in a systematic order. Dates should be in chronological order, whereas names of people, nomenclature of mechanisms, etc., should be in alphabetical order. This reduces the amount of searching necessary for the student to locate responses. It also negates the occasional student hypothesis that the test has been arranged so as to provide a pattern in the answers.

4. All items and options for a given matching exercise should be on a single page. This eliminates the possibility of students' overlooking options that may be on a second page. It also reduces the likelihood of random errors being made by students as a result of turning pages back and forth.

5. The number of items in a single matching exercise should be limited to five or six in the lower grades and to 10 to 15 as a maximum at upper levels. If more matches are desired, arrange for several matching exercises within a single examination. Ideally, each exercise should be limited to the prescribed number of items and should explore a different topic from other exercises, thereby providing a wider sampling of knowledge of the topic being studied.

6. Students should know exactly how the matching is to be done. Instructions should tell the student whether he can use an option more than once, whether each item has only one correct answer, and how the marking is to be done. With primary school children, marking is best done by drawing lines from the item to its correct answer although this procedure is difficult to score. With older children, a line can be drawn to the left of each item, with the letter of the selected option to be written on the line. This makes scoring by key quite easy. Here is a two-item portion of a matching test illustrating this procedure.

<pre>
  b
———1. Henry Clay   a) senator from South Carolina
———2. Daniel Webster   b) senator from Kentucky
</pre>

Variety in application of matching tests

Some suggestions for making the matching test more versatile seem appropriate, especially because it has so often been applied to rote-memory kinds of learning. Although the matching test does have wider application than this, it cannot be expected to be as widely applied as the multiple-choice item. Here are a few suggestions for breaking matching tests out of the paired-associate mold.

First, in the left-hand column, we can list as our items a group of principles such as we might study in science, mathematics, etc. The options in the right-hand column would be descriptions of practical problems, the solution to which could be found among the principles. Similar items could be formed around rules for operations, laws, etc.

Second, we could prepare a list of conditions as our items and a list of effects as our options. For example, in art we might list two colors to be mixed (items) and the resultant colors (options). Or, in home economics we might list items erroneously measured in a recipe. The options would describe the conditions of the completed food.

Third, we can also use matching exercises with diagrams, maps, and charts. The various parts are numbered, and these become our items. We list as our options the name of the part, or its function, or what it indicates, e.g., a symbol on a map. Or, we could provide a list of short, simple problems; the options would be a list of tools, objects, or processes that can be applied to this problem. For example, in wood shop I might want to cut a 45° angle in a piece of picture framing. The appropriate tool would be a mitre box.

These suggestions for applying the matching test to more than rote-memory situations are only samples, not an exhaustive list. It is hoped that you will generalize these suggestions to your own subject matter, expanding them to make the matching exercise even more adaptable to assessing the attainment of teaching objectives.

PROBLEMS

1. Several criticisms can be made of the following matching test. What are they?

    A

    ——1. George Washington

    ——2. Rapahannock River

    ——3. Boston, Mass.

    ——4. Bunker Hill

    B

    a) scene of a famous tea party

    b) Washington threw a dollar across it

    c) a revolutionary leader

    d) scene of an encounter between the British army and the Minute Men

2. Select a topic in your teaching area and write a matching test at the application level of the taxonomy of educational objectives.

ANALYZING TEST ITEMS

Every item in a test should contribute something to the assessment we are trying to make. In order to see if every item does indeed carry part of the load, some statistical analyses are necessary. The application of these procedures is called *item analysis*. Analysis of test items helps us to not only identify poor items, but also decide why an item is not functioning as we had planned. Hence, item analysis helps us become better test builders.

Here are some procedures we go through in order to build better tests. It should be noted that these methods are appropriate for norm-referenced, but not criterion-referenced, tests.

1. The item should discriminate between people who have achieved well in the topical area and those who have not. Professional test makers find this out by correlating item scores (right and wrong) with the total test score.* With a good item, most of the people who get the item right should be among the high scorers on the test, and most of the people who miss the item should be among the low scorers.

But we do not actually have to correlate items with total scores to get a fair idea of how well an item is discriminating between high and low achievement. A simple, quite serviceable procedure (Johnson 1951) follows.

a) First, we arrange the test papers in order of score, the highest-scoring paper on top, followed by the next highest, etc., throughout the

---

* The statistical procedure for doing this is called biserial correlation.

TABLE 6.1 The number of cases necessary to make up 27 percent of various-sized classes

Number in class	27 percent
25–27	7
28–31	8
32–35	9
36–38	10
39–42	11
43–46	12
47–49	13

entire class. Then, we count down until we have the top 27 percent of the papers; we will call these the "highs." A similar number is selected from the bottom of the stack; they will be called the "lows." We set aside the remaining papers and deal only with the "highs" and "lows." Table 6.1 tells how many papers to select from the top and bottom for various-sized classes. If your group is larger than the class sizes given here, find the number for half your class size and double it. For example, if your class has 50 students, find 27 percent of 25 and double it.

b) We now have papers for two groups of students—the high-scoring 27 percent and the low-scoring 27 percent. Our next job is to compare how the highs and lows marked each test item. To do this, we tabulate how many highs, and then how many lows, got item 1 correct. We do the same for items 2, 3, etc., until we have recorded this information for all items.

c) Next, we subtract the number of low rights from the number of high rights for each item.

d) We then divide the difference found in step (c) by the greatest possible difference to get the *index of discrimination*. How large is the greatest possible difference? If all the highs got the item right and all the lows missed it, the largest possible difference would be produced. This amount is also equal to the number of papers in either of the two groups, i.e., 27 percent of the class size.

For example, suppose there are 30 students in a class. Table 6.2 gives the frequency distribution of their scores, ranked from high to low.

At this point we are ready to begin tabulating for each item the number of highs and lows who got it right. A worksheet like that shown in Table 6.3 makes the job easier. Data for the four items in the test are

TABLE 6.2 A frequency distribution of scores for a classroom test

Score	Frequency		
51	1		27 percent of papers is 8 (Table 6.1)
50	3		
49	0	6	
48	2		
47	5	2	randomly selected highs
46	2	8	highs
45	4		
44	5		
43	2		
42	0		
41	1	8 lows	
40	2		
39	2		
38	1		
Total	30		

TABLE 6.3 Worksheet for tabulating how many highs and lows got each item correct

Item no.	High right	Low right	H-L	Discrimination index
1	7	3	4	.50
2	6	5	1	.12
3	5	3	2	.25
4	5	6	−1	−.12

reported on the worksheet format. The H-L value gives us the difference in number of correct responses between highs and lows. This value is divided by the maximum difference—in this case 8—and the result is the discrimination index.

The purpose of the discrimination index is to tell us if an item really is showing differences between capable students (as shown by total test score) and less capable students. The larger the discrimination index is, the better the item performs this task. But what is the minimum index for an acceptable item? Ebel (1965) has proposed the following criteria for item selection.

If index of discrimination is:	Do the following:
.40 or higher	Accept the item
.30 to .39	Accept, but scrutinize the item for improvement
.20 to .29	Scrutinize item for improvement; may be used as marginal item
.19 and below	Reject, revise item

It should be pointed out, however, that if a test is long (75 to 100 items), we can effectively use items that may be considered marginal on shorter tests (50 or fewer items). We should also note that the index of discrimination is applicable only to tests that have a norm-referenced base, i.e., when we are ranking students among their peers. It is not appropriate for criterion-referenced achievement tests. Item analysis in this latter group of tests deals with adequacy of the sample of behavior, lack of ambiguity of the task, and relation of the task to a success criterion, rather than with a statistical index.

After having completed our item analysis, we are then ready to look at our rejected items to see why they did not turn out the way we had planned. If the item is a multiple-choice item, did the people who missed the item cluster on one alternative? If so, why was that alternative attractive? Have we violated any of the rules of test construction? Was the item ambiguous? How shall we revise it? What shall we avoid in writing future items?

2. As noted earlier, for maximum discrimination the test should be sufficiently difficult so that each item should be missed by at least a portion of the class. One step in item analysis, then, is to establish the difficulty level of an item. This is usually done by merely computing the percentage of students who pass each item, i.e., the number who get an item right divided by the total number of students, times 100. In actual practice, a range of difficulty is allowed, e.g., between 40 and 80 percent for four-option multiple-choice items, and 55 to 85 percent for true-false items. These limits are admittedly arbitrary and are provided only as general guidelines.

If we are using tests to rank people on achievement, items that everyone gets correct do not show differences among individuals, hence contribute nothing to the ranking. This is also true for items that are too difficult. Therefore, we avoid both the very difficult and the very easy item. However, there is an exception to this procedure for noting difficulty. When we rank individuals and use the class mean as a point of departure, we are interpreting our test on a peer, or norm reference, i.e., we are assessing progress against what is average for the group. In this case, moderate difficulty is to be sought after. However, sometimes our test items are all made up of essential content (like the multiplication table), and everyone is expected to know the entire content area. We then assess achievement in terms of a minimum proficiency as shown by a criterion-reference test. In this case, we abandon the difficulty rule, do a careful job of matching test items to minimal levels of acceptable performance, and work toward 100 percent achievement.

3. Professional test makers utilize one additional procedure in item analysis; however, this step is too complex to apply to the typical classroom test without the aid of automated computing equipment. Every item should touch on a unique segment of the content area, a segment not entirely reflected by other items. Therefore, items should not correlate too highly with one another. Professional test builders actually correlate each test item with every other item and eliminate one item from any pair that intercorrelate too highly. In this way they keep the test length down while retaining a set of items, each of which contributes something unique to the total sample of behavior being assessed.

The purpose of item analysis is to identify the items that are doing the job we intend for them to do. Many teachers keep a test file of good items so that they may use them from year to year. This is a useful practice. However, the test file should never be allowed to control the content of instruction. Even statistically good items become obsolete in content and should be eliminated.

A further point should be noted before we leave item analysis. Item statistics, as described here, do tend to fluctuate from one group of students to another. You should not expect to get the same discrimination indices or the same difficulty level on this year's class as on last year's class.

PROBLEMS

Table 6.4 gives the total scores for a group of 25 students who took a 50-item test. We are going to do an item analysis on seven of these items. A "1" indicates that the student got the item correct; a "0" indicates that he missed it. Locate the items that discriminate between high and low achievers (use a criterion of .30). Locate the items that are too difficult and too easy (40% to 80%).

TABLE 6.4 Total and first seven item scores for 25 students

Pupil name	Total score	Item scores						
		1	2	3	4	5	6	7
Aye	47	1	1	0	1	1	1	1
Bee	46	1	0	1	1	1	1	1
Cee	44	1	1	0	1	0	1	1
Dee	44	1	1	1	1	0	1	1
Eey	43	1	1	0	1	1	0	1
Eff	41	1	1	1	0	1	1	0
Gee	40	1	0	1	1	0	1	1
Aych	38	1	0	0	0	1	1	1
Eye	37	0	1	0	1	1	0	0
Jay	37	1	1	0	1	0	1	1
Kay	36	1	0	1	0	0	1	1
El	36	1	1	0	1	1	0	1
Em	36	1	0	0	1	0	1	1
En	34	1	0	0	0	1	1	0
Owe	34	1	0	1	1	1	1	0
Pee	33	1	1	0	1	0	1	1
Kew	32	1	1	0	1	0	1	0
Ar	30	1	1	0	1	0	1	1
Es	30	0	1	0	1	1	0	0
Tee	29	1	1	1	0	1	0	1
Yu	28	1	0	0	1	0	0	1
Vee	27	1	1	0	0	1	0	1
Eks	26	1	0	1	1	0	0	0
Wye	25	1	1	0	0	1	0	1
Zee	24	1	1	0	0	1	1	0
Ans: Discrimination index		.14	.00	.30	.43	.14	.70	.30
Difficulty (%)		92	64	32	68	56	64	68

ESSAY EXAMINATIONS

The essay examination, which completely dominated the classroom measurement field for the first third of the twentieth century, has only grudgingly given ground to the objective test. Advocates of the essay test contend that it alone gets at the student's ability to employ higher mental processes, to be creative, and to organize material into a constructive solution to an expansive problem. Critics of the essay test, on the other hand, point to the unreliability of its scoring, the small sample of content it can assess, and the variety of variables—irrelevant to the subject being considered—that influence the score. Some exploration of the literature may be of assistance at this point.

The classic studies by Starch and Elliot (1913) showed that teachers could not agree on what constitutes a good paper, even in an objective area like mathematics. In one of several studies by Starch and Elliot, 116 high school mathematics teachers independently graded a common geometry paper. It was supposed that on a geometry paper, accuracy of procedure would be easily established and that considerable agreement among readers would result. However, the scores ranged from 28 to 92 percent.

In another study Ashburn (1938) had college professors read the same essays on two different occasions. He found lack of agreement among the professors on each reading and inconsistency between the two readings for a given professor. He concluded that "the passing or failing of 40 percent (of the students) depends, not on what they know or do not know, but on *who* reads the papers," and "the passing or failing of about 10 percent depends . . . on *when* the papers are read." (p. 3)

A number of other studies have continued to point to the unreliability of essay-test scores (Ruch 1929, Traxler and Anderson 1935, Finlayson 1951, Pidgeon and Yates 1957). These studies agree that reader reliability is relatively low for the essay tests. However, Coffman (1966) suggested that previous investigators have shown too much concern for reliability while ignoring the validity of essay tests. He has shown that in spite of apparent reliability problems, acceptable validities can be achieved for essay tests.

We quickly recognize that essay-test users may request a wide range of specificity in the answer. When the information called for is more specific, the agreement between readers increases (Stalnaker 1937, Grant and Caplan 1957). But if we increase specificity of response, we tend to destroy the claimed strength of essay tests, i.e., their latitude in allowing the student to formulate his own response.

Presumably, a competent assessment of a student's achievement would sample a number of behaviors, bits of knowledge, etc., that reflect competence in the basic subject matter. Scores should be free of influences from variables not relevant to the subject. However, Ruch (1929) showed that essay examinations sample less than half of the knowledge that the average pupil demonstrates on objective tests. Other studies have shown that irrelevant variables markedly influence the scores that readers give to essays. For example, quality of handwriting is an important variable in determining a student's score (James 1927, Sheppard 1929, Chase 1968, Marshal and Powers 1969). The order in which papers are read also appears to influence scores given by some readers, first tests read receiving higher scores than later tests read (Bracht and Hopkins 1968). Stanley (1964, p. 258) has summarized the role of the essay test as follows. It "overrates the importance of knowing how to say a thing and underrates the importance of having something to say."

Nonetheless, advocates of essay tests argue ardently for the use of essays to assess the higher-level cognitive skills presumed to be unassessable by objective tests. Some supporting evidence was presented in an early study by Weideman and Newens (1933), who suggested that skills assessed by the essay test go beyond those found in the true-false test. However, the nature of these skills was not identified. This question was investigated further by Bracht and Hopkins (1968), who on two occasions administered both essay and objective tests to 279 college students. Their analysis of the resulting data led them to conclude that "the findings of this study do not support the common supposition that essay and objective tests measure different abilities." In addition, the higher reliability of the objective test led the investigators to favor this tool. Of course, the findings noted in these studies, or in any similar study, are tied to the skill with which the two types of tests were constructed.

An interesting side issue in the Bracht and Hopkins study dealt with the belief held by some students that they do better on one type of examination than on another. This study found no significant relationship between preference for essay or objective tests and scores on these examinations. Many students, and some teachers, will see this as an interesting, if not controversial, finding.

Some teachers believe that students study more extensively for essay tests, noting the broad, pervasive issues and the integrating generalizations. Indeed, Meyer (1935) found that students did use different study techniques for essay and objective tests. However, French (1965) was not convinced that essay tests produce effective study habits, and Hakstian (1971) has shown that students who are faced with an essay test study about the same length of time, organize their materials in about the same way, and use essentially the same study methods as do students faced with an objective test. The evidence does not appear strong in supporting essay tests as a superior stimulant to study.

In summary, there is substantial evidence to indicate that there is a lack of agreement among competent readers as to what the score for a given essay paper should be. Further, the essay examination is a poor sample of the range of topics on which students could be requested to report, and irrelevant variables, such as handwriting, influence a student's score on an essay item. Also, it is not clear what the essay test measures beyond that which can be measured by objective tests, or that essay tests stimulate more effective study on the part of students. These conclusions from research evidence must be given careful consideration when we are thinking about using an essay examination.

Some advocates of the essay examination have suggested that the student's ability to guess the right answer on objective tests is a serious limitation. However, essays also encourage a type of guessing. No student who has even a faint idea about the topic will resist the temptation to write something, especially if he happens to be endowed with higher than average verbal abilities. Further, when a student is faced with a question he cannot answer adequately, essay examinations encourage outright bluffing. At this point, assessment of ability degenerates to a game unrelated to either the course objectives or the purpose of the examination. Under these circumstances it is not surprising that some students reject examinations as irrelevant to the purpose of education.

Ways to improve the essay examination

Although research evidence suggests that the effectiveness of essay examinations has its limitations, these tests still enjoy wide use at many levels of education. If we are going to continue to use essay tests, we must concentrate on constructing them carefully. Here are some suggestions to help us do that.

1. First and foremost, *we should restrict the use of this type of test to assessing those processes for which it is most applicable, and aim the questions directly at those processes.* Curtis (1943) listed 16 types of essay questions used in science textbooks. These types appear sufficiently general to be of benefit to test writers in many areas and are therefore summarized as follows:

a) compare and contrast

b) decision for and against

c) application of fact or principle to a new situation

d) classification

e) relationships involving cause and effect

f) example or illustration

g) statement of author's aim or purpose in the selection or arrangement of materials

h) criticism of adequacy, correctness, relevance of a situation, statement, or diagram

i) inference from data

j) discussion

k) outline

l) explanation or definition

m) simple recall

n) summary

o) observation

p) formulation of new questions

Curtis also noted that of these uses of essays, the most frequent were explanation or definition, and simple recall. These operations, along with outlining and classification, could also be well assessed by several types of objective tests. With these exceptions, however, this list provides suggestions for a number of tasks to which well-designed essay test items may be put. Limiting essays to these purposes is probably advisable.

2. Typically, *the breadth of an essay item should be clearly limited so that the answer can be brief and more specifically tied to a single objective or function.* Broadly stated items such as "What were the forces that led to the outbreak of the Civil War?" call on such a variety of operations—comparing and contrasting economic and social conditions in the North and South, evaluating foreign diplomacy, classifying political sentiments—that the writer must be expansive, and scoring becomes extremely complex. We immediately wrestle with questions of how many conditions are enough, and how much weight shall each condition receive in the score. How much elaboration on each condition is enough? If we had asked a more specific question, e.g., "Compare and contrast the role of agriculture in the economies of the North and South at the outbreak of the Civil War," we could aim it at a more specific objective, and the item could be evaluated much more simply. Additional items could get at other factors related to the war.

3. *All writers should be asked to respond to the same questions.* Since only a few essay items can be presented in the typical testing period, we always run the risk of asking the one thing that a given student is not prepared to handle. If our examination covers only five out of the many topics covered in an instructional unit, it is entirely possible that a student could be knowledgeable in most topics, but not in one of the five we ask him to pursue. His score then suffers a considerable amount, 20 percent. Oftentimes, instructors deal with this eventuality by presenting several items and letting the student select a specified subset on which to write. This practice must be questioned.

If we use measurement devices to compare people, all persons compared must perform the same tasks; otherwise, comparisons cannot be made. For example, suppose we ask students to perform two of the following feats: 100-yard dash, the shot put, and the high jump. We would not propose to compare a student who ran the dash and high jumped with one who high jumped and threw the shot put. True, our essay tasks are probably more similar than these physical events, but the basic principle is the same. We can compare people only to the extent that they have all "jumped the same hurdles." Allowing students to choose their own combinations of essay hurdles does not provide this common base for comparison.

4. *When students begin an essay examination, they should understand fully what it is that they are intended to do.* Test items must be carefully stated so as to define the task. The student should also know on what basis his essay will be scored. Are spelling and grammar being considered a part of the task? Is organization or quantity of supporting data the important consideration? All questions similar to these should be answered for the student before he begins writing. Once again, students should not have to rationalize a poor performance with the statement, "I didn't know what you wanted on that question." The question should clearly reveal what is wanted.

5. *Essays, like objective tests, should be scored by a prescribed method.* Sims (1933) has shown that two readings of an essay test will produce scores much more nearly alike if a prescribed scoring procedure is used than if prescribed methods are not used. There are two widely accepted procedures for scoring essays—the key method and the ranking method. In the key method, we list the elements of an outstanding answer, weighting the elements by giving them a set portion of the total points allotted to an item. For example, if we are allowing ten points for item 1, we may give three of these for element X, two for element Y, and 5 for element Z. We then read the students' papers, seek out X, Y, and Z, and record the points appropriately. One study (Chase 1968) indicated that with such a key, readers are less likely to be influenced by irrelevant conditions (such as quality of penmanship) than they are if no key is used. It should be noted that in using a key, one item should be read across all student papers before going on to the next item, e.g., item 1 should be read on all papers before item 2 is considered.

In the ranking method of scoring, we begin by reading through the first item on several papers to get some feeling for the variety of responses for that item. Then we begin to sort the papers into about five piles according to the quality of responses, the lowest quality going into the first pile, the next lowest going into the next pile, etc. Doubtful papers are laid aside for rereading after all other papers have been sorted on a given item. Points are then assigned to each pile, one point for the lowest-ranking pile, two for the next lowest, etc.

In any method of scoring, objectivity is promoted if we obscure the identity of the essay writer. This can be done in a variety of ways, the most common of which is to assign numbers to students and have their tests identified by number. A second procedure is to use essay booklets with the name on the front cover only. The cover is then folded back on all papers to conceal the names before scoring begins.

Adherence to the above procedures for constructing and scoring essay examinations should materially improve the use of this tool in many classrooms. However, considering the psychometric advantages of an objective test, one should carefully explore the extent to which he can achieve the instructional goal with an objective test instead of an essay examination. Only when it is clear that the goal cannot be assessed by objective means should we proceed with the use of the essay.

PROBLEMS

Criticize the following essay test in history in terms of the rules we have just set up for writing essay tests.

All students must write on four problems. Everyone must respond to the first three items, but may choose between items (d) and (e) for the fourth problem.

a) List the first four presidents of the United States and the vice president(s) that served with each.

b) How do you suppose the British subjects living in England felt about the revolution in America?

c) Compare and contrast the military stature of the British and the American armies of 1776, including supply problems, personnel, and leadership.

d) List four major battles of the Revolutionary War.

e) Why were the Articles of Confederation unsatisfactory?

SUMMARY

In this chapter we have reviewed the construction of the tests most widely used by classroom teachers. It is clear that test-writing is not a simple task. But test-writing can be done effectively with adherence to only a few basic rules.

Each type of test (true-false, multiple choice, etc.) can be applied to a variety of purposes and at a number of levels of Bloom's *Taxonomy of Educational Objectives*. The student is urged to try writing test items of all types that fit the higher levels of the taxonomy, thereby breaking the bondage of fact-oriented objective tests.

Research has shown repeatedly that the scoring of essay tests is unreliable. In addition, they are widely misused. Like objective tests, essays can do a better job for us if we follow a few simple rules in constructing and applying them.

Teachers must assess learning in one way or another. Whether we use criterion- or norm-referenced tests, attention to the rules of writing items will pay off in terms of fairness to our students and better judgments on our part. Assessment is bound to go in schools; why not do the best job we know how?

REFERENCES

Anderson, Scarvia B. "Sequence in multiple-choice item options," *Journal of Educational Psychology,* **43** (1952): 364–368.

Ashburn, Robert R. "An experiment in the essay-type question," *Journal of Experimental Education,* **7** (1938): 1–3.

Boynton, Marcia. "Inclusion of 'none of these' makes spelling items more difficult," *Educational and Psychological Measurement,* **10** (1950): 431–432.

Bracht, Glenn H. and Kenneth D. Hopkins. "Objectives and essay tests: Do they measure different abilities?" (Paper presented at the annual meeting of the American Education Research Association, Chicago 1968.)

Board, Cynthia and Douglas R. Whitney. "The effect of selected poor item-writing practices on test difficulty, reliability and validity," *Journal of Educational Measurement,* **9** (1972): 225–234.

Chase, C. I. "Relative length of option and response set in multiple-choice items," *Educational and Psychological Measurement,* **24** (1964): 861–866.

————. "The impact of some obvious variable on essay-test scores," *Journal of Educational Measurement,* **5** (1968): 315–318.

Coffman, William E. "On the validity of essay tests of achievement," *Journal of Educational Measurement,* **3** (1966): 151–156.

Curtis, Francis D. "Types of thought questions in textbooks of science," *Science Education,* **27** (1943): 60–67.

Dunn, Theodore F. and Leon G. Goldstein. "Test difficulty, validity and reliability as function of selected multiple-choice item construction principles," *Educational and Psychological Measurement,* **19** (1959): 171–179.

Ebel, Robert L., *Measuring Educational Achievement,* Englewood Cliffs, N.J.· Prentice-Hall, 1965.

Finlayson, D. S. "The reliability of marking of essays," *British Journal of Educational Psychology,* **21** (1951): 126–134.

French, John M. "Schools of thought in judging excellence of English themes," in *Testing Problems in Perspective,* ed. Anne Anastasi, Washington, D. C.: American Council on Education, 1965.

Gaffney, Richard F. and Thomas O. Maguire. "Use of optically scored test answer sheets with young children," *Journal of Educational Measurement,* **8** (1971): 103–106.

Grant, L. D. and N. Caplan. "Studies in the reliability of short-answer essay examination," *Journal of Educational Research,* **51** (1957): 109–116.

Hakstian, A. Ralph. "The effects of the type of examination anticipated on test preparation and performance," *Journal of Educational Research,* **65** (1971): 319–324.

Hughes, Herbert and W. E. Trimble. "The use of complex alternatives in multiple-choice items," *Educational and Psychological Measurement,* **25** (1965): 117–126.

James, A. W. "The effect of handwriting on grading," *English Journal,* **16** (1927): 180–205.

Johnson, A. Pemberton. "Notes on a suggested index of validity: the U-L index," *Journal of Educational Measurement,* **6** (1969): 97–101.

Kintsch, W. "Recognition and free recall of organized lists," *Journal of Experimental Psychology,* **78** (1968): 481–487.

Marshall, J. C. and J. M. Power. "Writing neatness, composition errors and essay grades," *Journal of Educational Measurement,* **6** (1969): 97–101.

McMorris, Robert, James O. Brown, Gerald W. Snyder, and Robert M. Pruzek. "Effects of violating item-construction principles," *Journal of Educational Measurement,* **9** (1972): 287–295.

Meyer, George. "An experimental study of the old and new types of examinations: II Method of study," *Journal of Educational Psychology,* **26** (1935): 30–40.

Mosier, Charles, M. Claire Myers, and Helen Price. "Suggestions for construction of multiple-choice test items," *Educational and Psychological Measurement,* **5** (1945): 261–271.

Pidgeon, D. A. and A. Yates. "Experimental inquiry into the use of essay-type English papers," *British Journal of Educational Psychology,* **27** (1957): 37–47.

Rimland, Bernard. "The effect of varying time limits and of using right answer not given in experimental forms of the U. S. Navy arithmetic test," *Educational and Psychological Measurement,* **20** (1960): 533–539.

Ruch, G. M. *The Objective or New Type Examination,* Chicago: Scott, Foresman, 1929, p. 54.

Sheppard, E. M. "The effect of quality of penmanship on grades," *Journal of Educational Research,* **19** (1929): 102–105.

Sims, M. "Reducing the variability of essay examination marks through elementary variation in standards of grading," *Journal of Educational Research,* **26** (1938): 637–647.

Solomon, Alan. "The effect of answer sheet format on test performance by culturally disadvantaged fourth grade elementary school pupils," *Journal of Educational Measurement,* **8** (1971): 289–290.

Stalnaker, John M. "Essay examinations reliably ready," *School and Society,* **46** (1937): 671–672.

Stanley, Julian C. *Measurement in Today's Schools*, 4th ed., Englewood Cliffs, N.J.: Prentice-Hall, 1964.

Starch, Daniel and Edward C. Elliott. "Reliability of grading work in mathematics," *School Review*, **21** (1913): 254–259.

Traxler, Arthur E. and Harold A. Anderson. "The reliability of an essay examination in English," *School Review*, **43** (1935): 534–539.

Weideman, C. C. and L. F. Newens. "Does the compare-and-contrast essay test measure the same mental functions as the true-false test?" *Journal of General Psychology*, **9** (1939): 430–449.

Wesman, A. G. and G. K. Bennett. "The use of 'none of these' as an option in test construction," *Journal of Educational Psychology*, **37** (1946): 541–549.

CHAPTER 7

MEASURING GENERAL ABILITY

In this chapter we shall deal with that large group of tools typically called intelligence tests. But the nature of these tests is varied, and the sample of behavior observed is characteristically heterogeneous, covering a wide range of intellectual activity. For this reason the tests are often referred to as tests of general ability.

STRUCTURE OF INTELLIGENCE AND TEST FORMAT

Although commercial test makers in the United States have been strongly pragmatic in their test-building efforts, they have not just sat down and written up a test. Rather, they followed a series of systematic steps. First, they formulated a detailed description of the trait to be measured, and then they decided what kind of behaviors should reflect this trait. Next, the stimuli—the test items—were arranged to elicit the behaviors to be observed as evidence of the trait.

From a technical position, the point of departure in building an intelligence test should be the description or definition of intelligence. Several theories have been proposed to provide such a description. Two theories of intelligence have most strongly influenced (they certainly have not controlled) test builders in putting together their tools: the group-factor theory and the two-factor theory. A number of definitions have also been submitted, but most of these can be subsumed under one of the two theories above.

Through the process of factor analysis (see Chapter 4), L. L. Thurstone (1933) evolved the *group-factor* theory of intelligence. According to this theory, intelligence is made up of several distinct and separate clusters of ability. Within each cluster are a number of highly related subskills. Each cluster of abilities is unrelated to the other clusters. For example, one group factor may be labeled "number." Here, we may have tests requiring the manipulation of quantities as managed in addition, subtraction, multiplication, and division. This factor is expected to be essentially uncorrelated with, say, the "space" factor, which would include a variety of tests involving conceptualizing and manipulating objects in three-dimensional space. Yes, we may attack number problems in a spatial context, but in solving these problems we draw on two factors of ability. The finesse with which we manipulate the number concepts involved should tell us nothing about how well we will handle the space problem, i.e., the factors are unrelated.

Thurstone concluded that there are seven "primary mental abilities": verbal meaning, word fluency, number, memory, reasoning, space, and perceptual speed. Although there is some evidence that Thurstone's factors are not entirely suitable (Bischof 1954), the group-factor approach has provided a theoretical framework for the construction of several intelligence tests. Thurstone began by producing the *Chicago Primary Mental Abilities*, typically referred to as the PMA. Successive revisions of this test produced the SRA-PMA, published by Science Research Associates. This test is composed of separate subtests within clusters that closely follow the Thurstone factors. Each factor produces a separate score, and the child's intelligence is interpreted from a profile of scores, each reflecting a fairly broad but distinct and not all-encompassing ability. For example, a child may score high in verbal meaning, low in number, about average in reasoning, etc. His behavior in tasks calling for these abilities would be expected to meet with success, relative to his status on the relevant factors.

In contrast with the group-factor model for test construction is the two-factor theory. Charles Spearman (1927), a British psychologist and statistician, believed that intelligence was first and foremost composed of a large, pervasive factor of general intellectual ability, which he called "g" to avoid labeling it as, in fact, intelligence. Supplementing "g" is a wide variety of specific intellectual abilities, or "s," which account for variation in intellectual capacities within a given individual. The "g" factor provides the basis for performance in all cognitive activities. However, we are not equally capable in all mental tasks we undertake. This is explained by variations in the quality of our specific mental abilities. Spearman eventually did acknowledge that some closely related "s" factors look like group factors, but he maintained that in any case, the general factor is of primary importance.

More definitions of intelligence appear to fit within the framework of the two-factor theory than within the group-factor theory. For example, Lewis Terman (1916) defined intelligence as the ability to think in abstract terms. Presumably, this ability pervades behavior regardless of the type of material with which one is dealing. George D. Stoddard (1943) described intelligence as the ability to undertake activities that are characterized by difficulty, complexity, and abstractness, and to perform these acts quickly and adaptively. Again, these performances are not unique to any cluster of mental tasks, but pervade all cognitive behavior.

46. The law of gravitation is —

    (66) obsolete   (67) absolute   (68) approximate   (69) conditional   (70) constitutional . . . .

47. Oil is to toil as (?) is to hate.

    (71) love   (72) work   (73) boil   (74) ate   (75) hat . . . .

48. If 4½ yards of cloth cost 90 cents, what will 3½ yards cost?

    (76) $3.15   (77) 86½¢   (78) 70¢   (79) 89¢   (80) 35¢ . . . .

49. Which number in this series appears a second time nearest the beginning?
    6 4 5 3 7 8 0 9 5 9 8 8 6 5 4 7 3 0 8 9 1

    (81) 9   (82) 0   (83) 8   (84) 6   (85) 5 . . . .

50. This ☆ is to this ✪ as this ◇ is to — (86) ✪ (87) ◇ (88) ◇ (89) ◐ . . .

51. If the first two statements following are true, the third is (?).
    Some of our citizens are Methodists. Some of our citizens are doctors.
    Some of our citizens are Methodist doctors.

    (1) true   (2) false   (3) not certain . . . .

FIG. 7.1 A sample of items from the *Otis Quick-Scoring Mental Ability Test*, Gamma Am, 1937, illustrating the variety of content and serial order of a spiral omnibus test. (Reprinted by permission of Harcourt Brace Jovanovich.)

A test built on the two-factor theory would emphasize behaviors that reflect the "g" factor. This means that the test would produce only a single, general score and that the test items would sample a wide variety of content, e.g., general vocabulary, number combinations, numerical reasoning, spatial relations, analogies, etc. Performance on separate items are added together to get a single, total estimate of general ability. A number of popular intelligence tests follow this format, e.g., the *Otis Quick-Scoring Mental Ability Test* and the *Henman-Nelson Tests of Mental Ability*. Both of these are of the "spiral omnibus" type, i.e., they include a variety of item types (space, verbal, etc.), which are first presented at a low level of difficulty and are repeated again and again at successively higher levels of difficulty (Fig. 7.1.)

Typically, tests that fit the two-factor theory produce a single, total score. However, some tests that assess general intelligence yield more than one score. Here, each score is presumed to reflect general ability, but it is obtained from test items that deal with a given category of behaviors. For example, the well-regarded *Lorge-Thorndike Intelligence Tests* produce two scores: verbal and nonverbal. The tests on which each of these scores is based are not presumed to sample specific, distinct components of intelligence. Rather, they are regarded as reflecting general ability, although in doing this job they employ a given category of skills, i.e., verbal and nonverbal. The *California Test of Mental Maturity* is similar in this regard.

It should be emphasized, however, that all tests that follow the Spearman format are not identical in content. Test makers differ in defining the classes of behavior that are reflections of intelligence. For example, Henman (1931) defined intelligence as the capacity for, and possession of, knowledge. The behaviors that this definition would require are much like those called for by some achievement tests. However, as noted above, Terman built his test around tasks calling for abstract mental operations, e.g., defining abstract terms, making generalizations about information, and interpreting proverbs. Nevertheless, both of these tests are presumed to tap "g."

Of what importance to teachers are the different approaches to building intelligence tests? We usually use general-ability tests to predict the level of general achievement we will see among students. Tests that sample a broad base of skills and are presumably sampling "g" usually correlate better with general indicators of achievement, such as grade-point average, than do tests with more specific content. However, if we wish to predict achievement in a rather circumscribed area, e.g., arithmetic, a test that has more specific content may do the job better, and for this purpose a group-factor test may be more appropriate.

But this view seems to avoid dealing with the question of what theory of intelligence is indeed the most adequate. The fact is that there are valid arguments in favor of each theory, and there are some that indicate that both theories may be inadequate. However, in the applied world we pragmatically capitalize on all procedures that allow us to do a job we have in mind. And tests based on the two-factor theory serve us well in many situations, whereas tests based on group factors may be useful in others.*

PROBLEMS

For each test below, decide which theory—two factor or group factor—is most likely being followed.

1. I have a collection of test items including vocabulary, arithmetic story problems, abstract reasoning, and abstractly manipulating forms in space. I present the items in a mixed order, score them right or wrong, and add up the right answers for a total mental-ability score.

---

* At this point it should be noted that Guilford (1959) has developed a very complex design of intellect which has generated much interest and activity among psychologists and educators. However, tests used in typical school programs have not yet been developed out of Guilford's theory, and therefore a summary of his position is not presented here.

2. I have divided my test into five subtests: vocabulary and verbal analogies, arithmetic operations, manipulation of objects in space, memory items, and speed of visual discovery of disparities in triads of abstract forms. I get a separate ability score on each of these subtests.

3. I believe that an intelligence-test score should discriminate between children who do well in school and those who do poorly. I collect a variety of item types and retain all items on which the students receiving good school marks do better than the students who are receiving poor school marks. I put these items together into my test. The child's score is the number of items he correctly completes in 20 minutes.

MENTAL AGE AND IQ

In his revisions of his original test, Binet arranged each item so that it appeared at the age level at which children were expected to pass the item. We very soon began thinking about a test score in relation to the age at which a child is expected to get that score. For example, suppose the average score on test X for children who are exactly eight years old is ten items correct. We would then say that a test score of 10 represents the mental development, or "mental age" (MA), of eight years. Regardless of a child's actual chronological age (CA), if he gets ten items correct on test X, he has a mental age of eight years. The mental age, then, is the average test score achieved by a given age group. An MA of 11 is the average score achieved by 11-year-olds; an MA of nine is the average test score achieved by nine year-olds, etc.

The child who has an MA of nine but is indeed only eight years old is maturing mentally more rapidly than is typical for his age mates. Similarly, the child who is ten years old and has an MA of nine is maturing mentally at a slower rate than is typical of his age mates. The MA, used in conjunction with the child's age in years (CA), can indicate a given child's *rate* of mental growth. This ratio of MA with CA, multiplied by 100 to make it a whole number, is the *intelligence quotient,* or IQ.

$$IQ = \frac{MA}{CA} \times 100$$

For a moment, let us go back to our elementary school arithmetic. There, we learned to find out how fast a car was going by noting how far it had gone and how long it took the car to get there. Our formula was

$$\text{rate} = \frac{\text{distance}}{\text{time}}.$$

Now, making the analogy between the formula for rate and for IQ, we see that MA tells us how far down the road of mental development a child has gone; CA tells us how long it took him to get there. IQ, therefore, is an indicator of rate of mental growth. Children who are developing more rapidly than is typical for their age mates will have an MA larger than their CA, and their IQs will be more than 100. However, children who are developing more slowly will have IQs below 100.

At this point we should note that there are several reasons to be cautious in using the IQ. One reason is that different tests may well produce different IQs for the same child. We have already seen that test scores may be related to test content. Also, a test score is interpreted in terms of the age level at which children typically achieve it. What were the children like on whom these standards were established? Chances are that the children used to standardize test A were not identical to those on whom test B was standardized. If this is so, norms on intelligence test A are not directly comparable to norms on test B. For example, the average score on a given test made by 200 ten-year-olds from Fargo, North Dakota is likely to be quite different from the average score made on the same test by 200 ten-year-olds from the inner city area of Chicago. Of course, the populations from which two makers of intelligence tests collect their data will not be this different in basic character. But differences do exist among the samples of the population on which various test-makers develop their examinations. These differences can produce disparities between MAs produced by two intelligence tests.

Further, IQs are often not comparable from one age level to another on a given test. If we put the IQs of all children of a given age into a frequency distribution, we expect the distribution to be bell-shaped. We can compute a mean IQ for the age (typically, about 100 IQ) and a standard deviation showing dispersion of IQs around the mean. But for a given test, the mean and the standard deviation of IQs at one age may not equal those figures for another age. This complicates our interpretation of IQ scores taken from time to time as the child grows older. For example, let us assume that we have a distribution of IQs for test A for the "population" of six-year-olds and another distribution for twelve-year-olds. Let us also assume that the standard deviation for our test at six years is 18 IQ points; at twelve years, 13 IQ points. Assume for convenience that the mean IQ at both ages is 100. John at age six has an IQ of 82, i.e., one standard deviation below the mean or just above the lowest 16 percent of the "population." At age 12 he has an IQ of 87. Has his score increased? As before, he is still one standard deviation below the mean, even though his score is now five points higher. This situation is shown in Fig. 7.2.

Similarly, IQs are often not comparable from test A to test B. Statistical characteristics that describe average performance and deviations from

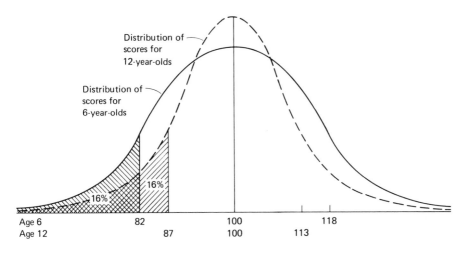

FIG. 7.2 Distribution of IQs at two age levels.

this average vary from a test made by one company to one made by another company. Let us assume that we have our two tests, A and B. Test A has a mean IQ of 100 and a standard deviation of 18. Test B also has a mean IQ of 100, but has a standard deviation of 12. Suppose also that John Wye, age 12, ranks in the "real world" above 84 percent of all children of his age level. We know from Chapter 3 that this puts John one standard deviation above the mean in a normal distribution. One standard deviation above the mean for test A is 100 plus 18, or an IQ of 118; for test B, one standard deviations above the mean is 100 plus 12, or an IQ of 112. Clearly, differences in the statistical characteristics of tests do not allow us to compare IQs directly from one test to another.

Do discrepancies between IQs in fact exist from one intelligence test to another? Lennon (1953) provided evidence that they do. For example, he found that an IQ of 130 on the *Terman-McNemar Test of Mental Ability* is equal to 123 on the *Otis Quick-Scoring Test* and 126 on the *Pintner General Ability Tests*. An IQ of 80 on the Terman is comparable to 83 on the Otis and 74 on the Pinter. These differences are obviously important ones. For example, with this last set of figures, the Pintner score may have led us to request further diagnosis of one child for possible placement in a class for the educable mentally retarded, but on the basis of the Otis or the Terman tests, we would have retained the child in a standard classroom. The skilled test user must rely heavily on knowing what a given test tells him in terms of a set of behaviors he wishes to predict. This means that extensive experience with a given test is essential before we can make our best judgments based on its scores.

In the example noted earlier, the distributions of scores for tests A and B could have the same average IQ but different standard deviations. If this is so, we must have different scores on tests A and B in order to achieve a given rank in the population. A score of 118 on test A showed the same rank in the population as a score of 112 on test B. An additional problem also arises with the ratio IQ. As one approaches adulthood, mental growth, like physical growth, levels off. The idea of an ever-increasing MA with passing years is misleading. To avoid these problems, the *deviation IQ* has been developed. With the deviation IQ, we assign a value of 100 to the average intelligence-test performance for a given age group. We then equate the standard deviation of the test to 15 IQ points.* With the deviation IQ, a person who ranks one standard deviation above the mean at one age will have the same IQ (115) as a person who ranks one standard deviation above the mean at other ages. Also, test scores can be compared between tests if both test makers have used this procedure for computing deviation IQs. But here is a word of caution. Although the deviation IQ score on one test may be statistically comparable with a deviation IQ on another, this does not guarantee that the scores are psychologically comparable in terms of test content and the characteristics of the people on whom the two tests were standardized.

PROBLEMS

1. Jack Witte has an MA of nine, although he is actually only eight years old. His IQ at this testing is 113. Which figure tells us the level of Jack's mental development at this point? Which figure tells us the rate at which he is developing?

2. Jim Quik had an IQ of 116 on the Zeta Intelligence Test. He then took the Omega Intelligence Test and came up with an IQ score of 120. Zeta has a mean IQ of 102 and a standard deviation of 14. Omega has a mean of 100 and a standard deviation of 20. What do you make of the difference in Jim's IQ between the two tests?

3. In the situation in problem 2, what would Jim's deviation IQ be on Zeta? On Omega? (Assume the deviation IQ scale has a mean IQ of 100 and a standard deviation of 15 IQ points.)

(ans: Zeta 115; Omega 115)

---

* A standard deviation of 16 points is used on the most recent revision of the *Stanford-Binet Intelligence Scale.*

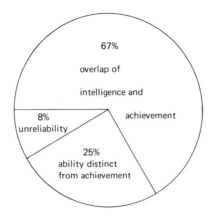

FIG. 7.3 Correlation of *Otis Quick-Scoring Mental Abilities Test* with an achievement test.

OVERLAP OF INTELLIGENCE AND ACHIEVEMENT-TEST SCORES

Look at the items in almost any intelligence test. Many, if not most, of the items will appear to be assessing achievement in a basic school instructional area. Take this item, for example.

Asbestos is produced from:

a) trees   b) mines   c) cotton   d) petroleum

This item could reasonably be found on either an achievement or intelligence test. It is in fact a revision of an item from an intelligence test. Some argue, of course, that a good indicator of what a child *can* learn is what he *has already* learned. Using this argument, a test maker would certainly include a sampling of achievement-type items in his test. However, this view requires us to assume that all children have had essentially equal opportunities to learn. We can readily reject this hypothesis.

Nevertheless, regardless of content, performance on intelligence tests overlaps, or is correlated with, achievement in school subjects. How much do we expect this overlap to be? On a group of 147 children from grades 4, 5, and 6, the Kuder-Richardson reliability for the *Otis Quick-Scoring Mental Abilities Test* was .92. The Otis correlated .82 with total scores on an achievement test. These data can be translated into the diagram shown in Fig. 7.3.*

* For a description of the procedure and an example with different data, see Lee J. Cronbach, *Essentials of Psychological Testing*, 2d ed., New York: Harper and Brothers, 1960, pp. 223–224. The data above were taken from a local evaluation study done by the author.

Is the overlap between intelligence tests and achievement tests too great? Coleman and Cureton (1954) argue that there is not enough distinct ability assessed by intelligence tests to distinguish them from general achievement. Certainly the two types of tests do overlap considerably, and we would be surprised if they did not. We expect the achievement of brighter children to be above average, whereas we expect that of duller children to be below average. These, of course, are roughly the ingredients for a substantial correlation between intelligence and achievement-test scores. This expected correlation has indeed led some test makers to use school performance, as assessed by several different yardsticks of success, as a criterion against which intelligence tests are validated, as we shall soon see.

If the two types of tests overlap so much, why do we use intelligence tests? For one reason, they are a quick estimate of a child's ability, and they allow us to make some reasonable judgments in the absence of other data. Also, they are diagnostic aids in dealing with learning disabilities. The discrepancies that appear between intelligence-test scores and achievement are often the first observation made by psychologists who deal with learning problems. Also, discrepancies between intelligence scores obtained by two types of tests (e.g., verbal and nonverbal) may give us important insight into a child's learning problems.

Reading ability and scores on general abilities tests

For the most part, general-ability tests are highly verbal in content. Even when number or spatial items are included, each of these types of items is typically accompanied by verbal instructions; or, the numbers or objects in space are presented in a verbal context. These items require reading ability. There are exceptions, of course, like the PMA spatial-relations subtest or the Lorge-Thorndike nonverbal subtest, but for the most part, group tests (and some individual tests) of general ability are highly verbal in content.

The dependence of test makers on verbal items appears to place a heavy demand on the reading skill of students taking the test. Clearly, some reading ability is a necessity for taking most group general-ability tests, but are these tests essentially tests of reading skill? Several studies have dealt with this question, but the results are equivocal. Hawthorne (1935) found that although remedial instruction improved children's reading-test scores markedly, no important change occurred in their intelligence-test score. He concluded that for upper-elementary age children, retardation in reading of up to three years does not have a depreciating effect on the IQ as measured by group verbal tests of general ability. Working with older adolescents, Blair and Kammon (1942) came to a similar conclusion. In their study of early adolescents, Barbe and Grilk (1952) found that reading rate may not be as important in group tests of intelligence as a subjective analysis would lead us to think. However, reading-comprehension skills did show a moderate correlation with intelligence-test scores. This study confirmed the conclusions by Strang (1943).

On the other hand, Lowry (1932) used a design similar to Hawthorne's and concluded that IQs on group tests may be largely reading scores. Durrell (1933) provided supporting evidence for this conclusion, whereas Manolakes and Sheldon (1955) found the relation between reading ability and intelligence to vary with the child's age.

Clear complications appear in the design of several of these studies, limiting the strength of their conclusions. The least that can be said is that the role of reading skill in achieving scores on intelligence tests has not been empirically established. Rate is probably not as large a factor as is comprehension. A certain minimum level of reading ability is clearly necessary to get high scores on group verbal-intelligence tests; however, it is not clear that successive levels of attainment, as shown by reading tests, will add proportionately to intelligence-test scores.

The speed factor in intelligence tests

The various definitions of intelligence often include speed of operation as a relevant factor. If two children can perform a given task, the one who can do it more rapidly is presumed to be the more capable. Most group intelligence tests, consequently, have a carefully-controlled time limit. How restrictive are these time limits? Would a child's score be appreciably different if he had been given more time? Eells' (1948) data indicated that for tests built on items of steadily increasing difficulty, additional time had very little influence on total scores. For example, when children between nine and ten years old were given 50 minutes to complete the 30-minute Henman-Nelson test, their scores increased by only 3.4 raw score points. Slightly older children taking the 30-minute Otis Beta increased their scores by an average of only 0.9 points when given 15 additional minutes to work. Apparently, most test makers have paced their tests so that the typical child has just about reached his maximum level of difficulty by the end of the allotted time. However, in individual cases this will probably not be true, and it is certainly not true for tests that contain a large rate-of-work component, such as the PMA-Number or the Verbal Fluency tests.

Social class and ethnic biases in general-ability tests

The widely read and often cited research by Eells, et al. (1951) directed considerable attention to the fact that intelligence tests are more demanding for lower-class children than they are for middle-class children. A casual skimming of many tests would support these findings. Many of the concepts are tied to experiences common to middle-class rather than lower-class families. For example, consider the following analogy.

Snow White is to the wicked queen as Cinderella is to:

a) the witch   b) the mother-in-law
c) the stepmother   d) the fortune teller

A child who succeeds on this item must have experienced a certain array of children's literature. A child who has not heard these stories, regardless of his verbal and reasoning abilities, probably will not get the item correct. Eells' data also show that lower-class children are about as handicapped on one kind of subtest item as they are on another, e.g., we do not expect class difference to be greater on a verbal subtest than on a performance subtest.

An added complexity is the matter of race. Lesser, *et al.* (1964) have shown notable differences among Jewish, Chinese, Negro, and Puerto Rican children in their abilities to deal with verbal, reasoning, numerical, and space subtests. No ethnic group was inferior on all types of test items, and no group was superior on all types. Clear differences also appeared between middle- and lower-class children within the same ethnic group.

The existence of differences among cultural groups in test performance is no longer a question. However, their meaning and what to do about them pose great problems. One attempt has been to develop "culture fair" tests, such as the *Davis-Eells Games.* However, the evidence (Ludlow 1956) appears to suggest that such tests do not eliminate cultural differences in test scores.

The relative function of environment and heredity in the development of intelligence has long been a source of controversy in education. Although much has been said about genetic controls on intelligence (Jensen 1969), the focus in recent years has featured the environmental factor somewhat more prominently than heredity. Hunt (1951) has argued that the child's capacity to process incoming stimuli and produce effective motor reactions to these stimuli is rooted in his earliest encounters with the world around him. If this is so, intelligence is not entirely a genetically fixed trait. It is a dynamic property that is tied to innumerable experiential factors. Environments rich in stimulating experiences would be required for optimum mental development.

Further, we cannot measure intelligence directly. Instead, we infer it from observing a class of behaviors we define as "intelligent." The definition will inevitably be stated in terms of cultural norms and values. It seems reasonable that what is classified as intelligent behavior in one culture may not be regarded as intelligent behavior in another.

It cannot be denied that the ghetto areas in large cities where many black Americans grow up do not provide the kinds of stimulation necessary for optimum cognitive development (Havighurst 1969, Schoggen 1969, Smilansky 1968, Hess and Shipman 1965, Bernstein 1961). This problem is true of all lower-class children as well, but is especially complicated by two factors among black children (Pettigrew 1964). First, society has imposed a limiting set of expectations on black children which diverts them from seeking many experiences and dilutes their motivation for others. Second, when the environment does pose demands on black children, it seldom stimulates behaviors that develop the abilities defined by the white middle class as intelligent. Therefore, it appears reasonable to conclude that cultural differences among the races and social classes have inadequately equipped black children to deal with tests that report behaviors appropriate for success on standard intelligence tests. This conclusion must temper our interpretation of general-ability test scores obtained on black children.

Most of the attention to this point has been focused on the development and definition of intelligence when cultural differences clearly exist. Little has been said about the ability of different cultural groups to deal with the criterion performances against which the tests were validated. If these performances favor one social class or ethnic group, then certainly valid tests must also favor that group (Thorndike 1971).

Since many intelligence tests are validated against a criterion of school success, the middle-class bias in schools must certainly influence test content. Because one of the leading uses of tests is to predict success in schools, a middle-class bias in tests will probably not only be evident, but is also appropriate. To predict success in a biased program, we must use tests with a similar bias. As the content of instruction in school changes, so must the tests used to predict success in instructional programs change if they are to continue to be valid.

Constancy of the IQ

A popular idea about intelligence is that it is a relatively stable condition throughout life. In other words, a child who is average at age five will be average at age 21; a child with an IQ of 130 at age five will have an IQ of 130 at age 21, etc. This, however, is not necessarily the case. In intelligence, as in other developmental traits, a given child grows at a different rate at different ages.

A carefully designed study of the stability of IQ was conducted by Honzik, Macfarlane and Allen (1949). They began a longitudinal study of 252 children from birth into adulthood. During the bulk of the school-age years, children were tested with the Stanford-Binet, an individual test of wide repute. Several findings are especially important to our interpretation of IQs. The older the child is, the more stable his IQ becomes. For example, the correlation between IQs taken at ages 4 and 6, a two-year span, was

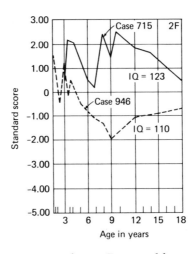

FIG. 7.4 IQ fluctuations of two students. (Reprinted by permission from Marjorie P. Honzik, Jean W. Macfarlane, and Lucile Allen, "The stability of mental test performance between two and eighteen years," *Journal of Experimental Education,* **17** (Dec. 1949), p. 318.)

.62, whereas the correlation between IQs taken at ages 8 and 14, a six-year span, was .85. Test scores taken on children during preschool years were of little value in predicting IQs during school-age years. In fact, IQs taken on children up to age five did a mediocre to poor job of predicting the IQ over even a one-year span.

The study provided several other interesting results. During the school-age years, ages 6 to 18, how much fluctuation should we expect in a typical child's IQ? If we followed a given child from year to year between ages 6 and 18 and took the difference between the highest and lowest IQs he scored in these years, how great would that difference be? Five points? Ten points? Honzik, *et al.,* found that the IQs of almost 60 percent of the group fluctuated 15 points or more. In addition, the IQ of one out of every three children in the group fluctuated 20 points or more, and the IQ of one out of every ten fluctuated 30 points or more. Only 15 percent of the group changed less than 10 points. It is clear that changes in IQ within a range of at least 10 points are common among children during their school years. An example of fluctuations in IQ in two cases from Honzik's study are shown in Fig. 7.4.

If fluctuation in IQ is to be expected, what can we say about the direction of change? Some children in the study showed consistent upward or downward trends, resulting in gradual changes that eventually accumulated up to 50 IQ points. The trends in IQ changes tended to be in the direction of the family level, as measured by parental education and socioeconomic status. That is, if a child with an initially high IQ has poorly educated parents who are in the unskilled labor market, his IQ would typically show a downward trend through the years to young adulthood. By contrast, if a child with an initially low IQ has parents who are professional people, his IQ would be expected to show an upward trend during his developmental years.

We often hear that emotionally charged situations in a child's life affect his IQ scores during periods of the emotional pressure. Honzik, *et al.*, noted that children whose scores showed marked fluctuations did have disturbing influences in their lives; however, it is significant to note that other children whose histories included highly disturbing experiences showed relatively little IQ change. It appears, then, that emotional pressures may be associated with IQ fluctuation, but they do not invariably precipitate such fluctuations.

The results of this study suggest that if we are to depend on IQs to indicate a given child's intelligence, we must have more frequent tests at early ages rather than in later years. Also, we clearly should expect the child's IQ to change from testing to testing during his school years. Most likely, over the years, the IQ will change in the direction of the family's educational and socioeconomic level.

PROBLEMS

Respond to each of the following comments made by a school patron.

1. "I don't believe that this intelligence test really gave Billy a chance. You know he's only an average reader, and this test had a lot of reading in it and not much time to do it in."

2. "The time limits on this test were tough! I'm sure Jill would have done much better if she could have had another 15 or 20 minutes to work."

3. "Yes, Melvin's lower-class background is a handicap to him in taking this intelligence test. I'm sure he'll do much better in this (middle-class-oriented) curriculum than his test score suggests he will."

4. "George had an intelligence test in the first grade and his IQ was 97; now in the fourth grade, it is 108. You just can't believe those tests!"

5. "IQ is like a bucket in your head with so much water being poured in when you're born, and that's the amount you'll have the rest of your life."

VALIDATION OF INTELLIGENCE TESTS

The basic procedure for establishing the validity level of general-ability tests is construct validation. In Chapter 4 we noted that the first job in construct validation is to establish a tightly knit theory of the construct and then to test out predictions about behavior from the theory. If the test is valid, it should provide results consistent with the theory. We noted that there are several basic kinds of data typically used to show to what extent the test results fit the theory: (a) differences between two classified groups, (b) correlations with other kinds of measures, (c) internal consistency, (d) studies of change after intervening experience, and (e) studies of test-taking process. Of these sources of support for claims of construct validity, only the first two, and possibly the third, are used widely by makers of intelligence tests.

Theories of intelligence suggest differences between at least two types of groups: those based on age of the child and those based on rate of progress in school. Typically, we expect older children to be more intelligent than younger ones. If our tests are valid, older children should get more items correct than younger children do. The Kuhlmann-Anderson Intelligence Test has in fact employed this procedure as one source of evidence for its validity (Kuhlmann 1952). Similarly, children who have moved ahead of their age mates in school should be more intelligent than children who have fallen behind their age mates. A valid test will provide higher scores for children who are accelerated in grade level compared to those who are retarded. The Kuhlmann-Anderson also calls upon this observation as evidence of the test's validity.

Probably no single source of evidence for construct validity is employed more than correlational data. Scores on general-ability tests are typically correlated with other tests of this type on the assumption that if the other tests are valid, so must this test be. Also, these tests are typically correlated with evidence of school success such as marks, teachers' ratings, and achievement-test data. For example, the verbal scale of the *Lorge-Thorndike Intelligence Test* was found to correlate .84 with the Otis, while the nonverbal scale correlated .71 with the Otis (Lorge and Thorndike 1962). The Henman-Nelson correlated with the Stanford-Binet at .737 (Lamke and Nelson 1959). These values are typical of the correlations we see between two, good, general-ability tests.

Some samples of tests correlated with school achievement will illustrate the predictive validity of general-ability tests. The Henman-Nelson correlated with the median scores on the *Stanford Achievement Battery* at .75, with average reading scores on the *Stanford Achievement* at .65, also at .65 with school marks in reading, at .57 with marks in arithmetic, and at .68 with total grade point. All these correlations were computed from data on midwestern sixth-grade children (Lamke and Nelson 1957). It should be pointed out that correlations tend to be lower for primary school children and higher for upper-elementary school children. If intelligence is an important factor in determining achievement, intelligence and achievement tests should correlate quite substantially. However, other variables clearly are involved in achievement, so especially high correlations between these two types of tests are not hoped for.

Correlational methods have also been expanded into factor analysis as a source of validity data for intelligence tests. Here, the objective is to illustrate that the ingredients that theory says constitute intelligent behavior are indeed in the behaviors sampled by the test and that ingredients unrelated to intelligent behavior are held to a minimum. As noted earlier, the *Primary Mental Abilities* test was developed from this point of view.

RELIABILITY OF GENERAL-ABILITY TESTS

General-ability tests are probably the most stable tools available to the psychometrist. Typically, reliabilities often run near .90, and occasionally above this point. Age of the pupil is, however, related to test reliability. Younger children tend to produce less stable scores than do older ones. (We noticed this in the data provided on constancy of the IQ.) For example, the Lorge-Thorndike, a carefully designed test, reported alternate-forms reliability of .91 for a group of first-grade children, but four-month retest data correlated at only .76 with the original test. For older children, the correlations between tests given as much as two years apart run in the vicinity of .75, and some are even higher. For the older children, the stability of scores over a two-year span was about what it was over four months for the first graders.

Although the generalization that the older the child, the more stable his test score will become appears to be true, we may have considerable error in estimating general ability even with older children if several years have elapsed since the score was obtained. The standard error of measurement cited in Chapter 4 will illustrate this point. Using the retest value of .75 given above and assuming that the typical general-ability test has a standard deviation of 15 IQ points, we can compute the following standard error:

$$\sigma_e = \sigma_t \sqrt{1 - r_{11}}$$
$$= 15 \sqrt{1 - .75}$$
$$= 15 \times .5$$
$$= 7.5.$$

You recall from Chapter 4 that the standard error may be interpreted as follows. For all children with a given test score, two-thirds will have *true* scores between ± 1.0 standard error. Hence, two-thirds of all children whose test scores produced an IQ of, say, 110 will in fact have true scores in the range of 102.5 to 117.5. Now this is quite a wide range of talent from which to make predictions. To complicate the matter, we cannot tell from looking at a given child's score if it is an overestimate or an underestimate of his true score. We cannot tell if John Ecks, whose test score produces an IQ of 110, has a true score of 103, 107, 110, 113, 117, or any other score within the range of 102.5 to 117.5. Also, a third of the pupils with test-score IQs of 110 will have true IQs *beyond* the range of 102.5 to 117.5. Our estimates of their ability will be even farther off. Therefore, the use of "old" general-ability test scores for making judgments about individuals is hazardous.

Recently administered tests (within a year of administration for upper-elementary age children and adolescents, within the month of administration for primary school children) are much more dependable, but even then we expect standard errors of measurement of almost five points. This possible error suggests that we seek out tests with the highest reliability available when we intend to make judgments about individuals. For judgments about groups, individual errors tend to average out, allowing us to utilize less reliable tools.

Now that we have seen the hazard of judgments based on intelligence tests, an additional point should be emphasized. Decisions based on information that may include a calculated range of error are clearly superior to those based on no information at all. Therefore, in the absence of other data to indicate a child's ability, even "old" intelligence-test scores may be of some use. In any case, decisions based on the results of intelligence tests are always best when supported by corroborating evidence, such as other intelligence tests, achievement reports, or teachers' testimonies.

PROBLEMS

I wish to build an intelligence test and have begun by accepting the definition of intelligence as "the ability to learn."

1.   What kind of content should I put into my items?

2.   How can I see if this test is valid—what criteria of validity could I use?

3.   If this test should some day rank among the "good" tests of intelligence, what size reliability coefficients should we expect it to produce? Will the reliability coefficients be higher for young children (first graders) or older ones (junior high school age)?

INDIVIDUAL TESTS OF GENERAL ABILITY

To this point, we have been talking about paper-and-pencil general-ability tests that are typically administered to groups of students simultaneously. The data on constancy of the IQ submitted by Honzik, *et al.*, is the one exception. However, educators have found considerable use for individual tests—tests that are given to a single person at a time. Carefully trained administrators are required in the use of individual tests. The necessary training of the psychometrist and the time involved in administering those tests make them expensive tools to apply. However, their precision and diagnostic quality make them most desirable for use in attacking an important segment of education problems.

Two groups of tests have dominated the individual testing field: the *Stanford Revision of the Binet Scales*—popularly referred to as the Stanford-Binet—and the Wechsler tests. We shall look at the Stanford-Binet first.

As we saw in Chapter 2, Binet's test was revised by Lewis Terman at Stanford University in 1916. Other revisions appeared in 1937, 1960, and 1973, respectively. Each of these revisions followed considerable research and practical experience with the test. Although no major internal changes were made in test format from the 1937 to the 1960 scales, it was becoming quite evident that several changes in the test were needed. In the 1937 test the standard deviation of IQs ranged from 20.6 points at age 2½ to 12.5 points at age 6, to 20 points at age 12. Sixteen points was taken as the ideal standard deviation. Clearly, this fluctuation in standard deviation from age to age presented a problem in interpreting the scores. A child one standard deviation above the mean at age 6 would have an IQ of 112.5, while at age 12 he would need an IQ of 120 to be at the same point in the population, i.e., one standard deviation above the mean. Similar fluctuations from age to age were also found in the mean. Also, some of the test items, including the vocabulary with which they were presented, were becoming obsolete. Other items no longer fit the age level at which they had been placed in 1937.

The 1960 Stanford-Binet has only one form, whereas the 1937 had two —forms L and M. The best items from L and M, as judged by statistical criteria, were combined into a single form and restandardized. This form became the 1960 revision. Item difficulty and discrimination were based on an up-to-date sample of increasingly aware children. As in the earlier test, each Binet item must show increasing numbers of children passing the item with each successive age level.

The 1937 Binet was criticized for having a middle-class bias in the sample of children on which the test was standardized. In the 1960 scale the sample was carefully stratified on a socioeconomic index to eliminate the middle-class bias of norms. In addition, to avoid the statistical problems involved in different means and standard deviation from age to age, a modified deviation IQ was incorporated into the 1960 revision of the Stanford-Binet. In terms of position in the group, an IQ of 116 at age six means essentially the same as does an IQ of 116 at any other age. The Binet IQ now has a mean of 100 and standard deviation of 16 at all age levels.

The 1973 edition continues the updating of content and norms which characterized the 1960 scale. No major changes were made in format, however.

The Stanford-Binet is an age scale, i.e., a separate set of items at appropriate difficulty is arranged for each age level. From ages two through five, a new set of tasks is provided for each six months of age. From ages five to fourteen, the tests are spaced at one-year intervals. Beyond this point there is one "average" adult test and three "superior" adult tests.

Age eight provides a typical example of the kinds of tasks included in the Stanford-Binet. There are six items at this age level:

1. *Vocabulary:* The examiner reads words aloud and asks the child to tell what each word means.
2. *Memory for stories:* A story is read to the child while he follows along on a separate copy. The child's copy is then taken away and several questions are asked about the content of the story.
3. *Verbal absurdities:* The child is given several absurd statements and is asked to tell why each is "foolish."
4. *Similarities and differences:* The examiner names two objects and then asks the child to tell how these objects are alike and how they are different. There are four sets of objects in this test.
5. *Comprehension:* A situation including a problem is presented, and the child is asked to provide appropriate action. There are six parts to this item.
6. The child is asked to name the days of the week.

A review of these six rather typical Binet tasks reveals that they depend heavily on abstract reasoning. Reading ability is not necessary, but verbal skills clearly play a large role in success on this test. This is one reason Binet IQs are relatively useful as predictors of school success in our typically very verbal middle-class school curricula.

The long-standing popularity of the Stanford-Binet has been seriously challenged by only one other group of tests—the Wechsler scales. The first of these scales, produced by David Wechsler in 1939, was called the *Wechsler-Bellvue Intelligence Scale.* The Binet had been criticized as not being as appropriate for adults as for children. The Wechsler was specifically designed for assessing adult intelligence. It was also intended to show deviant patterns of responses which characterized various types of psychopathology. Although it appeared abundantly logical that problems of mental health would affect performance on certain kinds of items on an intelligence test, considerable research has failed to establish clear response patterns on the Wechsler that characterize various psychological problems. Therefore, the greatest use of the test has been for the measurement of intelligence, not the diagnosis of psychopathology.

In 1949 the *Wechsler Intelligence Scale for Children* (WISC) was published. It covered ages five through fifteen, following the basic format of the Wechsler-Bellevue. In 1955 the Wechsler-Bellevue was revised and renamed the *Wechsler Adult Intelligence Scale* (WAIS). It was designed to begin where the WISC left off—age 16—and continue through adulthood. The most recent scale, the *Wechsler Pre-school and Primary Scale of Intelligence* (WPPSI),* was published in 1967 and is designed for children from ages four to six years, six months.

All the Wechsler tests use the same basic format. The WAIS and the WISC contain one set of six subtests that makes up the verbal scale, and a second set of five subtests makes up the performance scale. The verbal tests are information, comprehension, arithmetic, similarities, digit span, and vocabulary. The performance scale is made up of digit symbol, picture completion, block design, picture arrangement, and object assembly. The WPPSI has a similar formation, with some adaptations to accommodate the younger children for which it is intended. Items in each subtest of the Wechsler scales are arranged in increasing difficulty, but difficulty of any given item is not intended to correspond with the age at which it is to be passed. The test taker begins on a given subtest and works until he no longer can meet the criterion of success. Then he moves to the next subtest. In contrast to the Stanford-Binet, the test is scored by points for correctly answered items, not by months of mental age. A deviation IQ can be obtained for either the verbal or the performance scale, as well as for the total test. The mean IQ at any age is regarded as 100, with a standard deviation of 15 points.

The WISC was developed as an extension to the lower age levels of the Wechsler-Bellevue. The utility of the WISC as a measure of children's intelligence is essentially unquestioned. Its ability to produce a nonverbal, as well as verbal and total, IQ has had much to do with its popularity, especially as a tool to use with children who have language handicaps.

The WISC has, however, proved to be slightly difficult for work with preschool children, especially those suspected of being handicapped by mental retardation or by limited cultural backgrounds. Hence, the WPPSI

---

* The acronym is typically used in speaking about Wechsler tests. The WISC is pronounced "wisk," the WAIS rhymes with "mace," and the WPPSI is pronounced "wippsey."

was developed not only as an extension of the Wechsler scales to even younger children, but also as a test that provided a wider variety of items appropriate for more precise discrimination between children at the pre-school and first-grade levels.

The Stanford-Binet and the Wechsler scales both enjoy wide use as individual measures of intelligence. What is there to choose between the two?

Psychometrically, both tests stand up exceedingly well. Both have high reliabilities, both were carefully developed, and much research has gone into defining their application. The age-scale character of the Binet is preferred by many in assessing children's intelligence, but an age scale makes little sense for assessing adults. At this level the WAIS has a clear advantage.

The Wechsler scales are often selected because they provide a performance as well as a verbal IQ. This feature is especially important in dealing with persons from environments which limit verbal development, for persons from bilingual homes, or for persons who are illiterate.

But the selection of one test or the other may be more a personal matter for the test administrator than a matter of psychological importance. The correlations between scores on the Binet and the Wechsler scales are typically high, approaching the reliability of either test alone. For example, Wechsler (1958) reported that the full scale WAIS correlated .85 with the Stanford-Binet. The Wechsler's performance IQ typically correlates lower with the Binet than does the verbal IQ, but in any case considerable correspondence exists between the two tests.

A word of caution is appropriate at this point. The Wechsler tests and the Stanford-Binet are of value only in the hands of carefully trained test technicians. In the administration and scoring of these tests, many important decisions must be made. The accuracy of the score depends on how well these decisions are made. Only many hours of supervised training can produce test administrators with adequate knowledge to make the kinds of decisions that produce reliable results. Amateurs should not experiment with the Wechsler or the Binet tests.

PROBLEMS

1. What factors make the use of individual intelligence tests more expensive than group tests?

2. Contrast the Stanford-Binet (1960) with the *Wechsler Intelligence Scale for Children* as to: (a) the nature and organization of content, (b) kinds of scores that tests produce, (c) age placement of items in the test.

3.   Suppose you had a Mexican-American child in your class who spoke
     Spanish well but did not speak English very well. Knowing only this, do
     you suppose that the Binet or Wechsler test might be given first preference as
     a tool for assessing this child's general mental ability? Why?

SUMMARY

Builders of general-ability tests have generally followed one of two theoretical positions in constructing their examinations. They have either seen intelligence as composed of five or six separate and distinct abilities (such as
number, space, reasoning, etc.) or they have seen it as a global ability that
pervades all cognitive activity. Tests have been typically designed after
one of these two formats, with the latter probably the more common.

The IQ originally was defined as the ratio of mental age to chronological
age (multiplied by 100). However, the deviation IQ is now quite commonly
used. Here, the mean ability for an age group is set at 100, the standard
deviation of the group is set at 15 (or in some tests 16), and all scores are
translated in terms of one's deviation from the mean of his age group.

The items in general-ability tests assume a given set of cultural experiences. We are increasingly aware that this assumption is a false one for
significant segments of our population. This fact has tempered our use of
intelligence tests with certain social and ethnic groups and has restricted
the generality with which we interpret test results.

IQs are one kind of index of a child's development. Children develop at
different rates at different times in their lives. Hence, IQs are expected to
fluctuate from one age to another throughout a child's school-age years. In
fact, we may expect the IQ for one out of every three children to fluctuate
at least 20 points during ages 6 to 18.

General ability is a psychological construct. As such, construct validation procedures are relevant. Most test-makers use correlations with
achievement criteria and correlations with other general-ability tests as
evidence of validity. Some also use an increasing raw score with age as evidence. Several reliability procedures are used, but to the extent that
intelligence test results are used to predict behavior, retest reliability should
be reported.

Group tests of general ability are quite serviceable for many educational
requirements, but for diagnosis of difficult learning problems, individual
intelligence tests are preferable. These tests—given to one child at a time—
provide keener insights into a child's learning behavior than can be gained
from the typical group test. They are, however, expensive to use and require considerable training to administer.

SUMMARY OF SOME COMMONLY USED GENERAL-ABILITY TESTS*

1. *California Test of Mental Maturity.* Has forms for kindergarten through adult; produces eight scores, including language total and nonlanguage total. Use of subtest scores, other than language and nonlanguage, is probably not advisable, especially with younger children. Median reliability for language score was .90; for nonlanguage score, .86; for total test, .93. Takes about an hour and a half to administer. Short form available (about three-quarters of an hour to administer). Validity data more extensive on short form than on standard form where validity not well supported. Chart available relating CTMM (short form) scores to expected California Achievement Test scores. Published by CTB/McGraw-Hill.

2. *Cooperative School and College Ability Tests* (SCAT, Series II) Form for grades 2 through 14. Produces three scores: verbal, mathematical, and total. Verbal and mathematical scores correlate substantially (in vicinity of .70), indicating overlap in operations. Internal consistency reliability ranges from .87 (verbal, 2A) to .94 (total score). Takes about 50 minutes to administer. Norms sample carefully planned to be representative of nation's schools. Validity data largely correlations of SCAT with grades and the *Scholastic Aptitude Test* (SAT). Most such correlations are moderate (vicinity of .50), except for .83 with SAT-Verbal and .86 with SAT-Mathematics. Scores can be reported in bands of ± one standard error in width. Published by Cooperative Tests & Services, Educational Testing Service.

3. *Henman-Nelson Tests of Mental Ability.* Forms for grades 3–12 (30 minutes to administer) and a college-level form. Contains several types of items in spiral omnibus form. Standardization sample tied to United States Census Bureau data on areas and social class. Produces one score, which converts to deviation IQ, MA, grade equivalent, or grade percentile rank. Split-half reliability above .90; alternate-forms reliability above .90. Tests selected that discriminate between very successful and unsuccessful students. Correlates with other intelligence tests well (e.g., .737 with Stanford-Binet, .836 with *California Test of Mental Maturity*). Correlates with achievement tests in .50s and .60s. Published by Houghton Mifflin Co.

4. *Lorge-Thorndike Intelligence Tests.* Multilevel, with forms for grades 3–13. Administration takes almost two hours. Scores for verbal tests, nonverbal tests, and total. Nonverbal tests need no language. Multilevel edition—as student gets older, his starting point begins farther into test booklet. Reliability of alternate forms: verbal .83 to .91, nonverbal .80 to .88. Deviation IQs, with standard error provided for various raw score levels. Information on content, predictive, and construct validity provided

---

* Addresses of publishers are given in Appendix B.

in the manual. Scores correlate fairly well with achievement-test results (.60s to .70s). Published by Houghton Mifflin Co.

5. *Otis-Lennon Mental Ability Test*. Grades K through 12. Primary-level test takes about a half hour to administer; other levels take almost an hour. The latest of a series of Otis tests, test contains a variety of item types in spiral omnibus form. Aimed at verbal-educational aspects of Spearman's "g." Test produces a single score in deviation IQs, age and grade percentile ranks, and stanines. Standardization sample selected to represent school population, not population in general. Reliability from alternate forms ranges from .83 to above .90, generally increasing with age. Data provided for content, and empirical and construct validity. Test is simple to administer. Published by Harcourt Brace Jovanovich.

REFERENCES

Barbe, Walter and Werner Grilk. "Correlation between reading factors and IQ," *School and Society*, **75** (1952): 134–136.

Bernstein, B. "A sociolinguistic approach to socialization with some references to educability," in F. Williams, *Language & Poverty*, Chicago: Markham, 1970.

Bischof, L. J. *Intelligence: Statistical Concepts of its Nature*, Garden City, N.Y.: Doubleday, 1954.

Blair, G. M. and J. F. Kammon. "Do intelligence tests requiring reading ability give spuriously low scores to poor readers at the college freshman level? *Journal of Educational Research*, **36** (1942): 280–283.

Coleman, William and Edward E. Cureton. "Intelligence and achievement: the jangle fallacy again," *Education and Psychological Measurement*, **14** (1954): 347–351.

Cronbach, Lee J. *Essentials of Psychological Testing*, 2d ed., New York: Harper and Brothers, 1960, pp. 223–224.

Durrell, Donald D. "The influence of reading ability on intelligence measures," *Journal of Educational Psychology*, **24** (1933): 412–416.

Eells, Kenneth. "Social class factors in intelligence test items." (Unpublished doctor's thesis, University of Chicago, 1948.) Also cited in Cronbach, Lee J., *Essentials of Psychological Testing*, New York: Harper and Brothers, 1949, p. 173.

Eells, Kenneth, R. J. Havighurst, V. E. Herrick, and R. W. Tyler. *Intelligence and Cultural Differences*, Chicago: University of Chicago Press, 1951.

Guilford, J. P. "Three Faces of Intellect," *American Psychologist*, **14** (1959): 469–479.

Havighurst, Robert J. "Minority subcultures and the law of effect," Annual E. L. Thorndike Award Lecture, Division 15, American Psychological Association, Washington, D. C., August 1969.

Hawthorne, J. W. "The effect of improvement in reading ability on intelligence-test scores," *Journal of Educational Psychology*, **26** (1935): 41–51.

Henman, V. A. C. and M. S. Nelson. *The Henman-Nelson Tests of Mental Ability*, Boston: Houghton-Mifflin, 1931.

Hess, R. D. and V. Shipman. "Early experience and socialization of cognitive modes in children," *Child Development*, **36** (1965): 869–886.

Honzik, Marjorie P., Jean W. Macfarlane, and Lucille Allen. "The stability of mental-test performance between two and eighteen years," *Journal of Experimental Education*, **17** (1949): 309–324.

Hunt, J. McV., *Intelligence and Experience*, New York: Ronald Press, 1951.

Jensen, Arthur R. "How much can we boost IQ and scholastic achievement?" *Harvard Educational Review*, **39** (1969): 1–123.

Kuhlman, F. and R. G. Anderson. *Kuhlman-Anderson Intelligence Tests*, (6th ed.) *Master Manual*, Princeton, N.J.: Personnel Press, 1952.

Lamke, T. A. and M. J. Nelson. *The Henman Tests of Mental Maturity: Examiner's Manual*, Boston: Houghton Mifflin, 1957.

Lennon, Roger T. "Comparison of results of three intelligence tests," *Test Service Notebook*, New York: Harcourt, Brace and World, 1953, pp. 14–17.

Lesser, G. S., G. Fifer, and D. H. Clark. "Mental abilities of children in different social and cultural groups," Coop. Research Project No. 1635, Office of Education, U. S. Department of Health, Education, and Welfare, 1964.

Lorge, Irving and Robert L. Thorndike. *Technical Manual, Lorge-Thorndike Intelligence Test*, rev. ed., New York: Houghton Mifflin, 1962.

Lowry, Ellsworth. "Increasing the IQ," *School and Society*, **32** (1932): 179–180.

Ludlow, H. Glenn. "Some recent research on the Davis-Eells Games," *School and Society*, **84** (1956): 146–148.

Manolakes, George and William D. Sheldon. "The relation between reading test scores and language factors in intelligence quotients," *Elementary School Journal*, **55** (1955): 346–350.

Pettigrew, Thomas F. *Profile of the Negro American*, Princeton, N.J.: Van Norstrand, 1964, pp. 100–135.

Schoggen, M. *An Ecological Study of Three-Year-Olds at Home*, Nashville, Tenn.: George Peabody College for Teachers, November 1969.

Smilansky, S. "The effect of certain learning conditions on the progress of disadvantaged children of kindergarten age," *Journal of School Psychology*, **4** (1968): 68–81.

Spearman, Charles. *The Abilities of Man*, New York: Macmillan, 1927.

Stoddard, George D. *The Meaning of Intelligence*, New York: Macmillan, 1943.

Strang, Ruth. "Relationship between certain aspects of reading," *Educational and Psychological Measurement*, **3** (1943): 355–359.

Terman, Lewis. *Measurement of Intelligence*, Boston: Houghton Mifflin, 1916.

Thorndike, Robert I. "Concepts of culture fairness," *Journal of Educational Measurement*, **8** (1971): 63–70.

Thurstone, L. L. *The Theory of Multiple Factors*. Privately published by the author, 1933.

Wechsler, David. *The Measurement and Appraisal of Adult Intelligence*, 4th ed., Baltimore: Wilhems and Watkins, 1958, p. 105.

CHAPTER 8

SPECIAL APTITUDES

INTRODUCTION

Careful, painstaking Willie thinks he would like to be a draftsman. Sid believes mathematics would be an interesting pursuit, while exuberant Jane thinks that public relations is an attractive field. As an educator, you want to help students make informed decisions about these and a variety of other choices involving the future directions of their effort. What kind of data do we need to take our advice out of the visceral realm into the arena of probability? Would some aptitude tests help us?

In this chapter we look at a few of the aptitude assessments with which educators are most likely to deal. Therefore, this chapter will refer to a group of heterogeneous tools that deal with a broad class of behaviors which we believe reflect potential for growth in a given skill.

Generally defined, an aptitude test is a psychometric tool designed to predict how well an individual will profit from training in a special skill area. To a considerable extent, aptitude tests are also achievement tests, based on the assumption that the skill one has acquired incidentally is a good indicator of what one might do in a program of instruction specifically designed to advance that skill. However, aptitude tests do differ from achievement tests in the way they are validated. Whereas achievement tests are validated against the content of the instructional program, aptitude tests (theoretically, at least) are validated against some future indicator of performance, such as job success or final marks in a training program.

The concepts of aptitude and achievement are inextricably tied together. The moderate correlations (.50 and up) we find between certain aptitude tests and achievement suggest that high levels of achievement are likely to come with high levels of aptitude. This relationship tends to promote the idea that the complexities of a skill can be learned only by those who have high aptitude scores. However, Carroll (1963) has postulated that aptitude is revealed by the amount of time it takes a learner to achieve mastery on a given task. Such a position suggests that all students can achieve mastery of the learning task, given time and patient instruction. In this case eventual success on learning tasks can be hoped for by virtually all learners. Carroll's

166

idea is not only significant for educational practice, but also provides us with a valuable viewpoint for bringing meaning to aptitude-test scores. A moderate aptitude-test score does not necessarily mean a student should avoid a particular skill area. He must, however, be prepared to invest more time to gain achievement in the area than would students with greater aptitude.

Since educators typically deal with only a limited range of aptitude tests, we shall discuss only four types here: (1) general vocational batteries, (2) college entrance tests, and (3) tests of creativity. Although the procedures for developing tests in all these categories is quite similar, the tests in each category have some unique characteristics. Therefore, we shall deal with validation procedures separately for each of the four classes of tests.

GENERAL VOCATIONAL BATTERIES

As we saw in Chapter 2, the use of tests in batteries became widespread during and just after World War II. Test makers began to produce instruments made up of several subtests, all standardized on the same population and reporting scores on a common scale (typically, a T-score). Each of the subtests was designed to assess a largely unique segment of the individuals' spectrum of talents. For example, in a battery of five tests, one might find the following aptitudes assessed: clerical accuracy, clerical speed, mechanics, number, and verbal fluency. Tests of this type are often referred to as multifactor tests, although technically, the subscales are not "factors" unless they have been developed by use of factor-analytic methods.

Although evidence of validity for a multifactor test is drawn from several sources, a salient item is the extent to which tests in the battery, alone or in combinations, predict future performance of students. Typically, before we build a test for selecting people for a given job, the essential behaviors of successful persons on the job are listed and analyzed. From this analysis, hypotheses are made about the aptitudes that are prerequisite to developing these behaviors. Based on this analysis, a test is then developed for each of these aptitudes. Finally, the battery of aptitude tests is administered to a group of students prior to a given training program to see how well test scores predict success in the program.

Although many test makers use straight empirical validation procedures in developing aptitude tests, aptitudes themselves are psychological constructs. We observe a number of behaviors that appear to be related to one's ability to perform in a given skill area. We then develop a theory about this class of skills, hypothesizing a construct as the element that unifies the various behaviors within the class. Therefore, construct-validation procedures are relevant to developing aptitude tests. Under these conditions we will look for several kinds of data in aptitude-test manuals. First, we want evidence that the test will show differences between classified groups. For example, journeymen mechanics should score differently from shoe sales-men on mechanical-aptitude tests. Second, we expect to find that the test correlates well with other tests of the same aptitude, but not so well with tests of irrelevant abilities. Also, factor analysis of the test may be employed to identify its factor components. Third, our test, given before training, should show at least moderate correlations with measures of success in training. For example, a test of clerical aptitude should correlate well with grades in secretarial studies.

In terms of reliability, evidence of both stability and equivalence are relevant to analyzing aptitude tests. If such a thing as an aptitude exists, it is presumed to continue to exist within an individual without marked al-teration over a period of time. Hence, tests that actually measure aptitude will show stability. Also, if the test items adequately sample a relevant domain of behaviors, one sample of pertinent behavior should rank an individual among his peers about the same way as another sample of be-havior does, i.e., two concurrent measures should correlate well. For this reason we like to see reliability data developed on aptitude tests by more than a single method.

"Multifactor" aptitude tests

An excellent sample of a multifactor, general vocational aptitude battery is the *Differential Aptitudes Test* (DAT), published by the Psychological Corporation (Bennett, Seashore, and Wesman 1966). This test, designed for use in grades 8 through 12, contains eight subtests: verbal reasoning, numerical ability, abstract reasoning, clerical speed and accuracy, mechan-ical reasoning, space relations, and language usage (made up of two sub-tests—one in spelling and one in grammar). The combination of verbal-reasoning and numerical-ability scores is used as an indicator of general academic aptitude and correlates quite well (.70 and higher) with tests of general ability. It therefore seems inadvisable to administer the DAT and an intelligence test to the same group of students.

The statistical data on the DAT are unusually impressive and are cited as a model for other test-makers to follow. The careful sampling of students involved in the standardization took the test makers to over 50,000 indivi-duals who lived in 95 different cities and towns across 43 states. These data come about as close to being a national representation as can be expected. Norms are reported separately not only for sexes, but also for first-and second-semester testings. Norms can be reported in either percentile ranks by grade level or in stanines.

The DAT validity studies rest heavily on the predictive power of the subtests. Three major types of studies are reported: (1) prediction of specific course grades, typically one or two semesters after taking the test; (2) prediction of achievement-test results; and (3) prediction of vocational or educational success in post-high school work.

Some examples will illustrate the nature of the supporting data for the DAT (Bennett, Seashore, Wesman, 1966, Chapter 5). Assuming that a correlation of .50 or higher between test scores and English grades shows a useful predictive relationship, we find the following results. Forty-six percent of the studies on boys and 61 percent of those on girls produced correlations above .50 between English grades and the verbal-reasoning test. Fifty-five percent of the studies on boys and 70 percent of the studies on girls met our criterion for the correlation of English grades with the grammar subtest.

On the other hand, tests that are not expected to correlate well with English grades do not. For example, only five percent of the studies on boys and nine percent of the studies on girls produced correlations above .50 between English grades and clerical speed and accuracy. And 1.8 percent of the studies on each sex produced correlations at or above our criterion between English grades and mechanical reasoning. These data suggest that the subtests that appear logically related to a course performance may be useful in predicting success in the course. However, the tests may also be expected to have at least some ability to discriminate between courses in that not all tests correlate equally well with a common criterion.

Correlations between DAT subtests and achievement-test scores show a considerable parallel to those found between course grades and subtest scores. Achievement areas that have a strong verbal component (and this is true of most achievement battery subscales) correlate well with these achievement areas. While these data tend to support the validity, with exceptions, of the DAT as an aid to educational counseling, the data on the DAT as a tool for discriminating between vocational groups is less convincing. For example, salesmen do as well on mechanical reasoning as do draftsmen. Stenographers tend to do less well than do teachers on clerical speed and accuracy. In all fairness, however, some of the occupation-subtest relationships are indeed in the expected direction. For example, teachers tend to surpass clerks and stenographers on verbal reasoning, and factory workers tend to do better than do clerks on mechanical reasoning.

In scanning the many pages of data in the DAT manual showing correlations between the DAT subtests and course grades in various towns across the country, one is impressed with the fact that a given test does not correlate equally well with grades in a given course in all localities. For example, in an eleventh-grade class in Sacramento, California, the verbal-reasoning test correlated .80 with course grades in science. For a similar group in Tulsa, Oklahoma, the correlation was .42. Course content and procedures of instruction vary among study guides published across the

TABLE 8.1 Average (mean) intercorrelation coefficients of the DAT for Form L
(Reproduced by permission. Copyright © 1947, 1952, 1959, 1963, 1966, 1968 by
The Psychological Corporation, New York, N.Y. All rights reserved.)

BOYS (N = 913)	VR	NA	AR	CSA	MR	SR	Spell.
Numerical ability	.70						
Abstract reasoning	.68	.66					
Clerical S and A	.19	.36	.33				
Mechanical reasoning	.55	.50	.59	.16			
Space relations	.58	.53	.63	.28	.62		
LU — I: Spelling	.59	.60	.41	.29	.27	.31	
LU — II: Grammar	.74	.66	.58	.21	.46	.46	.65

nation. Also, the characteristics of students vary from town to town. Therefore, we believe that validity data in test manuals are essential to test
interpretation, but they cannot always substitute for a local try-out of the
test.

Typically, aptitude tests are used to help individuals make informed
decisions about themselves. Seldom do we use them to make decisions about
groups. Therefore, we cannot tolerate much error in test scores. To this end
we look for high reliability coefficients for aptitude tests, in the vicinity of
.90, if possible. Turning again to the DAT as an example, we find both split-
half and alternate-forms reliabilities reported by grade level and by sex
within a grade. Typically, coefficients run in the high .80s and low .90s,
with a few exceptions. Test-retest data are also provided.

If each subtest in multiple-aptitude batteries is really identifying a
distinct class of behaviors, the intercorrelation of subtest scores should be
low. Therefore, in analyzing multifactor batteries we look at the report of
subtest intercorrelations as salient data. We are trusting each subtest to
contribute something new and unique to our knowledge of the test taker.
If two tests correlate substantially, we may wish to regard them as alternate
forms of the same test, and the administration of both is probably unnecessary. After seeing the score on one of these tests, the score on the
other will tell us essentially nothing new. Therefore, we look for low
correlations among subtests on multifactor aptitude tests.

Again the voluminous data reported on the DAT provide us with an
example. Table 8.1 reports intercorrelations of DAT subtest scores for boys.
Two coefficients are .70 or greater, nine are .60 or greater, while only nine
of the 28 coefficients are less than .40. These data suggest that there is a
considerable overlap in the behaviors assessed by many of the tests in the
DAT. The interrelationship between verbal reasoning (VR), numerical
ability (NA), and abstract reasoning (AR) are substantial, suggesting a

common factor (general ability?) underlying success on each of these sub-tests. The perceptive student may wish to speculate from the data in Table 8.1 about factors common to other combinations of subscales.

These observations about the DAT lead to the following summary of multifactor vocational aptitude tests:

1. The battery should be based on behaviors believed to be relevant to job (or scholastic) success as shown by job analysis.

2. We expect the test manuals to provide evidence that the test does in fact correlate well with measures of quality of behavior following a specified course of training.

3. Since the test will be used for decisions about individuals, it should be highly reliable.

4. To insure that each subtest in the battery is contributing significant information beyond that given by other tests, we typically look for moderate to low correlations among the subtests in the battery.

Keeping these simple generalizations in mind will considerably aid educators in analyzing multifactor test batteries.

To this point we have used only the DAT as an example of a multi-factor aptitude test. There are several others that deserve mention. In its counseling of job seekers, the United States Employment Service (USES) has made extensive use of the *General Aptitude Test Battery* (GATB). This test, designed for grades 9–12 and adults, produces nine scores; intelligence, verbal aptitude, numerical aptitude, spatial aptitude, form perception, clerical perception, motor coordination, finger dexterity, and manual dexterity. A considerable body of research on the GATB has been accumulated by the Employment Service, and minimum cut-off scores for the subtests have been proposed for many occupations. With good reason, the USES carefully controls the GATB. However, it is available for use by selected nonprofit organizations in counseling clients for employment placement.

A second test in which the developers used some careful construction plans is the *Flanagan Aptitude Classification Test* (FACT). This test, published by Science Research Associates, is also designed for grades 9–12 and adults. It assesses 19 aptitudes: inspection, mechanics, tables, reasoning, vocabulary, assembly, judgment and comprehension, components, planning, arithmetic, ingenuity, scales, expression, precision, alertness, co-ordination, patterns, coding, and memory. Two illustrative items are given in Fig. 8.1. The FACT is based on careful job-analysis data. A number of jobs were first studied to identify the tasks that are critical to success on the job. Then, tests were built to assess the aptitudes related to success in the critical tasks. Finally, these tests were actually tried out against job success.

DIRECTIONS

This is a test of your ability to spot flaws or imperfections in small objects quickly and accurately.

Each problem consists of a series of 15 small parts. These parts are identical, except that some of them are perfect and some are imperfect. Your task is to inspect the parts in each problem and pick out the ones which are imperfect or contain flaws. In every case the *first* part in each series is a *perfect sample* of the material you are inspecting.

Look at the first part in each series, then at the remaining ones in the series. Make an X in the box under every part you find with a flaw. You will find *one or more* imperfect parts in every problem. *Mark the boxes for every imperfect part.*

In sample problems I and II below, the imperfect parts have been marked. Look at problems III and IV. Mark a cross in the box below those parts which are *not* exactly like the first one in each series.

SAMPLE PROBLEMS

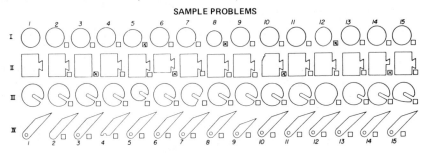

You should have marked boxes for parts 5, 7, 12, 13, and 15 in problem III, and parts 2, 4, and 9 in problem IV.

Remember, the first part in each problem is a perfect sample of the part you are inspecting. You will now have a timed practice trial on the next six problems. Mark a cross in the boxes where the parts are not exactly the same as the first one. Work as rapdily and accurately as you can. When the signal is given, you may begin.

This is a test of your ability to understand mechanical relations. Following each diagram in the test are a number of questions about that diagram. Each question has a choice of five possible answers. You are to choose the *best* answer and make a cross in the box to the left of that choice. Below is a sample problem:

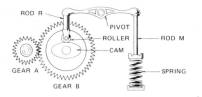

For every two revolutions of gear A, the spring is compressed

☐ A. once.
☒ B. twice.
☐ C. three times.
☐ D. four times.
☐ E. five times.

A cross has been made in the box corresponding to answer B since every time gear A turns twice, gear B and the cam make one revolution. Since there are two elevated points on the cam, the roller is raised twice for each revolution of gear B. This causes the spring to be compressed twice.

FIG. 8.1 Two sample items from the *Flanagan Aptitude Classification Test* (FACT) illustrating the types of tasks likely to be found on a multiple-aptitude test. Copyright © 1953 by John C. Flanagan. Reproduced by permission of the publisher, Science Research Associates, Inc.

Although the accumulated research on the FACT does not begin to approach the work done on either the DAT or the GATB, the test stands as an excellent example of careful test construction, following a procedure characteristic of proper personnel practices. The test is handicapped by its length (10½ hours for the total administration); however, the whole battery need not be used in all cases. Selected subsets of the tests in the battery may be used with considerable success in both academic and vocational counseling.

APPLICATION OF MULTIFACTOR APTITUDE TESTS

The success with which multifactor tests can be applied depends largely on two conditions: (1) how well the individual tests correlate with the criterion (academic and vocational proficiency), and (2) how well each subtest contributes relevant information distinct from that provided by other subtests. In interpreting these tests, we typically use the profiles produced by plotting subtest scores on a graph such as that shown in Fig. 8.2.

The profile shows that some aptitudes range higher than others and illustrates differences among subtest scores. How important are these differences? The *difference* between any two scores, like scores themselves, must be reliable before we can count on it. In the profile in Fig. 8.2, verbal reasoning is at the 90th percentile rank and numerical ability is at the 95th. Shall we say that this student is less capable in verbal skill than in numerical ability? That depends on how reliable (stable) that difference between the two tests is. Here is how we can compute the reliability of the difference between two scores.

$$r_{\text{diff}} = \frac{\dfrac{r_{11} + r_{22}}{2} - r_{12}}{1 - r_{12}}, \tag{8.1}$$

where r_{11} is the reliability of test 1, r_{22} is the reliability of test 2, and r_{12} is the intercorrelation of tests 1 and 2. From the DAT manual, we find the following information:

1. reliability of the verbal-reasoning test: .93
2. reliability of the mechanical-reasoning test: .93
3. intercorrelation of the verbal and mechanical tests: .70.

Fitting these figures into the Formula 8.1, we find

$$r_{\text{diff}} = \frac{\dfrac{.93 + .93}{2} - .70}{1 - .70}$$

$$= .77.$$

Name					Year*	Form	Grade	Sex
FIELD RALPH					63F	L	08	M

	Verbal Reasoning	Numerical Ability	VR + NA	Abstract Reasoning	Clerical Sp. & Acc.	Mechanical Reasoning	Space Relations	Language Usage Spelling	Language Usage Grammar
Raw Score	33	31	64	36	41	48	28	56	32
Percentile	90	95	97	80	40	75	70	55	85

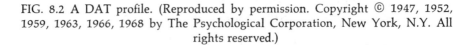

Norms Used_____(if no entry, percentiles are based on national norms)

*F — first (fall) semester testing and percentiles; S — second (spring) semester testing and percentiles.

FIG. 8.2 A DAT profile. (Reproduced by permission. Copyright © 1947, 1952, 1959, 1963, 1966, 1968 by The Psychological Corporation, New York, N.Y. All rights reserved.)

We interpret this coefficient quite like we do other reliability coefficients. Essentially, this coefficient tells us that the difference between the two tests in this case is moderately stable, although somewhat less so than either test score alone.

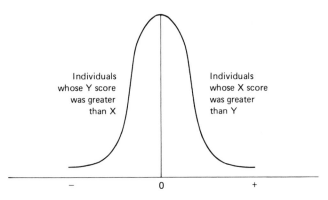

FIG. 8.3 A distribution which theoretically would result from subtracting test Y scores from test X scores for a large group of people, each of whom has the same skill in X as in Y.

Small differences between scores of two tests in a battery could be due to chance variations (errors of measurement) alone. This being true, we do not say that John is better in skill X than in skill Y if the difference between scores in X and Y is small. We realize that such differences could be due to chance alone.

How large a difference do we need, then, before we can feel quite sure that it is beyond chance? To answer this question, we first have to imagine that we have a large number of people, all of whom are equally adept in skills X and in Y. We give all of them test X and test Y. For most of them, the scores on the two tests will be much alike. For some of them, scores in X will be somewhat different from those in Y; for a very few, scores on X and Y will be very different. Since in our imaginary situation we began with people who were equally skilled in X and Y, if I find a person whose X score is not equal to his Y score, I know that the difference is due to errors of measurement.

In our hypothetical situation we could compute an (X-Y) value for all our test-takers and plot a frequency distribution of the resulting values. We would expect most of these (X-Y) values to be near zero, but many of the values would be larger than this due to errors of measurement. Such a distribution is shown in Fig. 8.3. Next, we might find the standard deviation of this frequency distribution. To distinguish this standard deviation from the one we compute on a set of scores, we call it the *standard error of the difference*.

Once we have the standard deviation of our large number of (X-Y) differences, i.e., our standard error of the difference, we can use it as a yardstick to say how far apart an X and Y score must be before it does not appear to be within the likely range of chance. Now, how many units on our yardstick must two scores be apart before we say that such a difference is not likely to be chance?

A good rule of thumb is that to be interpreted as comfortably beyond chance, the difference between scores of two tests in a battery should be equal to about two standard errors of the difference. With this difference, if your true ability on test X is in fact equal to your true ability on test Y, your two tests will produce scores that show a difference equal to the value of two standard errors of the difference only about five times out of 100 replications. Therefore, a difference this great between X and Y is not likely to be chance.

But how do we find a standard error of the difference? A useful approximation of this value is provided by Formula 8.2. We then double the result, and this is the amount that the two scores must be different if we are to be confident the difference is not a chance one.

$$\text{S.E.}_{\text{diff}} = \sigma \sqrt{2 - (r_{11} + r_{22})} \qquad (8.2)$$

In Formula 8.2, σ is the standard deviation of the tests in the profile* (if tests are based on T-scores with a mean of 50 and a standard deviation of 10 points, σ will equal 10), r_{11} is the reliability of the first subtest, and r_{22} is the reliability of the second subtest.

Now let us try this procedure on a practical problem. John Dublyoo has the following test profile on a fictitious aptitude test (Fig. 8.4). The scores are T-scores for each scale. We read in the test manual that the reliabilities are as follows: I .77, II .85, III .80, and IV .87.

Is the difference between John's mechanics and clerical scores comfortably beyond chance? We apply Formula 8.2 as follows:

$$\text{S.E.}_{\text{diff}} = 10 \sqrt{2.00 - (.77 + .85)}$$
$$= 10 \sqrt{2.00 - 1.62}$$
$$= 10 \times .616$$
$$= 6.16.$$

Now, twice the S.E.$_{\text{diff}}$ is equal to 12.32 score points. The difference between John's mechanics and clerical scores is only 11 points. We would be very cautious in saying that John is better in clerical tasks than he is in mechanical ones. We realize that due to the unreliability of the difference between

---

* It should be noted that tests in a profile will be on the same standard scoring scheme and will have equal means and standard deviations, based on the performance of people on whom the test was standardized.

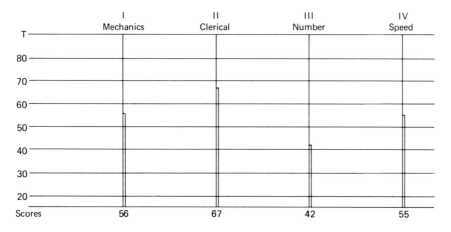

FIG. 8.4 Sample profile to illustrate application of the standard error of the difference.

the two tests, he could in fact be equally good in both aptitudes, yet still produce this test-score difference by chance alone.

These computations are simple enough, but oftentimes need not be done, because a general guide is sufficient in making decisions about differences between tests in a profile. Such a guide is presented in Table 8.2. The data here are derived from the ideas behind Formulas 8.1 and 8.2. Here, we find that if the average reliability of the two tests is .95, two tests must differ 6.3 points on a T-score scale to be interpretable as a "real" difference. If the intercorrelation between these two tests is .25, 61 percent of the students in a random sample will show interpretable differences. But if the two tests correlate as high as .75, only 38 percent of a random sample of students is expected to show interpretable differences. Therefore, this table also tells us that if intercorrelations of subtests in a battery are high, so

TABLE 8.2 Interpretable differences between test scores in a profile based on T-scores

Average reliability of the two tests being compared	Difference required for interpretation* (T-score scale $x = 50$, $\sigma = 10$)	Percentage of students showing interpretable differences if two-test intercorrelation is:		
		.25	.50	.75
.95	6.3	61	53	38
.90	8.8	47	38	22
.85	10.7	28	28	12

* An interpretable difference here is defined as one that would occur by chance in only five pairs of scores out of 100 pairs, assuming the true scores in the pairs are in fact equal (1.96 S.E.$_{diff}$).

few students will have profiles containing tests with interpretable differences that the battery may be of little value.

Let us take an example. If tests X and Y have an average reliability of .85 and an intercorrelation of .75, we should expect only 12 percent of a random sample of students to show interpretable differences between their X and Y scores. We expect this not because most of the children are in fact equally good in aptitudes X and Y, but because our test is not capable of showing the differences between X and Y to a more reliable degree. We will not entirely ignore differences that do not meet our criterion of interpretation. We will, however, regard the difference between the two tests with caution and look for supporting evidence to help us make a decision.

PROBLEMS

1. You read in the manual of the Scholarship Ability Test that there are two subtests: Verbal Aptitude and Numerical Aptitude. The reliability of the V-score is .90 for a group of 110 high school seniors; the reliability for the N-score is .85 for the same students. The correlation between V and N is .70. Scores are reported in T-scores, so each test has a mean of 50 and a standard deviation of 10. The following questions are based on these data.

    a) Jerry Mander has a V-score of 63 and an N-score of 54. Is the difference between Jerry's V- and N-scores greater than chance variation? (Use two standard errors as your criterion of a significant difference.)   (ans: no)

    b) Mary Wye has a V-score of 38 and an N-score of 51. Is the difference between her scores a significant one? (Use two standard errors as the criterion.)   (ans: yes)

    c) As you look over various students' scores on the test above, you note several students with wide differences between V and N, and some with very small differences. You wonder if this is a reliable picture of performance for your group. What is the reliability of the difference score $(V-N)$ on this test?   (ans: .58)

2. On the Flight Aptitude Test, I found the reliability of the hand-eye coordination test to be .92; the reliability of the digit-symbol test to be .88. The intercorrelation was .50. What percent of the flight-school applicants are expected to have interpretable differences between these two subtests? (Use Table 8.3.)   (ans: 38%)

COLLEGE APTITUDE TESTS

Although colleges use many tests to help predict success of entering students, two tests dominate the field: the College Entrance Examination Board's *Scholastic Aptitude Test* (SAT) and the *American College Testing Program* (ACT). We shall look briefly at these two instruments as examples of college aptitude tests. The comments that follow are of interest primarily to educators who work at the secondary and college levels.

We use tests because we can make better decisions with them than we can without them. Therefore, the nature of the test is important only to the extent that we understand better what the test will help us do. For this reason we shall look briefly at the structure of the SAT and the ACT, but we will spend most of our effort in looking at what the tests will help us do.

The SAT is a three-hour test that produces two part scores—verbal (V) and mathematics (M). The results of each test are reported in a standard scoring system that has a standard deviation of 100. The average performance is generally considered to be about 500. This scoring procedure is essentially a T-score, raised by a factor of ten. A T-score of 60 is one standard deviation above the mean, and about 84 percent of the group is expected to be below it. Similarly, a SAT of 600 is one standard deviation above the mean and illustrates a similar position in the population. It should be noted, however, that the population in this case is a wide sample of students who were applicants for college admissions.

One need not look hard at the test to see that a good deal of verbal skill goes into success in both the mathematics and verbal tests. The overlap in function between V and M is illustrated in intercorrelations between .65 and .70 (Angoff 1971, p. 31). Compared to the reliabilities of the two tests—typically in the high .80s range—the intercorrelation of V and M looks quite substantial. Referring to Table 8.3 and increasing the "Difference required for interpretation" by a factor of ten, we see that a student's V-score must be roughly 90 points (about one standard deviation) from his M-score before we have reasonable assurance that the two abilities are in fact different. We will also estimate that only about a fifth of the students will produce such interpretable difference.

In many high schools, the *Preliminary Scholastic Aptitude Test* (PSAT) is administered approximately a year before the SAT is to be taken. This is an abbreviated adaptation of the SAT, drawing items from obsolete forms of the parent test. The PSAT parallels the SAT in form and content and is intended to assist counselors and students with college planning. Many high school students already have in their records an indicator of general ability which, in conjunction with the student's academic rank in his high school class, provides a reasonably good estimate of his promise for success in college. Therefore, some counselors prefer not to use the PSAT. Other counselors claim that the PSAT provides test-taking experience for the time when the student will take the SAT, but the advantage of practice may be overemphasized.

On a second administration of the SAT itself, the average increase in scores is only about 10 scale points (Levine and Angoff 1958). On a test with a 100-point standard deviation, ten points is a relatively small gain. There is, in addition, evidence (Frankel 1960, French and Dear 1959) that a group having special coaching will not greatly increase its scores over a group that did not have this coaching. It therefore would seem that practice on the PSAT, which is abbreviated and slightly different in content from the SAT and is taken at least a year before the SAT, would produce little gain in SAT scores. Advantages in SAT scores to be had through practice on the PSAT, therefore, are very likely to be negligible.

If any advantage is to be gained at all, it appears to be in the educational growth that comes from postponing the taking of the SAT. From May of the junior year to January of the senior year, a 20-scale-point increase has been shown to occur in the V-score for both sexes, and an increase of 15 points for boys and 5 for girls in the M-score. If a course in mathematics is to be taken in the senior year, the advantage of postponing the test is especially great (Levine and Angoff 1958).

What will the SAT do for a student and for the colleges to which he is applying? The student gets an estimate of his test rank as compared to those for other students with whom he will be competing for not only admission but also academic considerations after admission. Before the student has a chance to perform in its curriculum, the college can compare an applicant's test data with performance records of students now in various campus programs. Colleges then try to admit students whose test scores look most like those of students who are currently successful in academic work. This is an attempt to maximize the likelihood of a student's being successful, once admitted, thus minimizing wasted time, effort, and the emotional pain of admitting students who very quickly find themselves in academic difficulty.

How well does the SAT correlate with academic performance? A typical correlation of the V-score with grade-point average is .33 for males and .41 for females; the M-score correlation with grade-point average is .30 for males and .36 for females (Angoff 1971, p. 127). A weighted combination of the two tests will produce slightly higher correlations. This figure indicates that although a positive relation between SAT and grade-point average does exist, a fair amount of whatever goes into making college freshmen differ from one another in grade-point average is not reflected in their SAT scores. In all fairness, however, we must note that college grades are a complex, heterogeneous criterion, influenced by variables other than academic ability. It is also interesting to note that high school record for the same group as cited above correlates with college grades at .47 for males and .54 for females. Both figures are higher than the correlations between SAT scores and grade-point averages. High school record continues to be among the best available indicators of college success.

How well does the SAT predict college success for minority groups? Several researchers have studied the hypothesis that tests discriminate against the black segment of the population. This hypothesis may not be true. For example, Stanley and Porter (1967) and Hills, Klock, and Lewis (1965) showed that the SAT is as valid a predictor of college success for students in predominantly black colleges as it is for students in predominantly white colleges. Thomas and Stanley (1969) found that the SAT predicted college grades for black students more accurately than did rank in high school class. They conjectured that this may say as much about the quality of grades for students from predominantly black high schools as it does for the validity of the SAT. Thomas and Stanley concluded that academic-aptitude tests are often better predictors of college success for black than for white students, but in any case, the best predictions are made when both aptitude tests and rank in the high school class are used together.

Similar findings were reported by Pfiefer and Sedlacek (1971). Although these investigators found that the combination of the verbal and mathematics SAT tests and high-school grades predicted college grades with essentially the same accuracy for white and black students, the SAT alone predicted grades for black students more accurately than did high school grades. But an additional point was noted in the study. A prediction equation based on a random sample of the student body at large produced overpredictions for black students, i.e., the equation predicted higher grade-point averages for black students than the students actually obtained. Similar findings were produced by Kallingal (1971), who used a different battery of tests.

It therefore appears that college entrance tests are likely to be about as useful in predicting academic success for black as for white students. However, prediction procedures should be constructed separately for the two races. Otherwise, the success of black students is likely to be overpredicted. Expectancy tables, such as described in Chapter 4, can be utilized in making these predictions.

The principal competitor of the SAT is the *American College Testing Program* (ACT). This three-hour test has four subscales: English usage, mathematics usage, social science reading, and natural science reading. Each subtest produces a mean ACT standard score of 15 for an unselected high school senior group; the mean for college-bound high school seniors is nearer 20. Although these tests require the student to demonstrate familiarity with basic subject matter, strong emphasis is placed on using information to solve problems. The tests are tied to basic subject-matter areas that underlie most academic programs, but the skills that lead to success on the tests are by no means separate and unique from test to test. The intercorrelations of the subscales run in the .50 and .60 range. With reliabilities in the high .80s, caution is advised in counseling students on the basis of small-to-moderate differences between any two subtest scores. We can again refer to Table 8.2. This time we must reduce the interpretable difference by .5, since the ratio of ACT subtest standard deviations to a T-scale standard deviation is 5:10. We find that we require a difference between two subtests of about five points before we can feel confident in saying that the student is better in one test skill than in another. Clearly, not many students will have this great a difference between pairs of scores. We would estimate from Table 8.3 that about one-third of the students might produce interpretable differences between pairs of test scores.

Validity coefficients for the ACT, with grade-point averages as the criterion, are very much like the SAT. Presumably, since the ACT has subject-area tests, it should have greater utility in predicting success in specific curricula than is true of the SAT. However, this is probably not true, especially when test scores are used in conjunction with high-school rank (Chase *et al.* 1963a).

The basis for selecting either ACT or SAT is primarily a matter of: (1) preference for one format over the other, (2) preference for the peripheral services, such as research, provided by one company or the other, and (3) demonstrated advantage of one of the tests in a unique college setting or in a unique program. For general prediction of college success, it is difficult to show a statistical advantage for either one test or the other. For example, Sassenrath and Pugh (1965), using a combined western and midwestern sample of college students who had taken both tests, found identical correlations (.53) between first-year GPA and SAT total, and first-year GPA and ACT composite. They also noted that the SAT total score correlated with the ACT composite in the midwestern sample at .86, a value essentially equal to the reliability of either test alone. On the basis of such data, one may wish to speculate that the SAT and ACT, in spite of format differences, are very similar samples of a common behavior domain.

Both the SAT and ACT are carefully constructed tests designed to predict success in colleges across the nation. But some institutions have been quite successful with locally assembled batteries and locally constructed examinations. For example, in one study (Chase, *et al.*, 1963b), a battery of commercially available tests acquired from several different companies produced as accurate a prediction of college success as either the SAT or the ACT. In another study (Juola 1962), a locally constructed test produced predictions with about the same accuracy as is typically found with the nationally administered college entrance examinations.

PROBLEMS

1. Would you say that college aptitude tests correlate with success in college (measured by GPA) at a low, moderate, or high level? What does this suggest about the accuracy with which we may predict a given student's college success from tests alone?

2. Compare and contrast SAT and ACT as to: (a) format of the test, (b) accuracy of predicting success in college, and (c) score form. Which do you think would present more useful information to a counselor advising a college freshman? Why?

CREATIVITY

Much has been written in recent years about ways teachers may nurture the creative talents of their children. Do you find some of it confusing and indefinite in definition and procedure? If your answer is yes, you are probably among a large group of colleagues who also feel as you do, because experts themselves are just beginning to uncover information about the nature of creativity.

One of the great handicaps we have in the study of creativity is that attempts to measure it have been quite inadequate. First of all, we do not have an extended "nomological network" defining what the construct of creativity is like. Hence, we are uncertain what hypotheses we can reasonably make about the effects of various treatments on creative talent. To complicate the picture, some writers have contended that creativity is one component of intelligence, whereas other writers see it as an ability apart from intelligence.

Regardless of our view of creativity as a construct, effective development of this aptitude will lead us promptly to methods of measuring it. We will evaluate tests of creativity by the same standards that we apply to other measuring tools, namely, looking at their ability to measure reliably and noting the extent to which they correlate with behaviors believed to reflect the characteristic being measured. On these two counts, tests of creativity typically do not come off well. Because of its wide use in research, the *Torrance Tests of Creative Thinking* will serve as our vehicle to illustrate this point.

The *Torrance Tests of Creative Thinking* were developed by Paul Torrance (1966) while at the University of Minnesota. These tests divide creative behavior into two areas: figural and verbal. Within each of these areas, skills called fluency, flexibility, and originality are assessed. The figural test has an additional score for elaboration. The tests may be used with children in grade 4 up into adulthood.

As with other measures, we will want to ask some questions about the psychometric nature of the Torrance tests—questions that are pertinent to not only the Torrance, but also all tests of creativity. First of all, we will want to investigate the theoretical basis for dividing creativity into the subclasses of behavior observed with this test. Guilford (1966) has proposed that creativity and problem-solving are part of the same mental process. Is this the way you typically think of creativity? Well, we had better decide what it is that the test is to reveal before we get too far along with using it. Torrance has defined fluency as the production of many ideas, regardless of quality; flexibility as shifting to a variety of approaches or categories; originality as unusual, in contrast to obvious, ideas; and elaboration as working out details of an idea. Is this what creativity is to you? Can this definition be supported with a substantial nomological net? A careful review of the literature would probably lead us to conclude that it could not be entirely supported. In other words, we do not clearly know what behavior we should observe when we are trying to measure creativity.

In validating tests of creativity, teachers' ratings are often used as a criterion against which we hold the test. However, halo effects adulterate this criterion. Teachers' ratings have been found to be much better criteria for academic achievement and leadership behavior than for creativity (Yamamoto 1965). Peer nominations have also been used as criteria in validation of creativity tests. But peers, like teachers, seem to be influenced by a variety of traits when making judgments. As a result, their nominations have not been especially useful as criteria for validating tests (Torrance 1959).

The question that emerges in selecting criteria for validating tests of creativity is: Are we assessing a *process* or a *product*? If we are interested in the process whereby unique things are evolved, the set of behaviors we observe may be quite different from that used if we are trying to decide how "creative" a given product is. In either case, the typical test of creativity may be defining creativity too narrowly (Crockenberg 1972). Fluency of ideas is not enough to account for the productions we see in people judged to be creative, but fluency weighs heavy in most tests of creativity.

How ever we define creativity, we shall certainly have difficulty achieving validity on a test if the scores are unreliable. How do tests of creativity stand up on this characteristic? Once again, let us turn to the Torrance tests. The evidence (Wodke 1964, Pugh 1968) appears to indicate that although the verbal test is more reliable than the figural, neither of these tests is sufficiently reliable for use in making judgments about individuals. Total creativity scores produce test-retest reliabilities in the high .70s, so total scores at the extremes of the score range may have value only in classifying individuals.

Clearly, more research is needed before we will be able to assess creativity with skill approaching that found in intelligence tests. The role of creative production in our society is a valuable one, and if schools can foster creative ability, everyone should benefit. However, much is yet to be learned before we can effectively teach for creativity and can accurately measure creative potential.

PROBLEMS

1. Do you see creativity as a product or as a process? Does this help you decide what behavior to record in assessing creativity?

2. List four or five criteria against which a creativity test might be validated. Do these criteria involve products or processes? Are these criteria consistent with your view in problem 1?

SUMMARY

Special-aptitude tests are designed primarily to assist students and counselors in making effective educational and vocational plans. To this end, these tests are intended to reflect the extent to which a student will profit from instruction in selected vocationally and educationally relevant skill areas.

One type of aptitude test widely used in schools is the multifactor test. This type of test, typified by the DAT, has a number of subscales in a battery. Each subscale is designed to assess a given aptitude area, e.g., mechanical, clerical, etc. Care must be taken in interpreting the results of these subscales. We cannot always trust the test title to tell us what skills actually account for performance on the items. Therefore, we need to know what criterion performances correlate with results of various tests.

We also must exercise caution in interpreting a profile of scores obtained on a test battery. How many points above test score B must test score A be before we can say that the difference is probably more than a chance variation? The answer depends on: (1) the reliability of tests A and B, and (2) the intercorrelation of the two tests. In profiles, we look for very reliable tests and low intercorrelations of tests. If we do not find these conditions, we must exercise caution in concluding that one test score is clearly higher than another.

College aptitude tests are widely used as an aid in making admissions decisions and in counseling students who are planning college programs. Combinations of subscales on college entrance tests and high school grades predict success in college moderately well (correlations near .50). However, much of what goes into success in college is not reflected in college-aptitude batteries.

Creativity is another special aptitude often encountered by teachers. At present, the construct itself is poorly defined, tests are relatively unreliable, and criteria against which they should be validated are difficult to identify.

REFERENCES

Angoff, William H. *The College Board Admissions Testing Program*, Princeton, N.J.: College Entrance Examination Board, Educational Testing Service, 1971, 181 pp.

Bennett, George K., Harold G. Seashore, and Alexander G. Wesman. *Differential Aptitude Tests*, Fourth Edition Manual, New York: Psychological Corporation, 1966.

Carroll, John. "A model of school learning," *Teachers' College Record*, **64** (1963): 723–733.

Chase, Clinton I., H. Glenn Ludlow, Martha C. Pomeroy, and L. Spencer Barrett. "Predicting individual course success for entering freshmen," *Indiana Studies in Prediction*, No. 2, Bloomington: Indiana University, Bureau of Educational Studies and Testing, 1963, 41 pp.

Idem. "Predicting Success for university freshmen," *Indiana Studies in Prediction*, No. 1, Bloomington: Indiana University, Bureau of Educational Studies and Testing, 1963, 47 pp.

Crockenberg, Susan B. "Creativity tests: a boon or boondogle for education?" *Review of Educational Research*, **42** (1972): 27–46.

Flanagan, John C. *Flanagan Aptitude Classification Test*, Chicago: Science Research Associates, 1960.

Frankel, Edward. "Effects of growth practice and coaching on Scholastic Aptitude Test Scores," *Personnel and Guidance Journal*, **38** (1960): 713–719.

French, John W. and Robert E. Dear. "Effect of coaching on an aptitude test," *Educational and Psychological Measurement*, **19** (1959): 319–330.

Guilford, J. P. "Basic problems in teaching for creativity," in C. W. Taylor and F. E. Williams (eds), *Instructional Media and Creativity*, New York: John Wiley, 1966, pp. 71–103.

Hills, J. R., J. C. Klock, and S. Lewis. *Freshman norms for the University of Georgia, 1958–1964*, Atlanta, Georgia: Office of Testing and Guidance, Regents of the University of Georgia, March 1960 to October 1965.

Juola, Arvo E. "The Scholastic Aptitude Test of the CEEB, a comparison to the CQT on difficulty and predictive validity at MSU," mimeographed, East Lansing: Office of Evaluation Services, Michigan State University, 1962, 8 pp.

Kallingal, Anthony. "The prediction of grades for black and white students at Michigan State University," *Journal of Educational Measurement*, **8** (1971): 263–264.

Levine, Richard S. and William H. Angoff. "The effect of practice and growth on scores on the scholastic aptitude test," *Research Bulletin*, Princeton, N.J.: Educational Testing Service, 1958, p. 22.

Pfeifer, C. Michael, Jr. and Wilham Sedlacek. "The validity of academic predictions for black and white students at predominantly white universities," *Journal of Educational Measurement*, **8** (1971): 253–262.

Pugh, Richard C. "Tests for creative thinking—potential for the school testing program," Bloomington: Indiana University, *Bulletin of the School of Education*, **44** (1968): 1–30.

Sassenrath, Julius M. and Richard C. Pugh. "Relationships among CEEB Scholastic Aptitude Test and American College Test Scores and grade-point average," *Journal of Educational Measurement*, **2** (1965): 199–205.

Stanley, Julian C. and A. C. Porter. "Correlation of Scholastic Aptitude Test Scores with college grades for Negroes versus whites," *Journal of Educational Measurement*, **4** (1967): 199–218.

Thomas, Charles L. and Julian C. Stanley. "Effectiveness of high school grades for predicting college grades of black students: a review and discussion," *Journal of Educational Measurement*, **6** (1969): 203–215.

Torrance, Paul. *Torrance Tests of Creative Thinking*, Princeton, N.J.: Personnel Press, 1966.

————. *"Explorations in creative thinking in the early school years: VI, highly intelligent and highly creative children in a laboratory school,"* Minneapolis: University of Minnesota, Bureau of Educational Research, 1959.

Wodke, Kenneth H. "Some data on the reliability and validity of creative tests at the elementary school level," *Educational and Psychological Measurement*, **24** (1964): 399–408.

Yamamoto, Kaoru. "Validation of creative thinking: a review of some studies," *Exceptional Children*, **31** (1965): 281–290.

CHAPTER 9

ACHIEVEMENT TESTS

If educators hold claim on any single type of test, it is the achievement test. They have developed its basic form, and their market has caused the achievement test to flourish. The advantages of achievement testing can be seen in a number of practical educational operations, and psychometricians have developed a variety of technical procedures from the demands of measuring achievement. On the other hand, the limitations that characterize these tests persist in large part because educators tolerate them. In strength and in weakness, the achievement test belongs to the educator.

How do we decide how useful an achievement test is? Obviously, the test has to tell us something about a child's status in a course of study if it is going to be useful. Well, then, when an achievement test in arithmetic places a child in the fourth month of the fifth grade, what does that placement tell us about the child's work? A close look at how achievement tests are constructed may help us answer these questions.

VALIDITY OF ACHIEVEMENT TESTS

Content validation is the standard procedure applied to development of achievement tests. This means that we take a careful look at the objectives of instruction and build our tests so as to assess these objectives in relation to their role in the instructional plan. Let's see how makers of achievement tests go about this. A look at some validity statements published in test manuals may help us here.

In creating the *California Achievement Tests,* or CAT (1963), a large pool of items had already been collected for use with the *Progressive Achievement Tests,* an achievement battery which preceded the California tests. The collection of items was submitted for review to "curriculum experts" (unspecified), research specialists, college professors, teachers, and personnel from the state departments of education. In their review, these experts put each item into one of four categories that indicated the importance of the skill or knowledge reflected in the item. Only items that were judged as fairly significant information were left in the test. Therefore, the judgment of "experts" established the validity of the content of the *California Achievement Test*.

The makers of the *Iowa Test of Basic Skills* (ITBS) (1956) took a slightly different approach. They began by analyzing courses of study, textbooks, and instructional procedures. After conducting "exhaustive" perusal of the research literature, they then selected items for "cruciality" and because more older children got them correct than did younger ones. The validity of this test is based on: (1) the judgment of the test makers in selecting information that appeared to be salient to the development of a topic, and (2) the increasing familiarity of topics to children as they get older.

A third battery is the *Sequential Test of Educational Progress* (STEP) (1957). The makers of these tests believed that application of information is the crucial skill, and they stated that validity is "best insured by relying on well-qualified persons in constructing the tests." This, of course, tells us very little about how content was selected, and at first reading it appears rather presumptuous. But how do we select a test for our own school? A group of "authorities" in our school's curriculum look over the content of a number of batteries and decide that test X presents the best sample of the objectives we are trying to achieve. On a somewhat more sophisticated level, this appears to be how the content of the STEP battery was selected.

Now let us look back over the three tests we have just noted in terms of our original question about how useful (valid) a given achievement test is for us. Are the statements of validity really of very much help to us? Probably not. We need to know to what extent the tests assess *our* objectives, and the judgments of "authorities" cannot tell us that. Only we can decide this.

There are, of course, large common threads of content that run through typical instructional programs, and these threads increase the likelihood that a test will have wide applicability. However, in the final analysis, the test will have content validity only if it fits our objectives. Only we can decide this. Therefore, the user must first decide what his goals of instruction are, and he must then analyze each achievement test to see how well it samples these goals. At this point we should note that achievement-test publishers strive to provide test content that is most common to all school programs. This should give their tests wide applicability. However, our own instructional objectives that differ from these common ones probably will not be assessed by the typical achievement test. But such objectives are most likely a smaller part of the total instructional program.

In making our analysis of test content, it may help us to note that makers of achievement tests generally follow one of two approaches to describing the components of the curriculum. They have either (a) tabulated the basic academic skills or (b) observed broad, general indicators of educa-

17. A store that offers toys ranging in price from $2.00 to $20.00 displayed this sign:

50 ¢ SALE

See Price on Tag

P A Y 50 ¢ L E S S

Which one of the following statements is true about the discount rate given in this sale?

1) The discount rate was a flat 50%.
2) The average discount rate was 50%.
3) The average discount rate was 10%.
4) The discount rate was higher for the more expensive toys.
5) The discount rate was higher for the less expensive toys.

FIG. 9.1 A sample item from the *Iowa Tests of Educational Development,* which calls for interpretation rather than recall of facts. (From the *Iowa Tests of Educational Development,* copyright 1952 by State University of Iowa. Reproduced by permission of Science Research Associates, Inc.)

tional development. Tests based on the analysis of basic skills typically include subscales in:

1. Reading: vocabulary and comprehension
2. Arithmetic: computation, concepts, and problems
3. Language: correctness of expression, mechanics
4. Work-Study Skills: references, maps, graphs, etc.

Examples of the basic-skills-type battery are the *Stanford Achievement Test,* the *California Achievement Test,* and the *Iowa Test of Basic Skills.*

Tests based on the analysis of general educational development emphasize generalization, interpretation, and application of knowledge. Tests in this group will have subscale titles that identify curriculum areas such as reading, mathematics, and science, but the items will call for complex mental processes beyond the mere reporting of facts. Items ask for conclusions from given data, for interpretations of information, evaluation of actions, etc., within the context of a given subject area (see Fig. 9.1). Typical tests of this type are the *Sequential Tests of Educational Progress* (STEP) and the *Iowa Test of Educational Development* (ITED).

Most school curricula include work appropriately assessed by the basic-skills battery as well as the general education development-type test. Therefore, neither approach to instrument development can be identified as most valid across all school systems. Instead, we must look at our own programs and decide which approach we believe best fits the educational objectives we have set for ourselves.

ACHIEVEMENT-TEST SCORES

Achievement-test makers try not only to sample the content of school programs, but also to report scores in a manner that corresponds with the typical school organization. Most school programs are based on an age and grade-level plan, so it is appropriate that achievement-test results be translated into age and grade scores. Several types of score conversions besides age and grade are now emerging, but of all types of scores developed for achievement tests, the grade norm probably has the widest use.

Grade scores

Suppose we see on a report form that Susan has achieved a 4.1 grade score on the arithmetic subtest of an achievement battery. What does this tell us? Well, the first number (4) represents grade level; the second (.1), months into that grade. Let us imagine that we have tested all children who were in their first month of the fourth grade. The resulting group of raw scores could be averaged to find the number of items the typical child got right. A raw score equal to this average is the 4.1 norm. In other words, Susan's score on the arithmetic test is equal to the average performance for the children in the standardization sample who were in their first month as fourth graders. The process is illustrated in Fig. 9.2.

Does this mean that test makers administer their tests every month to find out what a typical score is for fourth graders, fifth graders, etc., every month? No, it does not. They may administer the tests only twice during the year. For the months in between testing, they *interpolate* scores. Interpolation works like this.

Suppose we gave an achievement test in science to fourth graders on September 1st. Their average score was 15 items correct out of a total of 40 items. We gave the test again on March 1st, and this time the average

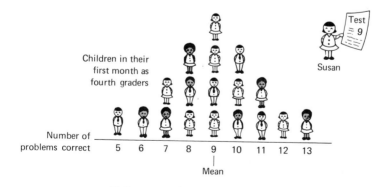

FIG. 9.2 Finding the grade norm.

was 27 items correct. During this six-month period, the fourth graders increased their scores by an average of 12 items (27 — 15). Therefore, we may speculate that they increased 12/6, or two, items per month. If this is true, we can now convert raw test scores to months in the fourth grade. The score of 15 would be the norm for grade 4, the first month (4.1); 17 would correspond to a grade placement of 4.2; 19 for 4.3, etc. The procedure is illustrated in Fig. 9.3.

One of the difficulties with interpolated scores is that they assume that an equal amount of achievement is gained for each month across the period of interpolation. This is probably not true. Certainly, children grow at different rates in any given month. Therefore, we will not think of interpolated months on grade scores as being absolute placements for a given child or, for that matter, groups of children.

In the example above, we have taken our children only up to March 1st. What about norms for April, May, and June to finish out the ten months on which grade scores are based? Between the two testings, we constructed a line in Fig. 9.3 to represent the course of growth during the six months covered. This line could be extended beyond our last testing, and norms for successive months could be established for the remaining months of the year. This process of projecting growth curves above (or below) the last point established by actual data is called *extrapolation*. Of course, extrapolation presents the same problems as does interpolation in that children's progress may not in fact correspond with the projected line of expected growth.

Grade scores have another problem in addition to the difficulties arising from interpolation and extrapolation. Look at the example above again.

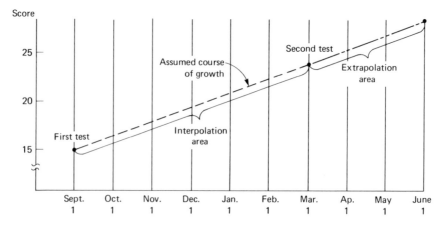

FIG. 9.3 Interpolating and extrapolating scores.

Any given month of work in science is represented by only two items of achievement. In a timed test, George may, under the tension of the moment, press too hard and break his pencil. He looks at the point, tries to piece it together, but decides it is a lost cause. Searching in his desk, he turns up his second pencil, but in so doing, forgets the question he was working on, hunts for it, finds it, and rereads it. As a result of all this, George has just lost the time he needed to complete another month on the grade-norm table.

The fact that on some achievement tests a month on the norms may be represented by as few as two items leads to considerable difficulty in precise interpretation of grade norms. Also, it may bring up grave questions as to the adequacy of the sample of content represented in the test. If you think this point is overstated here, get an achievement test. Look at the total number of items in a given subtest. Determine the number of months of school work covered by the subtest (at ten months per grade level). Divide this into the number of items, and you will be amazed to find a number of subtests in widely used achievement batteries in which a month's progress in norms is represented by only a very few test items.

Here is another problem with grade norms. Grade norms are calculated on the national sample of children the test maker selected for standardizing his test. Therefore, the adequacy of the grade norms on a given test depends on how well the standardization sample represents children across the nation. Since each test maker selects his own national sample of children, we may expect no two samples to be identical in any characteristic. Therefore, we may expect that two tests are likely to differ from each other in their placement of a given child. For this reason, direct comparison of a child's performance between tests is not advisable.

Further, a given grade placement on an achievement test does not mean the same thing for all children who achieve that score. Carol is a bright girl entering the fourth grade. She attained an arithmetic achievement score of 6.2. Mary, an average girl in the sixth grade, also achieved a grade placement in arithmetic of 6.2. Does this mean that Carol and Mary can do the same arithmetic problems? No, it is likely that Mary has some acquaintance with processes Carol has not even heard of yet. The same score of 6.2 means only that the two girls got the same number of test questions correct. It tells us nothing about what kind of questions each got correct. For example, let us imagine that a grade placement of 6.2 depends on getting 19 out of 30 questions correct. Carol could have got the first 19 correct, whereas Mary got the first 11 and every other one from there on. Carol did not get the more difficult processes at the end of the test, whereas Mary did get many items in that section. But since they both got 19 items correct, the test gives them a common grade placement, even though Mary has some ability to handle processes Carol cannot handle at all. Therefore, the grade placement for Carol does not represent the same skills as it does for Mary.

Another hazard in the use of grade norms is that users of test data often like to think that the units along a scale are all equal. This would mean that the difference in the amount of achievement between a grade norm of 4.2 and 5.2 is equal to the difference in the amount of achievement between 2.2 and 3.2. This could be true, but it is unlikely. We simply do not know how much achievement is made at various points in the educational process. Our standard for a given grade norm is the average score for children who are in that grade. But does the average child achieve as much between grade 4.1 and 5.1 as he does between 3.1 and 4.1? We cannot say. Therefore, we do not know that a difference of, say, six months of grade norms between two children in the intermediate grades represents more or less difference in skills actually performed than does a six-month difference in the upper-elementary grades.

Occasionally, test manuals report *modal* grade norms. This simply means that the norms were established by using only the children who were at the appropriate age for their grade level. Children who have been accelerated to a higher grade or who have been retarded in promotion are not included in modal grade norms.

Age norms

Age norms are very much like grade norms in their derivation in that they are based on the average test score for all children of a given age. Although age norms are still used occasionally, they are becoming less and less common. They suffer all the limitations of grade scores, plus another. Most schools have at least a core of work placed at a given grade. Children of several ages may be in that grade. Grade norms reflect content paced and sequenced by grade. Age norms would suggest that the content is leveled by age. This is clearly not true in most schools. Although age and grade are correlated, the relationship is something less than perfect in most schools.

Stanine

The word stanine comes from "standard nine." As we saw in Chapter 3 the base line of the normal distribution is divided into nine segments. This is achieved by beginning at the mean and moving up and down a fourth of a standard deviation. This cuts off a segment of the curve that is half a standard deviation wide, with the mean exactly in the middle of the segment. From the upper and lower boundaries of that segment, we continue to mark off additional segments, each a half standard deviation wide. The result is a distribution of scores with the base line divided into nine segments.* The upper boundary of the first stanine is at −1.75 standard deviations, and the lower boundary of the ninth stanine is at +1.75 standard deviations. The base line of the curve between these points is cut into seven equal units.

When a child's score is converted to a stanine, we can then interpret his performance in terms of his position among his classmates in his own grade level. For example, if a child's score falls in the seventh stanine, he scored higher than at least 77 percent of the children in his grade level in the standardization sample. We can see that the most common, and typical, performance is in the range of stanines 4, 5, and 6.

Stanines have several advantages. First, they show a child's position among his grade-level peers. We do not make the mistake of comparing skills of bright fourth graders with average fifth-grade children, as we might with grade-norms. Further, stanines are especially appropriate in reporting scores for high school students, where course content departs more clearly from grade level programing. Here, grade norms often appear quite inappropriate, but stanine scores can be used meaningfully and effectively. Also, a stanine is sufficiently broad to accommodate some error of measurement and still place most children within their proper stanine ranking. Although stanines are relatively new additions to the list of score conversions for achievement tests, their advantages have brought them increasingly into use.

Percentile ranks

In Chapter 3 we saw what a percentile rank is and how to use it. This method of score conversion is occasionally applied to achievement-test data. Percentile ranks, like stanines, have the advantage of allowing us to compare children with their grade mates in the standardization sample, forcing us to avoid intergrade-level comparisons. And, like stanines, percentile ranks are an appropriate way to report scores for students in high schools, where course content is less closely tied to grade level.

In Chapter 3 we noted several limitations on the use of percentile ranks. An additional one should be pointed out here. The 99-point scale that portrays the range of percentile ranks suggests that the test is really more precise than it actually is. To expect that children can be ranked into 99 levels of skill by the typical achievement test is sheer fantasy. Achievement tests are simply not that precise.

Some test makers report scores in "percentile bands." Each band marks off the range of ±1.0 standard error from the obtained score. This approach provides the test user the range of percentile ranks within which

---

* For a review of stanines, turn back to Chapter 3.

the student's true score is likely to fall. This procedure is a clear aid to realistic interpretation of scores.

PROBLEMS

1. Suppose you want to build an achievement test in automotive mechanics for high school students. How would you develop validity for this test?

2. On September 1, I administered my reading test to 300 third-grade children. Their mean was 15 comprehension items correct. This is my 4.1 norm. On December 1, I administered the test to these children again. This time the mean was 24 items correct. This is my 4.4 norm. By interpolation, find the raw-score equivalents for grade scores of 4.2 and 4.3; by extrapolation, find 4.5.   (ans: 18, 21, 27)

3. What is the hazard in using an interpolated or extrapolated norm?

4. After a recent parent-teacher conference a parent was heard to say, "My Willie is in the fourth grade, but his achievement test showed that his science score was 6.2. Can you beat that? Willie knows as much science as those sixth graders!

    a) In light of what you have just read about grade scores, how would you respond to this statement?

    b) If the achievement scores had been reported in stanines within a grade level rather than in grade scores, how would this have presented a different picture to the parent?

USES OF ACHIEVEMENT TESTS

The popularity that achievement tests have enjoyed is testimony that school people have found some important uses for their results. What are some of these uses?

1. Achievement tests are used to determine the status of local children's work compared to a "national sample" of children. We learn much about children's academic progress from teacher-made tests. We can rank children within a class, we can do some diagnosis of learning strengths and weaknesses, and we can get a fair idea about their readiness for the next procedure in a subject area. But teacher-made tests do not provide us with a base line against which to judge the status of our class. By providing us with norms based on grade levels, achievement tests do present us with that base line. For example, we can compare our fourth-grade class mean in arithmetic computation with the typical performance for the national sample of fourth graders. In this sense we will have a national base line of

achievement with which we can determine the status of our children's achievement.

2. Achievement tests also allow us to make a comparison between achievement and academic aptitude. We must, however, quickly note that this is not easily done using just any achievement or aptitude test. For accurate comparisons, the two types of tests should have been standardized on the *same* national sample. National samples of children used to standardize tests are not all alike. Suppose my achievement test is based on one sample and my aptitude test on another sample. If I rank higher in aptitude than in achievement, we cannot decide whether the difference in my performance is because I am not working up to my aptitude level or whether it is due to differences between the standardization groups with which I am being compared.

A further caution should be noted. The correlation between achievement and aptitude is less than perfect, and some variation between scores on these tests is normal. Comparisons are best made for class averages rather than for individual pupils.

3. Achievement tests are also used to analyze strengths and weaknesses in the curriculum. Achievement tests allow us to plot the average performance of children in each grade level in each of a variety of academic skills. An example of this procedure is shown in Fig. 9.4.

From Fig. 9.4 we see that Lakeside is doing somewhat better on reading than on language skills and somewhat better on work-study skills than on arithmetic. Eastline school is also having trouble with language skills, but is doing well in arithmetic as compared to other areas. By comparing across subject tests in a school, we can decide what curricular areas need more attention in planning, sequencing, and materials. We must, however, note that casual differences in skill areas on a profile should be ignored. Only when a given skill drags clearly below other skills on the profile will we investigate it for possible curricular revision.

4. Achievement tests may be used to study the progress of individual students, but caution must be used from the start on such a venture. Only scores on the longer subtests are sufficiently reliable to be of use in studying an individual child's achievement. Some tests dissect subtests into many component parts, each part being made up of only a few items. Clearly, scores on these parts of subtests are going to be too unreliable for any diagnostic work. A general-achievement test may well identify the broad skill in which a given child is having difficulty, e.g., reading, spelling, etc. However, it cannot be used very effectively in deciding *why* the child is having that difficulty. Tests that are more specific in nature may be called into use at this point to do a more detailed analysis of the learning problem.

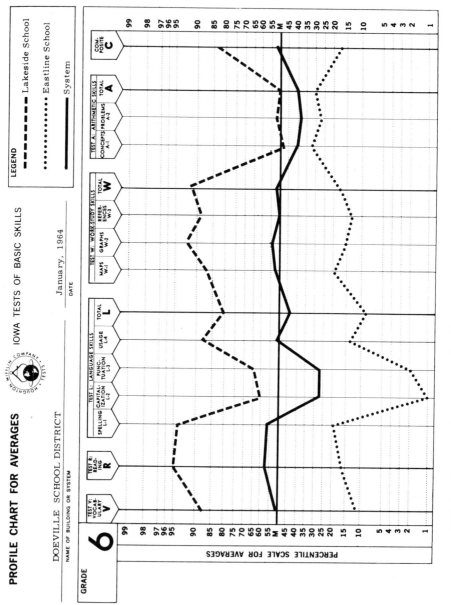

FIG. 9.4 School and system profile. (*Iowa Tests of Basic Skills—Profile Chart for Averages,* reprinted by permission of Houghton Mifflin.)

SELECTING AN ACHIEVEMENT TEST

Achievement tests are based on content validity, and the content of the curriculum to be sampled may well vary from school to school. For this reason, no test is best for all schools. Because they are most likely to know what the content of the curriculum is, teachers should be the ones to select the achievement tests. Having appointed a committee of teachers, with professional test people as consultants, many school administrators sit back to wait for the selection of the test to be announced. However, if the committee is to function well, some structure must be imposed on its operation.

We first need to know something about our instructional objectives. The taxonomy of educational objectives noted in Chapter 4 may serve as a competent guide. Our next step is to decide where we are in achieving these objectives. We already have a fair amount of information on this point in the form of teacher-made test results and other informal evaluations. Our questions now are "What additional information do we need?" and "What test will provide it best?" Only when we get to this last question will we actually be looking at sample tests. And certainly, much work is to be done before we get to this last question.

Of course, we are interested primarily in the adequacy with which a test samples the content of the curriculum. But we will also take note of other basic psychometric qualities of the test. If we intend to make decisions about children based on the results of the subtests we especially look for the reliability of subtest scores. We will also note the care exercised in getting a representative standardization sample and how nearly the qualities of that sample correspond with the characteristics of our students. For example, a test standardized on a large metropolitan sample may serve as a poor base line for estimating the status of a largely rural school system.

Then, too, there are administrative matters to consider. How easy is this test to administer? How many class hours will it consume, and can we afford to give up that many in exchange for the data we get? How easily can we get results, and what form will they be in?

It is preferable to use the same achievement test for all grades in a given school system. This facilitates a comparison across grades. Since scores at any given grade level depend on both the content of the test and the nature of the standardization sample of students, grade placement (or other types of scores) obtained from two different tests are not expected to be identical (Millman and Lindlof 1964). Therefore, if a group of children took test A in grade three and took test B in grade five, we have no basis for estimating the progress of these children from grades three to five. This problem is even more profound when we are dealing with an individual child, because errors of measurement influence an individual's score much more dramatically than they do the mean for the class.

Well, then, if a school wishes to change from one achievement test to another, how can it best be done? The new test should be phased in at the lowest grade level in which achievement tests are given. With the next school-wide test administration, the new test is moved to the next higher grade level, until all grades are finally taking the new test. In this manner a given child has scores on his record from only one achievement test, and class progress from year to year becomes somewhat more meaningful than would be true if the new achievement test were introduced across all grade levels at one time.

Achievement tests should also have the characteristic of employability, as noted in Chapter 4. When thousands of tests are to be used and administered by people with varying talent, employability of a test becomes a large economic, ethical, and practical characteristic to consider.

PROBLEMS

1. A penny-wise member of the school board has advocated doing away with achievement tests. He claims that everything we do with achievement tests can be done with other data already on hand. How would you rebut this argument?

2. Describe how an achievement test is used to determine which of the subject areas (reading, mathematics, etc.) may need a curriculum review and revision.

3. Eisenhower Elementary School has decided to select a new set of achievement tests.
   a) How should this be done?
   b) How will the new test be phased into the program?

LIMITATIONS OF GENERAL-ACHIEVEMENT TESTS

School people should be careful not to overvalue the results of achievement tests, because these instruments have clear limitations. They are, first of all, a small sample of the total content of the instructional program. A given skill area may be assessed by 40 or 50 test items, and when a skill area is broken into several subtests, the size of the sample of information within a single subtest is even more restricted. Clearly, many outcomes of instruction are not touched by so small a sample of behavior. Children can perform many specific skills not required by the tests at all. This limitation in content sampling, of course, is the principal reason why general achievement tests are not diagnostic instruments.

Achievement tests also tend to standardize instruction. They seem to place a "required" stamp on the content of the test, suggesting that other material is less central or important. Since children will be asked to perform the skills sampled by the test, teachers will devote time to these skills. Hence, strong emphasis on achievement testing inhibits efforts on the part of both teachers and students to explore unique interests or items of primarily local concern, unless they can be used as vehicles to teach the basic skills assessed by general-achievement tests.

Overemphasis on achievement tests not only constricts the range of topics taught, but also tends to influence the level of abstraction promoted by instruction. Many, but not all, achievement tests lean heavily on factual content. If children are to do well on tests, they must accumulate a large supply of facts. This influences not only the conceptual level of instruction, but also the mode of study. Factual materials, especially isolated facts, promote rote-learning methods. Under these conditions the levels beyond "knowledge" in the taxonomy of instructional outcomes will get less attention than good teaching would otherwise provide.

Lastly, achievement tests are only one type of information among several types teachers have accumulated on a child; therefore, they should not be overvalued. They should be interpreted in the context of all other data. Too often, achievement-test results are interpreted as the major, if not the only, valid source of information about how our children are doing. Clearly, this is wrong. General-achievement tests are broad surveys of skills. They do not provide the diagnostic clues that well-written, teacher-made tests can reveal. They do not present the insight that a review of a child's work books might produce. And a host of educational objectives are not even presumed to be assessed by achievement tests. Achievement tests provide their own unique information on children, classes, and schools, but this information is only one of many kinds of data and should be interpreted in that context.

ACCOUNTABILITY, PERFORMANCE CONTRACTS, AND ACHIEVEMENT TESTS

The popular literature in education has recently featured the idea of accountability. According to this idea, teachers are held responsible for seeing that children make specified gains in basic skills throughout the course of the year.

Performance contracting is a type of accountability in which private organizations contract with school systems to teach a group of children—

typically, inner-city classes. The contracting agency guarantees a specified amount of gain in skills and accepts payment only in proportion to the number of children who do indeed show the specified gains.

When the experiment of performance contracting was introduced, it caught the eye of many educators and school patrons. What could be better than to contract with a teaching organization to pay only when definite levels of advancement were achieved by the children? But how are we to assess the extent of advancement? Shall we use standardized achievement tests?

There are several reasons why achievement tests are not ideal instruments for use in accountability situations and with performance contracts (Stake 1971). First, students are typically tested in the fall and again in the spring to show gains. Differences between these two sets of scores are used to indicate the number of children who have achieved a given amount of growth during the term of the contract. But we saw in Chapter 8 (Formula 8.1) that difference scores are typically less reliable than either of the two scores from which the difference was obtained. For example, suppose we have a reading subtest of an achievement battery that has a reliability of .85 for each of two forms. One form is given in the fall, the other form in the spring. The correlation between fall and spring tests is typically about .75. Putting these data into Formula 8.1 we have:

$$r_{\text{diff}} = \frac{\dfrac{.85 + 85}{2} - .75}{1 - .75} = .40.$$

The reliability of the difference score is only .40, not as high as we would like to see it for most careful psychometric work.

There are other reasons why achievement tests are not satisfactory for use with performance contracts. We saw earlier that a month's gain (or more) on the norms of an achievement test might be acquired by getting as little as one additional item correct. This fact, coupled with the reliability problem above, means that we cannot accurately place children with these tests. Further, this limited sample of behavior further complicates the picture. If we need only ten new skills to get a year's progress on the norms (i.e., one item per month), it should be simple to teach these few skills if broader (noncontracted) objectives of the school can be ignored. We may teach enough to equal a year on the norms, but this does not mean that we are doing a good job of teaching in general.

One further problem should be noted in the use of achievement tests in assessing gains under performance contracts. There is a phenomenon called "regression effect" (Lord 1963). Briefly, the regression effect is a name for the fact that persons whose initial scores were toward either extreme (very low or very high scores) tend to score nearer to the mean on retest than they did on the original test. Performance contracts typically have dealt with low-achievement schools. The regression effect would say that with these children on the low end of the distribution, we should see movement upward toward the population mean on retesting, even without intervening instruction. If this is so, our achievement test should show some children progressing according to contract specifications, but the progress might well be a test phenomenon rather than a reflection of teaching excellence.

With these problems to overcome, can we use achievement tests to assess the fulfillment of performance contracts? The answer is yes, if . . . (Wrightstone, Hogan, and Abbott 1972). The "if" is tied to a number of complicated measurement and statistical questions that are beyond the scope of this text. Without expert advice on experimental designs, on the calculation of regression effect, etc., it seems risky to use standardized achievement tests for accountability purposes. Even with expert advice, some of the limitations in achievement tests will persist. It then becomes a question between contractor and school corporation as to the amount of measurement error that each can tolerate in managing the contract.

ACHIEVEMENT TESTS IN THE HIGH SCHOOL

In grade schools achievement tests can be made to correspond with the essential core of most instructional programs. However, high schools provide a diversity of courses and programs not characteristic of elementary curricula. Therefore, it is somewhat difficult to build tests that assess the "essential core" of the high-school program.

Test builders have attempted to deal with this difficulty in two ways. Some have used the basic-skills approach in that continued progress in skill areas is essential to success in many curricular areas in high school. For example, reading and number skills are required by many courses in high school. Students who are deficient in these basic tools may well be headed for academic adversity. To this end, basic-skills tests are more useful in assessing a student's readiness for high school courses than for measuring outcomes of the high school experience.

Some tests attempt to assess knowledge in high school curricular areas such as science and social studies, but these tests are even more subject to problems of content sampling than are elementary-level batteries. How well can a 50-item examination assess knowledge in social studies among students who have taken ancient and modern history, geography, government, and maybe sociology and psychology? To complicate the matter, some students have selected one subset of such courses, while others have chosen another subset. What constitutes a common core for high school students is obscure, and adequate sampling of appropriate content across the entire area is very difficult to accomplish. Tests that attempt to do this are best suited to schools that follow a fairly traditional plan and that have a rather narrow range of offerings.

School people may find that tests that follow the general educational-development approach to curriculum analysis may be more nearly suited to the instructional objectives of high schools than are tests based on the basic-skills approach. High schools that teach subjects from a problem-solving approach find the tasks called for by general educational development tests quite appropriate for many of their instructional objectives. The problems posed are not content-specific in that the skills necessary to deal with a situation can be developed in any one of several types of courses. For example, the methods of science can be learned through several different courses. The ability to analyze information on a social issue can be gained through a variety of social studies experiences. Because the broad cognitive skills required by general educational development tests can be acquired through diverse curricula, and because the problems in the tests tax higher-level abilities than simple knowledge, these tests find favor for assessing outcomes of many modern high school programs. Tests like the STEP and ITED deserve the careful attention of secondary school teachers and administrators.

TRENDS IN ACHIEVEMENT-TEST CONSTRUCTION

The content of achievement tests has not been static over the 50 years since the first standardized tests appeared; however, changes in content have been slow in coming. The early tests were limited primarily to the three R's and were heavily factual in content. How much better a job are we doing today?

Although many achievement-test items are still quite factual, there is increasing effort to assess the child's ability to apply knowledge. For example, the *Sequential Tests of Educational Progress* (STEP) present situations calling for utilization of knowledge and application of information given. Recall of a collection of factual details does not appear to be of major importance in this test. (Before selecting STEP however, teachers should note whether their curriculum also has this orientation.)

A second trend in achievement tests is the wider sampling of curricular content. Several batteries now include subtests that assess the ability to gain information through the use of dictionaries, maps, graphs, and other reference materials. In these days of information explosion, the content of a given field changes rapidly. The ability to find information becomes increasingly important, and some achievement tests are reflecting this fact.

There are also some statistical changes in test-building that have appeared in recent years. First, the sample of students on which norms are based is expanding and becoming more representative. This is not universally true, but several of the more commonly used tests draw their standardization samples from a wide variety of geographic areas, representing almost all conceivable variations in community characteristics. There is also some effort to make available separate norms for various subgroups in the population; unfortunately, however, there seems to be little demand for this trend among test users.

Test users have, however, begun a clear trend away from the singular dependence on grade norms. Achievement tests are providing several types of norms, e.g., grade norms, stanines, and percentile ranks within a grade. In addition, test builders are advising that use be made of scores other than the traditional grade norms. Noting the limitations of grade norms, we must welcome the use of scores, such as stanines, that rank a child within his own age or grade level.

A section on trends in achievement-test construction cannot be closed without emphasizing the fact that changes in style and content of standardized achievement tests are less than sweeping. Many achievement-test items still tap the recall of basic factual material, and the three Rs still consume by far the greatest share of the working time that goes into many achievement batteries. Further, grade norms are probably still the most popular type of norms for reporting achievement-test results. These conditions are true largely because our curriculum has not undergone sweeping changes requiring similar alterations in test content. However, the few changes that have been made in both the curriculum and its assessment through achievement testing are encouraging.

PROBLEMS

1. Respond to each of the following situations.

   a) A teacher was heard to say, "All of my classroom tests show Jill to be doing at least as well in arithmetic as in her other subjects, but her achievement-test scores show her to be below par in arithmetic. I guess I haven't been measuring her very accurately on my classroom tests.

   b) "At last I've had a chance to look over the *Iowa Tests of Basic Skills*. Now I know what I'm supposed to be teaching my sixth graders."

   c) "I've been teaching a lot of things my children really didn't have to know this year. A lot of what we've done is not on the achievement test."

2. Do you feel the new trends in achievement tests fit the tests more closely to the modern curriculum, or are they essentially attractive frills designed to improve the test-makers' sales? Why?

SUMMARY

Achievement tests are a tool of the educator. He has developed them to their present status, he gains from their service, and he endures their limitations.

Validation of achievement tests is typically based on a content analysis of the curriculum. Two approaches have typically been used by test makers in describing the content of the instructional program. They have sorted instructional objectives into basic skills to be acquired by the child, and they have described objectives in terms of broader abilities to analyze, to make conclusions, etc. This latter method of describing curricular content is an analysis based on general educational development.

Achievement tests typically provide scores converted to one of the following: age norms, grade norms, percentile ranks within grade, and stanines within grades. The latter two score conversions have much to recommend them in that they avoid the problems of comparing children across age and grade levels, and they allow us to describe a student's standing among his peers without making the assumptions required by the use of grade norms.

Achievement tests have several uses not common to teacher-made tests. They allow us to compare our children's performance with a "national sample" of children. In addition, some tests allow us to compare achievement with ability. Achievement tests may also provide a basis for curriculum assessment, and they can be used to a limited extent to assess the relative progress for a given child across several subject areas.

Achievement tests also have their limitations, however. They are a restricted sample of a child's behavior and as such should not be overvalued in the total assessment of a pupil's performance. They tend to standardize the curriculum by identifying certain topics as essential content. This fact tends to constrict individual initiative on the part of both students and teachers in exploring unique and innovative topics or procedures. Achievement tests are only one of many sources of information about children and should be regarded as such.

The use of achievement tests in support of performance contracts is probably not satisfactory. The unreliability of fall-to-spring differences, the limited sample of behavior represented in subscales, and the regression effect—all contribute to the inadequacy of achievement tests as a measure of contract objectives.

In most school systems the achievement test, if carefully selected to match teaching objectives and with proper interpretation of scores, can be a very useful educational tool. However, if it is haphazardly selected and its scores are misinterpreted and exaggerated, the achievement test can well bear harm. The outcome of the matter clearly depends on the skill with which the educator uses the tool.

SUMMARY OF SOME WIDELY USED ACHIEVEMENT TESTS

1. *California Achievement Tests*—1970 edition. Forms available for grades 1.5 through 12. Produces 13 or 14 scores: reading (vocabulary, comprehension, total reading); mathematics (computation, concepts, problems, total arithmetic); language (mechanics, usage and structure, spelling, total language) listening test for grades 1.5 and 2; entire test total. Time for testing—1 hour 45 minutes at lowest level up to 2 hours 33 minutes at the highest level. Designed to assess understanding of content, application of knowledge, and level of performance. Jointly standardized with the Short-Form test of Academic Aptitude, providing achievement expectancy in relation to age, grade, sex, and mental ability. Reliabilities in .80s to .90s. Extensive profile may be too unreliable for individual student diagnosis. Published by CTB/McGraw-Hill.

2. *Iowa Tests of Basic Skills*—1964 multilevel. Ranges from grade 3 to 9; four forms available. Subtests in vocabulary, reading comprehension, work-study skills, and arithmetic skills. Working time ranges from 60 minutes (arithmetic) to 80 minutes (work-study skills), with a total of over 4½ hours for the entire test. Four work sessions recommended. Scores reported in grade equivalents, grade percentile ranks for individuals, and grade percentile ranks for school averages. "Multilevel" in that one test covers many grade levels—as student moves from one grade to the next, his starting point in the test is further and further into the test. Validity based on analysis of courses of study, textbooks, and instructional procedures. Reliabilities (split-half) range from .70s to .90s. Test contains much factual material, with some content from higher cognitive levels. Published by Houghton Mifflin Co.

3. *Iowa Test of Educational Development*—1963. For grades 9 through 12. Nine subtests intended to measure understanding and the application of knowledge rather than the recall of extensive factual content. Tests in understanding basic social concepts, general background in the natural sciences, correctness and appropriateness of expression, ability to do quantitative thinking, interpretation of reading material in social studies, interpretation of reading materials in natural science, interpretation of literary materials, general vocabulary, and use of sources of information. Two forms of the test available. Short forms available for all tests except uses of sources of information. Full-length tests require 50 to 65 minutes working time each; short forms require 40 minutes. Reliabilities in .80s and .90s, computed at each grade level. Content, empirical (predictive and concurrent), and construct validity reported in test literature. Best evidence is on content and predictive validity. Twelfth-grade composite score correlates .80 to .87 with College Board score. Scores can be converted to standard scores for each grade level and percentile ranks by grade level.

Expectancy tables provided for predicting College Entrance Examination Board tests and for predicting success in college. These tables should be used cautiously. Norms are based on over 50,000 students distributed over 39 states in 1962. Schools were stratified on geographical location and school size. Published by Science Research Associates, Inc.

4. *Metropolitan Achievement Tests*—1970 (High School Battery—1964). Tests for K.6 to 9.5; three forms at each level. Content varies with grade level of tests, e.g., primer: listening for sounds, reading, and numbers; primary I: word knowledge, word analysis, reading, mathematics computing, and mathematics concepts; primary II adds spelling and math problems; elementary adds language but drops word analysis; intermediate and advanced contain word knowledge, reading, language, spelling, mathematics computing, mathematics concepts, mathematics problem-solving, science, and social studies. Time limits range from 1 hour 10 minutes at the Primer level to 4 hours 30 minutes at the intermediate level. Content tends to follow traditional curriculum, with considerable emphasis on factual knowledge. Scores are reported in standard scores within grade levels, grade equivalents, percentile ranks, and stanines within grade levels. Validity based on topical summaries of leading textbooks, syllabuses, state guides, and "other curricular sources." Items developed proportionate to topical appearance in the summary of materials noted. Reliability (internal consistency) in high .80s to .90s. Published by Harcourt Brace Jovanovich, Inc.

5. *Sequential Tests of Educational Progress* (STEP)—1963. Tests for grades 4 through 14, with two forms at each level. Contains several subtests at each level: reading, writing, mathematics, social studies, science, listening (individually administered), and essay (four forms available for essay subtest). The essay test is scored on a scale described by the local school. Working time for total test ranges from $7\frac{1}{2}$ hours to 8 hours 20 minutes. Reliabilities (Kuder-Richardson) range in the .80s. Evidence of content validity and predictive validity. Content aimed at higher levels of taxonomy of educational objectives and at broader orientation than basic skills. Substantial correlation between STEP and SCAT, suggesting that they are tapping largely common skills. Scores reported in percentile bands (obtained score plus and minus one standard error of measurement). Has student report form to advise the student in making his own interpretation of results; has teacher's guide. Clearly a test that has broken tradition in the area of achievement testing. Published by Cooperative Test Bureau, Educational Testing Service.

6. *Stanford Achievement Tests*—1964. Tests for grades 1.5 through 9.9. Subtests at grades 1.5 to 2.4 include word reading, paragraph meaning,

vocabulary, spelling, word-study skills, and arithmetic; at grades 2.5–3.9 word meaning added (word-reading dropped) arithmetic separated into concepts and computation, science and social studies concepts, and language added; at grades 4.0–5.4 arithmetic applications added. Word-study skills dropped at 5.5, word meaning dropped at 7.0. Time for working runs from 2 hours 7 minutes at primary level to 4½ hours at intermediate (4.0–5.4) level. Content based on analysis of widely used textbooks, courses of study, and literature in area of children's concepts, experiences, and vocabulary. Is fairly traditional in orientation. Reliability (split-half and Kuder-Richardson) in high .70s to .90s. Published by Harcourt Brace Jovanovich, Inc.

REFERENCES

Cooperative Sequential Tests of Educational Progress, Technical Report. Princeton, N.J.: Cooperation Test Division, Educational Testing Service, 1957.

Gronlund, Norman E. *Measurement and Evaluation in Teaching,* 2d ed., New York: Macmillan, 1971, Chapter 12.

Lord, Frederic M. "Elementary models for measuring change," in *Problems in Measuring Change,* Chester W. Harris, ed. Madison: University of Wisconsin Press, 1963, pp. 21–38.

Manual for Administrators, Supervisors, Counselors, Iowa Test of Basic Skills, Boston: Houghton Mifflin, 1956.

Mehrens, William A. and Irving J. Lehmann. *Standardized Tests in Education,* New York: Holt, Rinehart and Winston, 1969, Chapter III.

Millman, Jason and John Lindlof. "The comparability of fifth grade norms of the California, Iowa, and Metropolitan Achievement Tests," *Journal of Educational Measurement,* **1** (1964): 135–138.

Stake, Robert E. "Testing hazards in performance contracting," *Phi Delta Kappan,* **52** (1971): 583–588.

Tiegs, Ernest W. and Willis W. Clark. *Manual, California Achievement Tests, Complete Battery, Advanced,* Monterey, Cal.: California Test Bureau, 1963.

Wrightstone, J. Wayne, Thomas P. Hogan, and Muriel M. Abbott. "Accountability in education and associated measurement problems," *Test Service Notebook* 33, New York: Harcourt Brace Jovanovich, 1972.

CHAPTER 10

ASSESSING PERSONALITY

INTRODUCTION

Teachers and administrators rarely will see the results of a personality test, and certainly they will not select or administer one. These tests are typically the province of specialists such as guidance counselors or school psychologists. But personality inventories are continually appearing in many places on the educational scene; they are promoted by vendors, used as a measure of dependent variables in educational studies, and are written about in the popular and professional press. If educators are to react intelligently to these encounters with personality inventories, they need to know something about them. It is therefore the purpose of this chapter to describe personality inventories and to point out their complexities as a deterrent to the casual use of these instruments.

Ms. Wilson, supervisor in language arts in Central City, has just read a study in which method A for teaching creative writing was shown to produce no better products than did method B. However, children who took method B showed changes in a positive direction in self-concept as assessed by inventory X. Shall Ms. Wilson alter her language-arts program to accommodate method B? That depends—can we really put stock in personality test X, how much, and under what circumstances?

A school psychologist has just organized a class for emotionally disturbed children. Under what circumstances has he decided that these children are emotionally disturbed? A mistaken placement of a single case could have a crushing effect on that child. As an educator, the methods involved in structuring that special class are your concern. Do you need to know a little bit about personality inventories before you react to the special class proposition?

Incidentally, the term personality "inventory" rather than "test" has been used here, because "test" suggests stimulating the test taker to perform at his maximum level, such as on an intelligence test. However, when we assess personality, we are not putting the individual into high-stress situations and asking him to show how well he can integrate his personal traits to cope with the stress. Instead, we are characterizing the individual by tabulating behaviors and attempting to estimate where a given individual stands on these behaviors relative to a described reference group. This kind of tabulating is best called inventorying.

TYPES OF PERSONALITY INVENTORIES

Personality inventories seen in educational settings are of two types: the problem checklist and the general-adjustment inventory. Problem checklists are just what the name implies. A long list of problems often reported by students is accumulated. Each of these problems usually falls into one of a half dozen or so categories, e.g., social relations, study habits, and courtship. The student's job is to check those problems with which he is wrestling. The problems can then be either dealt with separately by a counselor or classified by category and the problem area identified. For example, items like these may appear:

> I have trouble with my eyes.
>
> I have frequent conflicts with parents.
>
> My reading ability is not adequate.

The first item could come from the general category of physical development and health; the second, from home and family relations; and the third, from adjustment to school work. The *Mooney Problem Check List* is among the better-known tools of this type.

Typically, checklists provide no scores as such other than a tabulation of problems within appropriate categories. Profiles are not typically drawn, and norms are not an important aid to their use. Checklists do provide an *entré* to counseling by identifying areas where the student's problems appear to emerge. It is then up to the counselor and the student to see why these problems arise and to determine what can be done to solve them.

The second type of inventory—the general-adjustment inventory— is somewhat more structured. Examinees are given long lists of statements describing various personal feelings, attitudes, and responses. The student's job is to note which statements characterize him and which do not. These statements have been *a priori* assigned to subscales in the inventory, although statements are typically presented in a random order. The subscales are normed, and a student is ranked with the standardization sample to determine his status on each subscale. A profile of his subscale scores is typically constructed, illustrating his relative standing on several characteristics of personal and social adjustment. An example of this type of inventory is the *California Test of Personality* (CTP). A typical profile from the CTP is shown in Fig. 10.1. It should be kept in mind that subscale

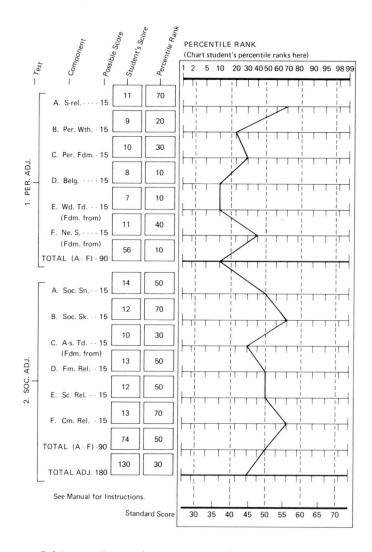

FIG. 10.1 *California Personality Test Profile.* Subtests are: (1) Personal Adjustment (Self-reliance, Personal Worth, Personal Freedom, Belonging, Withdrawing Tendencies, Nervous Symptoms, Total Personal Worth); (2) Social Adjustment (Social Standards, Social Skill, Anti-social Tendencies, Family Relations, School Relations, Community Relations, Total Social Adjustment.) (From *California Test of Personality* devised by Ernest W. Tiegs. Copyright © 1942, 1953 by McGraw-Hill, Inc. Reproduced by permission of the publisher, CTB/McGraw-Hill, Monterey, CA. 93940. All rights reserved. Published in the USA.)

scores are "high" or "low" relative to scores made by the persons on whom the inventory was standardized. Such scores simply do not reflect absolute amounts of a trait.

LIMITATIONS OF PERSONALITY INVENTORIES

Before we measure a given trait, we need to define it with sufficient precision so that our clientele knows what it is we are putting the yardstick to. But personality proves to be a slippery characteristic when we try to prescribe its bounds. A dozen writers are likely to submit a dozen definitions. Allport (1932), for example, located almost 50 definitions of personality in the literature. The range of ideas reflected by these definitions indicates that personality is not easily defined. If it is not well defined, how shall we agree on what it is that we are measuring?

Another limitation with personality assessment is the magnitude of the job of taking an inventory. Personality inventories are typically much longer than a group intelligence test. For example, the *Edwards Personal Preference Schedule* has 225 items, and the *Minnesota Multiphasic Personality Inventory* has 566. On the other hand, the *Otis Quick-Scoring Mental Ability Test* has only 80 items. Clearly, the amount of reading alone that goes into many personality inventories is extensive. This is of particular consequence when the test taker is not a good reader. One may wonder if after an hour's work, the slower reader is not tempted to begin marking items rather casually just to get on with the job of finishing.

Why are personality inventories so long? Personality, however defined, is a complex characteristic, and many samples of behavior are required to get at all of its components. For each component of personality, we need a subscale on our inventory. If our subscales are to be reliable, we must have more than a few items covering each component being assessed. (We saw in Chapter 4 that longer tests tend to be more reliable than shorter ones.) In total, then, this means that many items are required to produce adequate samples of the complex behaviors we are trying to measure by personality inventories.

Aside from the magnitude of the reading task, there is the problem of interpreting what the items say. My response to an item depends on how I interpret the words before me. For example, an inventory item may say, "I often have terrible thoughts." How frequently is "often"? You may think once a week is often, whereas your neighbor thinks "often" is daily. And how bad is "terrible"? The job of interpretation has to be difficult with items such as these. However, we shall, in all fairness, soon see that when the inventories are empirically validated, the matter of interpretation is not quite as profound a problem as it may at first appear.

Another problem with personality inventories is that one must look at one's self rather analytically in order to respond to many of the items. To look at one's own behavior and decide whether a given inventory item describes it requires a degree of objectivity that may not characterize normal, not to mention emotionally disturbed, individuals. Many normally functioning people have built extensive behavior systems which fog their self-perceptions. If these systems lead to inconsistent responses to personality items, the reliability of personality inventories must be affected.

Similarly, two individuals might give the same response to an inventory item, but do so for quite different reasons. For example, to the item "I like to be alone," one individual may say yes because he feels awkward and anxious in a group. Another individual may say yes because he accomplishes his work more efficiently without the distractions of company. To the item "I like to travel," one person may say yes because he likes the anonymity he has in strange settings. Another person may say yes because of the intellectual stimulation and excitement new surroundings can produce. Thus, two different personality structures could reasonably produce a common response to an inventory item. If this is true, we might expect to find considerable difficulty in getting personality inventories to discriminate consistently between classified personality types. And we do in fact have this difficulty.

Another problem with personality inventories is that most people can decide on many of the items which of the responses will make a test taker look good or bad, however they wish to make themselves appear. We say that items of this type are "visible," or "transparent." These items make an inventory highly fakable. A number of studies have illustrated that responses on personality inventories can be faked to fit the view the responder wishes to present for himself (Green 1951, Wesman 1952, Borislow 1958, Dickens 1959). In a review of 25 studies, Ellis (1953) found that subjects successfully faked results to personality inventories in 22 instances. The experimental evidence strongly supports the conclusion that if a subject wishes to achieve for himself a given image on a personality inventory, his chances of doing so are very good.

Clearly, the validity of personality inventories depends on the honesty of the examinee. But emotionally disturbed individuals probably will be least capable of reporting straightforward answers. They may report rationalizations or attempt to avoid responses, the endorsement of which may arouse unseemly emotions carefully tucked away in the unconscious. As a result, the persons for whom many inventories are developed may well be the least suited to produce usable data.

Psychometrists have attempted to deal with faking in two ways. They have tried to build "unfakable" inventories, and they have built subscales within an inventory designed to identify the fakers.

A widely used device for building "unfakable" tools is the forced-choice item. Here, two (or more) statements are presented, and the test taker must select the one that is most like him. For example:

a) I like to collect stamps.

b) I like to read novels.

The test taker chooses the item that is most like him, even though he may like both or neither of the options listed. When both options appear to be equally socially desirable, the test taker has difficulty selecting the one that makes him look good.

In the example above, is stamp collecting or reading the more "acceptable" behavior? It is very difficult to say. This makes the item hard to fake. But if an inventory maker included this pair of statements in a scale, he would be prepared to show that personality type A typically chooses one of the options whereas personality type B very well may choose the other option. Hence, keys for scoring these inventories can be developed empirically. We begin by identifying several clinically different groups. We then select pairs of statements, one of which is often selected by one of our groups, whereas the other is more likely to be preferred by some other group. However, from the outset we should note that the forced-choice format has not been entirely successful in eliminating faking (Feldman and Cerah 1960).

There are some other limitations to forced-choice items. Some users do not like them because the decisions to be made in many items are artificial. For example, you may not like *either* collecting stamps or reading novels, but you must endorse one or the other. This annoys certain people and occasionally encourages them to fall into random marking. This behavior will then lower the reliability of the inventory.

Another limitation on the use of forced-choice items is that they are time-consuming. To respond to 100 items, each of which requires a decision between two options, obviously will take more time than to respond to 100 items which ask us to decide about a single option only. As a result, fewer behavior samples can be collected in forced-choice inventories than in other types of inventories.

Another way test makers deal with the faking problem is to build "lie" subscales into their inventories. These scales are designed to identify persons who are trying to distort their inventory image. For example, the *Minnesota Multiphasic Personality Inventory* (MMPI) includes four scales designed to detect the test taker's efforts to distort the results. The statements used in "lie" scales typically describe behavior which may appear unseemly, but is so common that almost everyone must in truth endorse it. For example, one such item might be "I never think an evil thought." Since the frustrations of life lead most people, at least occasionally, to wish ill of someone or something, one who says no to such a statement may be attempting to look "good." At least unlikely responses to a number of such items may provide cause for the counselor to entertain the possibility of attempted distortion in the test taker's responses.

As attractive as the "lie" scales are, they are not entirely foolproof. Studies (Ellis 1953) have shown that "lie" scales are only partially successful in catching the test taker who is faking his responses. However, enough positive data are available to warrant the continued investigation of these scales as aids to the interpretation of inventory profiles.

There are other types of response peculiarities in addition to faking good or bad. For example, some people tend to prefer agreeing rather than disagreeing to responses to inventory statements (Cronbach 1950). If the statements are to be marked "true" or "false," these people would select an unusually large number of trues. Other people are indecisive and select large numbers of "cannot say" responses when that option is given. These kinds of response biases complicate the validity of personality inventories; however, they may also reflect a personality characteristic of the client (Gage 1957). The person who likes to be agreeable and the noncommital person are both demonstrating something of their personalities, albeit not ideally correlated with the typical validation criteria. The extent to which response biases influence inventory scores is under debate (Bentler, Jackson, Messick 1971, 1972; Block 1971). However, it appears likely that response biases do reduce the validity of many personality assessments.

Another limiting condition in some, but not all, personality inventories is the problem of *ipsative* scales (Clemens 1966). Suppose you have 100 marbles to distribute into five jars. If you distribute them evenly among the jars, you will have 20 marbles per jar. But suppose you put 60 marbles into one jar. This leaves only 40 to distribute among the remaining four jars. In other words, when we build up the content of one jar, we reduce the possibility of building up the content of other jars. Now suppose you have 100 points to distribute among four subscales in an inventory. If you pile up points on one subscale, you do so by reducing the number of points available for other scales. When an inventory has this characteristic, we call it an ipsative scale.

When I have a forced choice between two statements, one of which gives me a point on subscale A and the other on subscale B, I have an ipsative situation. To select the statement favoring A means I must avoid B, and this therefore reduces the possibility of a high score on B. Well, what is the problem with that? Life is like that, isn't it? If you choose to go bowling, you also choose to avoid studying. That's the way our lives run. We live in an ipsative world.

The problem is a psychometric one. Ipsative scales, by giving us high scores on one scale at the expense of scores on other scales, show us which among several personality traits is more prominent in an examinee, but they tell us little about how strongly he evidences the prominent characteristic. Such scales say only that one trait stands out more than others do.

Ipsativity also complicates our comparison of two individuals on a given scale. Suppose we have personality scales for three traits, A, B, and C. Jones scores highest on trait A. Smith has the same scores on these traits as Jones. Can I say that trait A is equally prominent for Smith and Jones? No! Smith might have got his high A score because although none of the three traits was really conspicuous with him, trait A was more prominent than B or C. Jones got his A score from the prominence of all three areas, with A slightly more conspicuous than B and C. I can say that each individual ranks trait A over B and C, but I cannot say from an ipsative scale how Jones and Smith compare on trait A.

PROBLEMS

1. When you think of personality inventories, what characteristics of human behavior do you consider? Look at some of the inventory reviews at the end of this chapter. Do the subscale titles appear to label categories of behavior that meet with your concept of personality?

2. Read the following personality inventory item.
   "I seldom attend parties."
   a) How do you define "seldom"?

   Do you suppose your neighbor defines it the same way?

   b) List two different reasons that could explain why this item might be marked "true."

3. Suppose you are taking a forced-choice inventory in which you encounter the following pair of statements from which you must select one.

   _____"I would like to learn how to play the tuba."

   _____"I wish I knew more about taxidermy."

   a) Which statement is most like you?

   Is that statement very much or only remotely like you? If I encounter a number of pairs of statements, neither of which seems to fit me well, do you suppose this will reduce the extent to which the inventory appears *to me* to be valid?

4. Suppose you are applying for a job as an elementary school teacher. You have to produce "normal" inventory scores before you can be hired. Here

are some of the items to be marked yes or no. How would you mark them if you want to be sure to look good to your prospective employer?

"I often feel lonely."

"I have always had very good health."

"I worry a lot."

Would you say that these items are "visible" and fakable?

RELIABILITY OF PERSONALITY INVENTORIES

Several of the problems with personality inventories were seen to contribute to lower reliability. In personality inventories, reliability certainly becomes more troublesome than it is in either achievement or intelligence measures. Personality is not generally considered to be as stable a characteristic as are some other traits. Moods fluctuate from day to day and from situation to situation. Also, our behavior tends to vary from one circumstance to another. For example, a person may choose to cheat at cards, but be scrupulously honest with money. Items about honesty could get different responses from this individual, depending on the arena—cards or money—we chose as a reference for his behavior.

Also, characteristics of inventories themselves tend to reduce scale reliability. For example, statements in inventories are often rather general. This opens the possibility that a given statement may not mean the same thing to me today as it did last week. For example, look at this item:

I worry about my health.

I could say, "Yes, I'm interested in good health, but is this worry?" "Worry means an extended anxious concern," you tell me. I respond by arguing that worry does not have to be that intense. Our discussion could go on, but suffice it to say that because of its nonspecific nature, the item allows for a range of interpretations. But in an achievement test, $2 + 4 = ?$ can be interpreted in very few ways. The range of variations in interpretations of items in personality inventories could lead examinees into seemingly inconsistent responses and hence reduce scale reliability.

Since many personality inventories produce a profile of scores on subscales which assess various personal traits, we are interested in the reliability of not only the total inventory, but also the individual subscales. This fact introduces the problems in reliability that come with shorter scales, namely, shorter scales tend to be less reliable than longer ones. It also poses the problem we noticed in Chapter 8 when we looked at profiles of aptitude tests. There, we noticed that the importance of a difference between two profile scores depends on: (a) the reliability of each of the

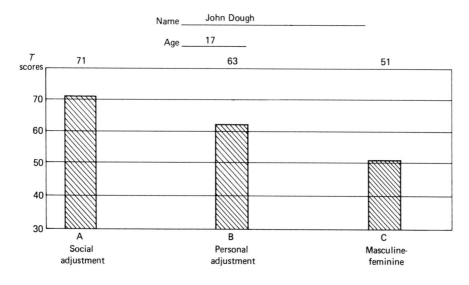

FIG. 10.2 Fictitious profile.

two scales, and (b) the correlation between the scales. These considerations loom large in the use of personality inventories, because profiles are the common vehicle for expressing scores. Suppose the profile given in Fig. 10.2 were presented to us. Is John more solidly established in "Personal Adjustment" than in "Social Adjustment"? We cannot say for sure from the profile. The difference could be due to errors of measurement that characterize unreliable scales. We would need to know how reliable each subscale is.

Table 8.2 on page 177 gives us a clue to interpreting the above profile. If we should find in our test manual that the average reliability of the subscales A and B is .85, and many personality inventories will have scales that fail to reach a reliability of .85, we need a T-score difference of 10.7 for an interpretable difference between the two scales. Since John Dough's profile does not show that great a difference between scales A and B, we cannot feel confident that the difference is more than a chance fluctuation of the two scales on which John in fact ranks equally high. Provided the reliability of test C is also .85, we can feel a little more confident about the differences between scales A and C, and B and C. However, if the intercorrelation of A and C, or B and C is as high as .50 (and this is quite common for personality inventory subscales), Table 8.2 says that only about one-fourth (28%) of the students are likely to have interpretable differences on these scales.

How is reliability determined for personality inventories? Since personality is expected to change with experience and to fluctuate with mood, we do not expect highly consistent scores over time. Therefore, we typically use one of the techniques applicable to single administration of an instrument. The split-half technique is widely used with personality inventories; however, where subscales are aimed at unitary traits, the Kuder-Richardson methods are also employed. Test-retest data are not commonly utilized by inventory builders. When this technique is used, it typically indicates that scores on personality subscales do not stand up well with the passage of time (Kelly 1955).

VALIDATION OF PERSONALITY INVENTORIES

Although reliability is often a cause for caution in the use of personality inventories, validity is likely to be an even greater problem. Personality traits are constructs, and construct-validation techniques are typically employed in validating personality inventories. However, as noted in Chapter 4, construct validation borrows heavily from the methods of other validation procedures. Three sources of validity data have typically been used by personality-inventory builders: empirical tests of discrimination between previously classified groups, correlational study (including factor analysis), and logical keying.

Since personality traits are constructs, inventory-builders must begin by circumscribing the behaviors that characterize the construct. When a nomological network of supporting evidence has been put together to make the construct appear viable, we can then turn to test construction. From the nature of the construct, we make hypotheses that can be tested. If our test is valid, it will produce findings consistent with the hypothesis. For example, let us say that our definition of personality allows us to hypothesize that persons who have problems in the behavioral area we call trait X will also have difficulty with the perceptual task of organizing colored blocks into various patterns. If it is a valid measure of X, our inventory should produce higher scores for persons who quickly form the block pattern than it does for persons who have problems organizing the patterns. In addition, our theory of the construct would probably tell us with what others measures our inventory should (and should not) correlate, and it will probably allow us to sort out (on a logical basis) behaviors that should indicate deviance.

Some builders of personality inventories have exploited empirical-validation techniques. If one group of subjects can be clinically identified as having an abnormally high frequency of deviant behavior, why not use this group empirically to select items that distinguish "abnormal" people from "normals"? We can produce a body of items and administer them to a clinical sample and again to a nonclinical sample, and form into a scale all items on which the clinical group responds differently from the nonclinical group.

We noted earlier that variations in interpretation of inventory items may be a problem for both the reliability and validity of our scales. However, we also noted that when empirical methods are used, the problem of interpretation is reduced. We do not ask *why* clinic patients respond differently from nonclinic patients to a given item; we do not ask *why* delinquent girls respond differently from nondelinquents. We note only that there is a statistical difference between the responses of one classified group compared to the other. How individuals in these groups interpret the statements in the inventory may be a clinically relevant question, but it is not important to the psychometrist who is validating the test. To him, the important consideration is whether or not two behaviorally different groups respond differently to the item. If two clinically different groups of clients respond to an item in clearly different ways, we may very well ignore the reason why. For example, take the item

"My eyes get tired very easily."

Suppose that 85 percent of a group of delinquent boys in a correctional institution responded yes to this item, while 75 percent of a nondelinquent sample said no. We do not have to wonder why the individuals in each group responded the way they did. We wish only to place the item into or out of a delinquency-proneness subscale. If we get the results above, we can place the item in the scale, regardless of why the delinquents said yes and the nondelinquents said no. The makers of the *Minnesota Multiphasic Personality Inventory* and the *California Psychological Inventory* leaned heavily on empirical methods in building their tools.

Several tests have utilized correlational analyses as evidence of validity. The extent to which an inventory measures the same thing as an established inventory is accepted as evidence of validity. An example of this type of data is given in the manual of Bell's *Adjustment Inventory.*

Also, a number of test makers have built inventories by the use of factor analysis. With this technique we collect a large group of items, administer them to a sample of people, and use factor analysis to sort out the traits assessed by these items. All items that load well on the first factor are grouped into one subscale, all items that load well on the second factor are grouped into the next subscale, etc. Each subscale is then defined by the common element that appears to thread through the items grouped under that factor.

Several well-known inventories have used factor analysis as a basis for validation. Cattell's *16PF* (personality factors) is based on one variation of factor-analytic techniques. The *Guilford-Zimmerman Temperament Survey* and the *Thurstone Temperament Schedule* base their validity on the results of factor analysis.

In logical keying, the inventory builder begins with a theory about the structure of personality. This theory defines the characteristics, or traits, of the individual. The inventory builder then constructs items that describe behaviors that portray each of these defined traits. Edwards, in constructing the *Edwards Personal Preference Schedule*, began with Murray's theory of personality. This theory emphasizes the interplay of "needs" and "presses." Edwards' inventory employs a forced-choice format to identify 15 needs, e.g., achievement, order, exhibition, affiliation, etc. The structure of the items is logically consistent with Murray's theory, and the items are also internally consistent (as shown by Kuder-Richardson data) within each need scale. However, the scales are ipsative, which poses difficulty in interpretation.

Because personality characteristics are constructs, and competent construct validation typically calls for more than a single type of evidence (see Chapter 4), we should ask that inventory publishers provide more than one type of validation data. For example, if a manual indicates the success with which the inventory has identified previously classified groups of individuals, we should look for additional information, like a moderate to high correlation of the scale with other tools that purport to measure the same characteristics and low correlations with tests that measure unrelated traits. The more types of evidence for validity and the more replications of validation studies we have, the more confidence we have in our ability to make reasonable use of the inventory.

PROBLEMS

1. In the manual for a personality inventory, would you prefer test-retest data for reliability over internal consistency data? Why? Would you most want total scale reliability or subscale reliability? Why?

2. I have a personality inventory with the following profile for Mary Goe. Is Mary's "Home Adjustment" score really superior to her "School Adjustment" score, or could this difference have occurred by chance? (Note Chapter 8.)

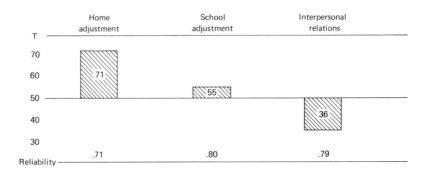

3. I have built an inventory to assess degree of test anxiety. It correlates with a widely known anxiety inventory at .63. I have had clinical psychologists interview and classify 200 children according to their relative status on test anxiety. From these, I select the 50 rated highest and the 50 rated lowest. My inventory shows that the mean for the highs is not significantly greater than the mean for the lows. What would you say about the validity of my inventory?

PROJECTIVE TESTS

Up to this point we have looked only at personality inventories, but a second very important approach to assessment of personality is found in a group of instruments called projective tests. These tools present relatively unstructured stimuli, such as the ink blots of the Rorschach and picture series of the *Thematic Aperception Test*. The test taker is given a blot or picture or similar stimulus. He is then asked to tell about what he sees in the stimulus. Systematized ways have been developed to categorize responses and to arrive at a diagnosis based on the manner in which a client distributes his responses over the various categories.

Projective tests rarely have a place in a typical school operation; therefore, we shall not explore them at length. Briefly, two trained clinical psychologists looking at the responses recorded for a given individual may very well come up with a common diagnosis for that person, but empirical attempts at validation have not been that successful (Zubin *et al.* 1956). Projective tests appear to be useful tools in the hands of a skilled and sensitive clinician, who incidentally gains many clues about the client's behavior in the course of the test interview. But these tools have not fared well under the scrutiny of rigorous psychometricians.

SUMMARY

Although teachers are not users of personality inventories, they are continually encountering these instruments in the literature, in discussions with counselors, and in the popular press. Some basic knowledge of the structure and limitations of personality inventories seems important to a well-rounded professional educator.

Personality-assessment tools used in schools are typically of two types: the checklist and the inventory. Checklists are long columns of problems that are often found among students. The examinee checks those problems which he believes characterize him. The inventory is a list of statements describing actions, feelings, and beliefs. For each item, the examinee is asked to positively or negatively endorse the condition described.

Personality inventories have a number of limitations that the expert user must note. First, the definition of personality varies widely among test makers. Also, the job of reading the many statements that make up an inventory is a large one, especially for poor readers. Beyond this, the interpretation of items—often written in general terms—is difficult.

Inventories are also fakable. Students can make themselves look good or bad on many available tools. To get around this problem, test makers have used two techniques: the forced-choice approach (where students must choose between two or more events that are equated on social desirability), and the "lie scale" (a set of items specifically designed to identify inconsistent marking patterns). Neither procedure has been entirely successful.

Some personality scales also suffer from being ipsative in nature. Ipsative scales may indicate the relative status of various traits *within* an individual, but they do not tell us much about the status of an individual among his peers.

Personality inventories typically are not as reliable as are intelligence or general-achievement tests. Moods fluctuate and the domain is complex and difficult to sample adequately. Similarly, personality scales are difficult to validate. Scale-assessed traits are constructs, and although the techniques of construct validation are appropriate, they are often underexploited by test makers.

In short, personality inventories may be useful tools in expert hands. But they can be dangerously misused by the unsophisticated amateur.

SOME COMMONLY USED PERSONALITY INVENTORIES

1. *The Adjustment Inventory*—rev., Hugh Bell. One form for grades 9–16 (one form for adults available). Student form has six subscales: home, health, submissiveness, emotionality, hostility, and masculinity. Total inventory has 200 items to be answered by marking "yes," "no," or "?," and takes about 30 minutes to complete. Some items selected for predictive validity (correlated with other tests); some items based on logical validity. Subscales correlate well (.70s) with similar scales in other inventories. Split-half reliabilities in .80s. Norms on scales based on small sample (fewer than 300 boys, fewer than 400 girls in grades 10, 11, 12). Supporting statistics about as good as any high-school-level personality inventory; scales also relevant to many adolescent adjustment problems. Published by Consulting Psychologists Press.

2. *California Psychological Inventory*. One form for ages 13 and up. Provides 18 scores: dominance, capacity for status, sociability, social presence, self-acceptance, sense of well-being, responsibility, socialization, self-control, tolerance, good impression, communality, achievement via conformance, achievement via independence, intellectual efficiency, psychological mindedness, flexibility, and feminity. Scale has 480 statements to

be marked "true" or "false." Empirical validation used extensively to support scales. Test-retest (one year apart) reliabilities for high school students were .65 for boys, .68 for girls. Reliabilities over shorter period, or internal consistency types, probably would be higher than this. Norms based on 6000 males and 7000 females selected from a broad geographic area, across several social and age strata. Total scores presented for 30 special groups for each of the 18 subscales in the inventory. Instrument, designed for use with normal students, is as carefully planned as any available. Takes almost an hour to administer. Published by Consulting Psychologists Press.

3. *California Test of Personality*—rev. 1953. Forms available for K to adulthood. Produces 16 scores: self-reliance, sense of personal worth, sense of personal freedom, feeling of belonging, withdrawing tendencies, nervous symptoms, total personal worth; social standards, social skills, antisocial tendencies, family relations, school relations, occupational relations (adult), community relations, total social adjustment; total adjustment. Kuder-Richardson reliabilities from .51 into .80s for primary level; at other levels, from .70s to .90s. Intercorrelation of subscales is moderate. Differences between subscale scores must be interpreted with great caution. Validity tied largely to logical approach in scale development. Takes 45 minutes to an hour to administer. Published by CTB/McGraw-Hill.

4. *Mooney Problem Check-List*—rev. ed. Junior high form produces seven scores: health and physical development; school; home and family; money, work, and the future; boy-girl relations; relations to people in general; and self-centered concerns. High school form produces 11 scores: health and physical development; finances; living conditions; employment; social and recreational activities; social-psychological relations; personal-psychological relations; courtship, sex, marriage; home and family; morals and religion; adjustment to school work; the future—vocational and educational curriculum; and teaching procedures. College form has same areas as high school. Adult form also available. Items in checklist selected from a collection of statements of problems made by students, from a survey of the literature, and from counseling experience. Takes about 30 minutes to complete; student checks only items he is concerned with. Checklist approach does not fit usual reliability-calculation procedures. Typical normative data also not suited. Designed to identify problem areas for students as aid to counseling. Published by Psychological Corporation.

5. *Sixteen Personality Factors Questionnaire* (16 PF).—Raymond Cattell, *et al.* 1949–1970. Produces 22 scores, 16 primary-factor scores: reserved vs. outgoing, less intelligent vs. more intelligent, affected by feeling vs. emotionally stable, humble vs. assertive, sober vs. happy-go-lucky, expedient vs. conscientious, shy vs. venturesome, tough-minded vs. tender-

minded, trusting vs. suspicious, practical vs. imaginative, forthright vs. shrewd, self-assertive vs. apprehensive, conservative vs. experimenting, group dependent vs. self-sufficient, undisciplined self-conflict vs. controlled, relaxed vs. tense, plus six additional scores. Scales established by a variation of factor analysis. Low-literacy form available. 1970 handbook is an extensive aid to use of test. Correlations between forms (four forms available) is only moderate at best, limiting extent to which validity data on one form can be generalized to other forms. Hence, general validity data (other than factor base) are difficult to establish. Coefficients of equivalence among forms runs from .20s to .70s. Interpretation of profile differences should be done with extreme caution. Published by the Institute for Personality and Ability Testing (IPAT).

6. *SRA Youth Inventory*—1953. Covers grades 7 to 12. Yields eight scores: my school, looking ahead, about myself, getting along with others, my home and family, boy meets girl, health, and things in general. A general-adjustment indicator, called basic difficulty, is also available, but users are cautioned not to interpret it too widely. Total inventory takes 30 to 40 minutes to administer. Reading difficulty and level paced at upper-elementary grades. Items in inventory based on problems reported by students in anonymous essays. Items clustered into subscales and correlated with subscale score to determine relevance in subscale. Most item-subscale correlations were moderate. Internal consistency (Kuder-Richardson) reliabilities range from .75 into .90s, most in .80s for seniors, slightly higher for combined seventh- and eighth-grade levels. Validity tied to student reports of problems. Has student interpretation guide with profile. Caution should be used in interpreting profile differences. Categorizing of student problems may be useful *entré* to counseling. Published by Science Research Associates.

REFERENCES

Allport, G. W. *Personality: A Psychological Interpretation,* New York: Holt, 1937.

Bentler, P. M., Douglas N. Jacksen, and Samuel Messick. "Identification of content and style: a two-dimensional interpretation of acquiescence," *Psychological Bulletin,* **76** (1971): 205–210.

————. "A rose by any other name," *Psychological Bulletin,* **77** (1972): 109–114.

Block, Jack. "On further conjectures regarding acquiescence," *Psychological Bulletin,* **76** (1971): 205–210.

Borislow, B. "The *Edwards Personal Preference Schedule* and fakability," *Journal of Applied Psychology,* **42** (1958): 22–27.

Clemens, William V. "An analytical and empirical examination of some properties of ipsative measures," *Psychometric Monographs,* 1966, No. 14.

Cronbach, Lee J. "Further evidence on response sets and design," *Educational and Psychological Measurement,* **10** (1950): 3–31.

Dickens, C. F. "Simulated Patterns on the EPPS," *Journal of Applied Psychology,* **43** (1959): 372–378.

Ellis, Albert. "Recent research with personality inventories," *Journal of Consulting Psychology,* **17** (1953): 45–49.

Feldman, M. J. and N. L. Cerah. "Social desirability and the forced-choice method", *Journal of Consulting Psychology,* **24** (1960): 480–482.

Gage, N. L. "The psychological meaning of acquiescence set for authoritarianism," *Journal of Abnormal Social Psychology,* **55** (1957): 98–103.

Green, R. F. "Does a selection situation induce testees to bias their answers on interest and temperament tests?" *Educational and Psychological Measurement,* **11** (1951): 503–515.

Kelly, E. L. "Consistency of adult personality," *American Psychologist,* **10** (1955): 659–681.

Wesman, Alexander. "Faking personality test scores in a simulated employment situation," *Journal of Applied Psychology,* **36** (1952): 112–113.

Zubin, Joseph, Leonard D. Eron, and Florence Sultan. "A psychometric evaluation of the Rorschach experiment," *American Journal of Orthopsychiatry,* **26** (1956): 773–782.

CHAPTER 11

INTERESTS AND ATTITUDES

INTRODUCTION

Certainly, school people want to know about the interests and attitudes of the students with whom they work. Influencing these characteristics is a big part of the school experience. Whether or not we intend to, we are molding the interests and attitudes of our class members. Ms. Jenkins, who teaches literature with little enthusiasm or imagination, may incidentally be leading her students to avoid reading and to dislike literary work. Mr. Wilson, by the way he structures his shop class, may be developing mechanics with a devotion to their trade, or he may be teaching them to avoid vigorously mechanical work.

If attitudes and interests are going to develop out of the myriad activities in which students are involved, why do school people not seize every opportunity to capitalize on these characteristics as vehicles for promoting learning? The answer is that we typically do not know what our students' interests are or what their attitudes may be. We rely primarily on intuition and the expressions on the faces of our students to give us a hint. Surely, we can assess attitudes and interest more effectively than this. This chapter will provide some brief descriptions of how we might do the job.

School counselors are continually dealing with interests and attitudes. They help students become aware of their feelings about various vocational and social topics, and they help students make decisions that square with these feelings. But teachers and administrators also need to know about interests and attitudes. How else can we adapt our instructional programs to our students? How can we judge the current value of programs in the students' world? How can we communicate with students unless we get at least a peek at the world as they see it?

Attitudes and interests both deal with likes and dislikes, but the terms are not synonymous. An attitude is a predisposition to accept or reject, in a consistent manner, groups of individuals, social systems, or other social objects. It is tied up with emotional responses to social objects (Krech 1962). For example, when you hear the term "radical," what psychological state does this create for you? Just off-hand, do you have an accepting or rejecting feeling about persons who fit this classification?

Interests, on the other hand, are tendencies to participate in an activity. Shall I read a novel tonight or watch a drama on television? If I choose to read a novel, the subject I select to read about will be tied in with my attitudinal system, but my preference for the activity of reading reflects an interest. The essential distinction between attitudes and interests in this case is that attitudes identify our predisposition for emotional responses to social objects, whereas interests are tied to activities. Attitudes say I will react positively or negatively toward a given group or institution, but there are many kinds of activities from which I may select to evidence my feeling toward the social object involved. The activity I select shows my interest.

Although there are at least four different approaches to assessing interest (Super and Crites 1962, p. 377ff), only one, the interest inventory, will be discussed in this chapter. Similarly, there are a half dozen approaches to assessing attitudes (Edwards 1957), but only two widely used methods will be presented. The fact that the other methods of assessing attitudes and interests are not discussed here should not be construed to mean that they are not useful in educational settings. Certainly, educators need to work from as large a data base as possible. The methods presented in this chapter were selected only because they have wide currency in research and practice and are, therefore, most likely to be the procedures educators will encounter and employ.

INTEREST INVENTORIES

Builders of interest inventories have used three basic approaches to constructing their instruments:

1. They have developed homogeneous clusters of activities and labeled each cluster as an interest area;
2. They have collected into a scale the items to which people in occupation X provide a level of endorsement clearly different from that of people in other occupations;
3. They have grouped inventory items on the basis of a logical analysis of the variety of facets of a given job area.

The first method provides a clustering of activities much like that resulting from a factor analysis, the second method is like empirical validation, and the third is similar to content validation. We shall look at each procedure separately.

We could begin to build an interest inventory by collecting a number of items that appear on the surface to fit a given vocational area, e.g., outdoor work, mechanical work, or clerical work. This collection of items could be carefully edited and designated as a scale for the vocational arena.

However, we cannot have confidence in the extent to which a group of items does in fact cluster together until we have run some statistical analyses. We could begin by computing a reliability coefficient for internal consistency. Or, applying factor analysis at this point would also help us sort items into a common area.

Some test makers have used simpler correlational methods for grouping items. Items were grouped together if they all correlated moderately or better with one another, but correlated poorly with items from another vocational area. The interest area identified by this group of items was rationally identified by looking for a common thread of activity within all items in the group. This approach is called "homogeneous keying."

A set of widely used inventories based on the homogeneous keying approach has been built by G. Frederic Kuder. We shall use these inventories as examples of this procedure for instrument development. The original edition of the Kuder scales appeared in 1939, and three editions (B, C, and E) have followed. We shall look only at the *Kuder Preference Record—Vocational* (Form C) and the *Kuder General Interest Survey* (Form E). These two are very much alike, the latter being a downward extension of the former. Form E uses a simpler (fifth-grade level) vocabulary than does Form C, and it avoids use of occupational titles which have uncertain meanings for young people. Also, Form E has norms for junior high school, as well as for high school students. However, because it is a more recent development (1964) than Form C (1948), Form E does not have as broad a research base as does Form C.

Forms C and E have the same format and produce information on the same interest areas. Statements are presented in sets of three, or triads. Each item is therefore a triad of statements rather than a single statement. For each item, the test taker makes two selections. He chooses which of the three activities he likes most and least. For example, suppose the following triad were in the inventory.

    a. Write a letter to a friend.

    b. Make arrangements for a party.

    c. Collect overdue bills from customers.

The student's job is to select the one item he likes most and the one he likes least. Each item (a total of 184 in Form E) is made up of similar forced-choice triads.

The use of triads leads to a number of tough decisions for the test taker. In some cases none of the three options look attractive; in others, they all look attractive. This method of presenting items makes the job of completing the inventory far from simple. Also, each of the statements in a triad is likely to be keyed on different occupational-area scales, resulting in ipsative scores. We shall cite this problem again later.

In both Forms C and E, the Kuder inventories produce interest scores in the following areas: outdoor, mechanical, computational, scientific, persuasive, artistic, literary, musical, social service, and clerical. The earlier manual provided advice for "self-interpretation" of scores. Lists of actual vocations corresponding with each interest area and with combined interest areas were provided. The student looked at his profile to identify his high-interest area or areas, then consulted the vocational listings. In the later Form E, however, actual vocational listings were not provided, probably due in part to the fact that the empirical evidence did not strongly support the job selections provided. Also, since Form E is designed for younger students who will not be making specific vocational choices immediately, a job listing is less relevant for this audience.

A second method for building interest inventories is known as empirical, or criterion, keying. In this method, used in building the *Strong Vocational Interest Blank*, items in a given vocational scale are identified by field tests. If people in one vocational area do in fact respond differently to a set of items from people in other vocations, we retain the items for our scale. For example, suppose that a group of janitors and a group of truck drivers have been asked to mark three items as "like," "indifferent," or "dislike." In addition, we ask a group of men unselected by occupation to mark these same items. The responses of these three groups are shown in Table 11.1.

TABLE 11.1 An example of empirical keying such as used in the *Strong Vocational Interest Blank* (L = like; I = indifferent; D = dislike)

Items	Truckers			Janitors			"All Men"		
	L	I	D	L	I	D	L	I	D
1. Attending a boxing match	64*	32	4	3	24	73	30	41	29
2. Backyard gardening	10	24	66	70	25	5	38	29	33
3. Writing letters to a friend	70	20	10	0	32	68	70	21	9

* Data are given in percentages.

By comparing the pattern of responses of the truckers with that of a group of men representing many different job areas, we can find the items that truckers endorse differently from unselected men. We then put these items in a truck-driver scale. Similarly we can locate items for a janitor's scale. Item 1 in Table 11.1 shows that both truckers and janitors deviate from men in general. However, to differentiate truckers from janitors, a "like" response would be scored "plus" on the truck driver's scale and "minus" on the janitor's scale. Similarly, item 2 shows deviations for both groups, but this time a "like" response would be scored negatively for the truckers and positively for the janitors. Item 3 is discriminating for the janitors, but does not show the truckers as deviating from men in general. Therefore, a "like" response to item 3 would subtract a point on the janitor's scale, but would be scored zero on the trucker's scale. Thus, on item 1 a trucker would get a +1 for marking L and a −1 for marking D; on item 2, a +1 for marking D, a −1 for L; but item 3 would not be scored on the trucker's scale. A janitor would get a −1 for L on the first item, a +1 for D; on item 2, a +1 for L, a −1 for D; and on item 3 a +1 for D, a −1 for L.

Empirical keying, then, is simply a matter of identifying a set of activities that a given occupational group endorses differently from people in general. These activities are then put into a scale for that occupation, and they are scored in the direction of the differential endorsement.

The *Strong Vocational Interest Blank* is a widely used inventory based on empirical keying. It has a separate inventory for men and women; however, both inventories use the "Like," 'Indifferent," "Dislike" format for responses. Keys on the male form were developed by selecting out items on which the distribution of responses among the L, I, and D categories for men in a given occupation differed clearly from the L, I, D selections made by men in general. Scales on the women's inventory were developed in a similar manner. The procedure is purely an empirical-validation technique.

The stability of Strong scores has been striking. Extensive longitudinal data are available for the men's inventory. The more recently developed women's scales provide less extensive data. Test-retest reliabilities for men produce a median value across all scales of .68 over a three-year period, and a median value of .67 over 22 years (Strong and Campbell 1966, pp. 28, 29). Other sources show the median test-retest correlation across scales to be as high as .74 over a period of 22 years (Strong 1955, pp. 64–65).

It should be noted, however, that in these impressive studies the first testing occurred when the subjects were late adolescents and adults. Although Tyler (1964) has shown that certain vocational interests begin to "crystalize" between ages 10 and 14, other writers (Canning et al. 1941) have shown that Strong scores taken in the sophomore year in high school correlated only between .48 and .66 with scores taken in the senior year. Interests assessed by the Strong inventory do not appear to become sufficiently reliable until examinees reach late adolescence.

A third method of building interest inventories is known as logical keying. This method is much like content validation. First, the components of the job—in terms of personal characteristics of employees—are established from authoritative sources. Then, based on the educated judgments of personnel specialists, items are constructed to indicate the behaviors believed to reflect the desired personal qualities. For example, the job description for a tool-and-die maker will include a demand for precise measurements and subsequent construction of the tool within very exacting limits. Personnel specialists constructing items for the tool-and-die maker scale would include statements that reflect a concern for accuracy in work, patience with detail, and pride in accomplishing a job that demands attention to minute detail.

An inventory that uses the logical keying approach is the *Lee-Thorpe Occupational Interest Inventory*. The authors began with a list of occupations from the *Dictionary of Occupational Titles*. From this list they created six broad categories of occupations: personal-social, natural, mechanical, business, arts, and sciences. The inventory produces a score in each field for three types of interest (verbal, manipulative, or computational). Also, three levels of interest or responsibility are reported (high, medium, or low).

The basic scoring structure of the Lee-Thorpe is indeed intriguing. The scoring format is, however, more impressive than the data available to support the inventory. The principal claim for validity is based on the content analysis of the job areas. Data on external verification of the adequacy of the content analysis are slim, although at least one study (Bridge and Marson 1953) does suggest that the job was fairly well accomplished. The amount of research on the Lee-Thorpe is diminutive compared to the work on the Kuder and Strong inventories. The conclusion at this point must be that although the Lee-Thorpe may be a valid tool for identifying the interests of late adolescents and adults, the quantity of currently available data on the scales is too small to state with any degree of assurance that the tool is capable of doing the job intended.

PROBLEMS

1. Test makers who use homogeneous keying usually come up with scales that "assess" rather broad areas of activity, e.g., outdoor, clerical, mechanical. Do you see anything inherent in the method of homogeneous keying that would encourage development of broad scales? Could scales designed to assess broad areas of activity also be developed empirically?

2. What do you see as a disadvantage of logical keying compared to empirical keying?

3. In any of the three most commnoly used methods for building interest inventories (empirical, logical, and homogeneous keying) is it necessary to develop the construct of vocational interest? Why?

Interpretation of interest scores

Like all psychological measurements, interest inventories can best serve their user when certain precautions are noted. We shall investigate five limiting conditions that bear on interpretation of interest-inventory scores: fakability, ipsativity, motivation for making choices, the role of client experience, and the relation of aptitude to interest.

Like personality inventories, interest inventories can be faked (Longstaff 1948, Wesman 1952). Curiously, it appears easier to fake high interest on the Strong, whereas it is easier to fake low interest on the Kuder. In any case, persons who have reason to make themselves appear to have certain types of interests can alter their scores in the desired direction. This appears to be true despite the fact that some inventories (Kuder, Lee-Thorpe) use a forced-choice format. One's motivation for taking an interest inventory is therefore relevant information in interpreting scores. Was this inventory taken to produce an image contrived to look impressive to an employer, an academic department, or one's mother? The client may only occasionally be aware of his effort to bias results. Responses can represent rationalizations of behavior or can indeed be tied to unconscious motivations (e.g., in rejecting parental authority, a boy whose parents want him to be a physician produces a very low score on the "Physician" scale of the Strong). Therefore, interest-inventory scores are best interpreted by counselors who are trained to investigate motivations as well as to deal with vocational selections.

Like personality inventories, interest inventories also must deal with the problem of ipsative scales. Suppose I have a set of 50 items like these:

> "I like team sports."
>
> "I find reading dull."
>
> "I prefer walking to model-building."

I have two scales on my inventory—"Outdoor" and "Solitary." Each time I mark one of the items "agree," it counts on the "Outdoor" scale; similarly, "disagree" counts on the "Solitary" scale. Each time I mark an item "agree," it increases my "Outdoor" scale, but reduces my chance of getting a high score on the "Solitary" scale. It is therefore impossible to score high on both scales. Also, I may not like activities in either area particularly well, but consistently give "Outdoor" a slight edge. I will get a "high" score on the "Outdoor" scale, just like the person who is enthusiastic about outdoor activities. For this reason inventories with ipsative scales are very difficult to interpret either for a given individual or in comparing individuals (Clemens 1966, 1968).

Another complicating factor in taking interest inventories is the assumption that students have enough occupational and avocational experience to know what kinds of activities they like and dislike. Before I can say with assurance that I like collecting rare coins, for example, I need to know something about the hobby. "Would you like, dislike, or be indifferent to being an aviator?" Many people will respond to such an item without even having flown in an airplane, let alone know anything about flying the machine.

As students become older, their interest scores begin to stabilize. One reason is that their range of experiences expands and allows them to make choices of activities on something more than a very superficial impression.

But further problems arise in taking interest inventories. Two students may well make the same selection of an activity for very different reasons. Would you like, dislike, or feel indifferent to being a jockey? One student may like the job because of the persistent challenge to man and beast to win races. Another student may like it because he sees glamour and public acclaim as a central part of the occupation. Two students may mark an item the same way, but their reasons for doing so can be quite different. Possibly, we could identify the interests of students more precisely if we knew more about their motivation for making the selections they make.

It should be noted, however, that when tests are empirically validated, we do not ask why a given occupational group endorses a given activity. Rather, we are concerned only with finding statements that persons in this occupation endorse with a frequency clearly different from that of other people. However, the responses of the validation samples of employees who have been in their work for a period of time cannot be equated with responses of students who are clearly more naive about the experiences described in the inventory.

Finally, interest scores cannot be construed to mean that the client has aptitudes commensurate with his interests. If Mary has a high interest in the "Musical" area on the Kuder, it does not mean that we have discovered in her a latent talent for music. If Tom has a high score on the "Accountant" scale on the Strong, it does not mean that he has the academic ability to graduate from a college program in accounting. Although some evidence shows that Strong inventory scores are related to professional success (Kelly and Fiske 1951), other studies show that inventories have not been good predictors of academic achievement (Robinson and Bellows 1941, Jacobson 1942, Berdie 1944, Melville and Frederiksen 1952).

Advising a client on vocational selection clearly requires more data than that provided by an interest inventory alone. We can expect an interest inventory to serve us best only when used as one item of information in a broad assessment of a client's characteristics. For example, suppose I have a student whose Strong scores rate him high on the "Physician" scale. Shall I recommend a strong science core to his high school and college work? I need more information. What is his general academic ability? Can he make it through an undergraduate program with sufficient success to be admitted to medical school? What is the nature of his personality? Is he sufficiently mature and stable to assume the responsibilities and bear the stresses of a rigorous training program? Clearly, the student's interests alone are only one component of the data required for vocational counseling.

But interest inventories have wider possibilities than providing a base for counseling individual students. What kinds of programs shall we provide for our students? Is the answer to this question partly tied to the interests of our student body? Would knowledge of student interests help us decide how to approach the teaching of literature, sciences, and social studies? Educators have not yet exploited the curricular and methodological uses of interest-inventory data, but we should begin to do so.

PROBLEMS

1. In the problems that follow, we are dealing with interest inventories.

    a) I have built an interest inventory with two subscales, A and B. The inventory has 40 items, each of which is made up of two statements. In each pair of statements, one scores on scale A, and the other scores on scale B. Test takers are asked to select the one statement from each pair that is most like themselves.

       Is it likely that I could get a high score (e.g., 1 + standard deviation above the mean) on one scale and a low score (1 + standard deviation below the mean) on the other scale? Is it likely that I could get two high scores and no low score? Two low scores and no high score? What does this tell you about ipsative scales?

    b) A parent recently said to the band teacher, "Our Jenny received a high interest score in Music. We want you to start her on the violin so that she may develop this talent." How would you respond to this parent's statement?

2. I wish to make an interest-in-teaching scale. Describe how I would validate it by using (a) logical keying and (b) empirical keying.

ASSESSMENT OF ATTITUDES

In accordance with our earlier discussion about attitudes, we may wish to see attitudes as one's set of action tendencies associated with a social object. Suppose I say to you, "I've got an acquaintance I want you to meet—he's a labor union leader." Because of an action tendency you have that leads you to either approach or avoid labor leaders, you probably have some predisposition toward my acquaintance before you meet him. In other words, you have an attitude about labor leaders.

If attitudes are sets of action tendencies, how can we assess them? We cannot see them, and we do not know what people are likely to do (their tendency to act) until the situation inciting action arises. Attitudes are inferred from behavior, so by identifying a person's pattern of responses to a class of behaviors, we make up our minds about what his attitude is. But we cannot push a person into a wide variety of "real life" situations and observe his behavior, so typically we pose hypothetical situations and ask the individual to tell us how he thinks he would respond to them. We make our inference about behavior from what the client says he would do.

Of course, there are hazards to this approach. What a person reports he will do is not always what he actually will do (Corey 1937). Edwards (1957, Ch. 1), however, defended the questionnaire approach by asserting that people feel freer to express themselves in the privacy of an inventory than they do in open social settings. In face-to-face questioning, people may be somewhat reluctant to relate their personal feelings. Also, behavior is influenced by variables other than attitude. For example, a man who strongly prefers a sales tax over the income tax may not wish to argue with his hostess, who prefers the income tax. Thus, behavioral observations also are limited as indicators of attitudes.

Attitudes are learned. Learning, presumably, is what goes on in schools. We learn not only bookish content there; we also acquire a set of attitudes toward all kinds of people, organizations, and social endeavors. Is it not the business of educators to assess these learnings along with the assessment of cognitive abilities? Krathwohl *et al.* (1964) believed that the interest/attitude/emotional side of a child's development is clearly a concern for educators. To this end, they prepared a taxonomy of educational objectives in the affective domain. This taxonomy may be used both as a guide for instruction and the subsequent assessment of students' affective characteristics. Briefly, the taxonomy, in order of complexity, is as follows.

Class or category	*Related behaviors*
1. Receiving—the student attends to phenomena and stimuli (lowest level on this taxonomy).	Observes objects, listens attentively, shows sensitivity to differences in personal characteristics of peers, follows class instruction.
2. Responding—the student reacts to objects and events, he participates as a contributor, and finds satisfaction in reacting.	Completes assignments, follows rules, gets involved in class discussion, volunteers for projects, and reads and questions to pursue interests.

3. Valuing—deals with the worth a student places on objects and events, ranging from accepting values to assuming responsibility for developing direction for the group.

Attempts to promote rules giving all people equal opportunity, promotes quality modes of expression (literature, art, etc), and shows concern for welfare of others.

4. Organization—the student puts together different values, resolves conflicts between values, begins to form a consistent value system.

Balances freedom and responsibility, accepts responsibility for own behavior, makes long-range life plans, shows consistent behavior toward social objects.

5. Characterization by a value or value complex—student has organized a complex of values with sufficient stability to have developed a life style.

Demonstrates constructive approach to group activities, shows cooperation, leadership, industry, self-discipline, practices self preserving health and safety routine.

Attitudes are woven in at all levels of this taxonomy. The events described above can be observed in all schools, but how well have we assessed the child's progress in moving through the levels of this taxonomy? Not very well.

Since most teachers are better able to make an achievement test than an attitude scale, let us take a look at how attitude scales are built. They really are not so complex that teachers should avoid them. Here are the basic procedures to follow.*

We will look at two different approaches to constructing attitude scales: (1) the summated ratings, or Likert scale, and (2) the equal-appearing intervals, or Thurstone scale. Although there are several other procedures for building attitude-assessment tools, these are two of the most widely used methods and are the ones you are most likely to encounter.

The Likert scale

The Likert scale, or summated ratings, is built by accumulating a number of statements, about half of which reflect a negative attitude toward a psychological object and half of which are positive. We then give these statements to a group of subjects and ask them to either agree or disagree with the statements. For each statement we allow the subjects to express

---

* The student who wishes to construct an attitude scale is referred to a more detailed text on the topic, e.g., Allen Edwards, *Techniques of Attitude-Scale Construction*, New York: Appleton-Century-Crofts, 1957, 256 pp.

their response in only one of five categories: strongly agree, agree, un-decided, disagree, strongly disagree. An example might look like this:

	SA	A	U	D	SD
My school is a stimulating place.	——	——	——	——	——
School work is boring.	——	——	——	——	——

Our next job is to weight the categories of response. We want the category that reflects the most favorable attitude to get the greatest weight. We have five categories, and we can weight them 0, 1, 2, 3, and 4. In the first example above, the weight of 4 would be assigned to the SA category, (strongly agree), 3 to A, 2 to U, etc. In the second statement the weight of 4 would be assigned to the SD category, 3 to the D category, and so on.* If I marked the first item under A and the second under D, my summated score for these two items would be 6, i.e., 3 + 3. Of course, we will not settle for only two items in a scale; we will probably want about 30 items.

After our sample of people has responded to the items by checking the categories that best reflect their feelings, we apply our weights (0 to 4) to the items. I can then get a score for any given person by adding together the weights of the categories he has checked. If our items are doing their job, the people with the highest scores will be those with the most favorable attitudes toward the psychological object involved.

Not all of our original statements will be good ones. An item analysis will be necessary to select out the best items. Psychometricians will do this by correlating the scores on each item with the total scale score. For example, suppose we have a scale on attitude toward school. John Ecks has a total score of 68 points. On the first item he chose the SA response, which gave him 4 points. To see how well item 1 correlates with the total score, the psychometrician would begin with these two measures on John, i.e., 4 and 68. He would complete the correlation procedure by looking at the same two bits of data—item 1 score and total score—for all students in-volved. From these data for all students in the try-out sample, the cor-relation between item 1 and the total scale could be computed. If item 1 is accurately assessing the attitude that the entire scale is measuring, the correlation should be at least moderate (.50 or more). If the correlation is low, we should drop item 1 from the scale, because it would not appear to be assessing the same attitude as is the total scale.

As a substitute for actually computing correlations between items and the total score, we can do a very rudimentary item analysis by "eye ball,"

---

* More complex weighting is based on the deviates corresponding to proportions of a normal curve. However, Likert (1932) found a high correlation (.99) be-tween simple weighting as above and normal deviate weights.

as follows. First, arrange the total scores from high to low. Locate the papers with the scores in the highest third of the group; then locate those with scores in the lowest third. For *each item*, tabulate the number of responses in each SA, A, U, D, SD category made by the high scorers; just below, tabulate the responses made by the low scorers. The result might look like the following for item 1 of the attitude-toward-school scale administered to a group of 60 students.

	SA	A	U	D	SD
Papers in high ⅓ of total scores	11	7	2		
Papers in low ⅓ of total scores		1	3	7	9

Clearly, item 1 brought different responses from high- and low-scoring students, i.e., it is a discriminating item.

Here are two items that aren't quite so neat.

	SA	A	U	D	SD
Papers in high ⅓ of total scores	5	6	4	4	1
Papers in low ⅓ of total scores	4	4	6	4	2

	SA	A	U	D	SD
Papers in high ⅓ of total scores		5	10	5	
Papers in low ⅓ of total scores		3	5	10	2

These, and many other varieties of patterns, do not show the high scorers on the total scale choosing response categories markedly more favorable or unfavorable than those of the low scorers. Therefore, these items are probably not assessing the same trait as is the total scale, or are ambiguous, and such items should be dropped from the scale.

Once we have tried out our scale on a group of students and have dropped out the poor items, do we rescore the scale for our try-out group, using only the good items? We do not. Our try-out sample of students is used only for scale-construction purposes. We now have what we hope are some pretty good items, and we are ready to apply them with another sample of students, once again checking the items for discrimination. A split-half reliability may also be interesting to compute on this second sample of students. If the reliability looks good and our items still appear to be discriminating satisfactorily, we are ready to use the scale to assess attitudes.

The steps are, then: (1) collect positive and negative statements about the psychological object involved; (2) try out the statements on a sample of students and do an item analysis, (3) select the items that appear to be measuring what the total scale measures and arrange these items into a new scale; (4) administer this new scale to a second group of students and once again calculate discrimination values for all items; and (5) apply the new scale to the students whose attitudes we wish to assess.

The Thurstone scale

A second approach to building an attitude inventory is described by Thurstone and Chave (1929). In this procedure we begin by collecting a set of statements about a psychological object; these statements range across the entire spectrum from extremely favorable to extremely unfavorable. About 40 to 50 statements will be needed. We then give these statements to a group of judges. Thurstone said 300 judges were needed, but Rosander (1936) produced good results with as few as 15 judges. Each judge places the items, one by one, on a scale like that below.

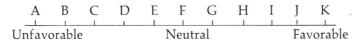

The location of the statement on the scale depends on how *favorable* the statement appears to the judge in reference to the psychological object involved. The judge does *not* rate the item as to whether he agrees or disagrees with the statement. He only places the item on the scale of *favorability* in terms of his perception of how positively the statement reflects the attitude being assessed.

For example, suppose we are building a scale to assess attitudes toward Little League baseball. The first item is:

"I think Little League baseball should be abolished."

Judge A looks over the item and decides it reflects an unfavorable, but not extremely unfavorable, attitude toward the Little League. Judge A does not consider whether he disagrees with the item. He thinks only about how favorably the item reflects the subject involved. He marks the scale as shown below.

```
    A    B    C    D    E    F    G    H    I    J    K
    |____|____|____|____|____|____|____|____|____|____|
    Unfavorable  X         Neutral              Favorable
```

This process is repeated for every item we have prepared for our scale.

When all judges have independently placed each item along the scale, we will have for every statement a set of judges' placements. We can convert these placements to quantities by assigning number values to the letters in the scale, as follows.

```
    A    B    C    D    E    F    G    H    I    J    K
    |____|____|____|____|____|____|____|____|____|____|
    1    2    3    4    5    6    7    8    9   10   11
```

Now suppose that the statement about the Little League got an A placement by two judges, B by seven, C by eight, and D by three. We could then compute a median rating for all judges.* This median could become the *scale value* for the statement.† If judges rated the statement about the Little League as cited, the scale value would be as shown in Table 11.2.

TABLE 11.2 Computing the scale value

Category	Value	No. of judges	Limits of value intervals	
D	4	3		$1/2 \times 20$ judged $= 10$; to make a
			3.5	total of 10 cases we need one case
C	3	8		from the interval 2.5 to 3.5, or 1/8
			2.5	of interval which is one point in
B	2	7	9 judges	width, or $1/8 \times 1$, or .125. This
A	1	2		we add to the bottom of the inter-
		20		val, $2.5 + .125 = 2.625 =$ the
				scale value for item.

After we have computed medians for each of the statements, we can then place the items along the favorability continuum. It is desirable to have a set of statements whose scale values (median ratings) range from near one end of the continuum to near the other so that all gradations of the attitude from negative to positive are represented. We probably will find that a few items cluster at several points along the scale. We typically thin out these piles by selecting the one statement from the cluster on which the judges had the closest agreement. For example, judges' placements of the two statements X and Y are as follows.

Item X		A	B	C	D	E	F	•	•	•
No. of judges		0	2	7	10	1	0	•	•	•

Median 3.60

Item Y								•	•	•
No. of judges		1	2	6	6	3	2	•	•	•

Median 3.67

```
       A    B    C    D    E    F    G    H    I    J    K
      |____|____|____|__|_|____|____|____|____|____|____|__ Scale
                     ↑↑                                    placement
```

---

* The student who needs a review of the median should turn back to Chapter 3.
† Edwards (*op. cit.*, pp. 90–92) proposed a graphic method for computing the scale value, and Jurgensen (1943) used a nomograph for obtaining scale values which he claimed could be developed in ten minutes for any given set of judges.

Although the scale values are not identical, they are very close. We would therefore wish to use only one of the statements in our final scale. We would probably select item X because the 20 judges were more closely in agreement on the placement of this statement than they were for Y. Item Y would be dropped from the scale.

When we have scale values for the statement and have eliminated scale pile-ups by taking out those items with a wide range of judges' placements, we are ready to use the scale to assess the desired attitude. We provide our students with a list of the statements arranged in random order. Students are asked to mark statements as "agree" or "disagree." We then look only at a given student's "agree" items and compute the *average scale value* for these statements. This average scale value places that student on our unfavorability-favorability continuum.

To review, the steps in building a Thurstone scale are: (1) collect statements, some representing very unfavorable attitudes toward the psychological object, some moderately unfavorable, some neutral, etc., throughout the entire range of favorability-unfavorability; (2) have judges place these items on an 11-point scale of favorability; (3) compute the judges' median rating for each statement—this is the scale value for the statement; (4) place the scale values on the 11-point scale to see (a) if we have items across the favorability-unfavorability range, and (b) which items pile up at points on the scale so that we may eliminate less desirable items; (5) list remaining items randomly on a page and ask students to mark each item "agree" or "disagree"; and (6) find a given student's attitudinal position on the favorability range by averaging the scale values for all items with which he agreed.

There are advantages to both the Likert and Thurstone types of scales. The Likert scales are typically more reliable (Edwards 1957, p. 162) and are less difficult to construct (Edwards and Kenny 1946) than are the Thurstone scales. However, the Thurstone procedure places the student on a definite scale of favorability, whereas the Likert method does not. The Likert procedure merely allows us to rank people without regard to the extent of favorable or unfavorable affect.

Use of attitude inventories

A number of questions dealing with student, parent, or teacher attitudes arise in any school (or for that matter, in any class). We seldom assess these attitudes, however, because we do not have the necessary tools. Instead, we find ourselves making decisions with only visceral-level information. We can do better than this.

Part of a teacher's job is helping children develop skills, but these skills will seldom be called upon if the student holds a negative attitude toward the subject area. Another part of instruction must be directed toward developing positive attitudes toward the skill area. How well do we do this? Who knows? We just do not assess attitude changes. But why not? It is not that difficult.

A school flourishes only when it has the support of its clientele. What is the attitude of parents toward ungraded classes, toward substituting conferences for report cards, toward raising a bond for building a new gymnasium? Administrators also need to assess attitudes, and their operations are successful only when they have a good sense of the feeling of the community. Using the procedures for developing formal assessment of attitudes described in this chapter, educators could remove hypotheses from the hunch category to a data-based probability level.

PROBLEMS

1. I have written items for a Likert scale and have asked 90 students to respond to it. I have taken the 30 highest and 30 lowest on total-scale score and have distributed their responses among the options. I plan to do a visual inspection of the items to select those that appear to be working. The results of the first four items are given below. Which ones would you retain for the next administration of the scale?

Item A	SD	D	U	A	SA
High 1/3	18	7	4	1	0
Low 1/3	10	4	4	12	0

Item B	SD	D	U	A	SA
High 1/3	4	1	7	8	10
Low 1/3	11	13	4	1	1

Item C	SD	D	U	A	SA
High 1/3	1	9	10	5	5
Low 1/3	7	14	4	5	0

Item D	SD	D	U	A	SA
High 1/3	3	16	8	2	1
Low 1/3	0	6	5	14	5

2. I have just made a list of statements for a Thurstone-type scale and have given it to 30 judges to get favorability ratings on the statements. The judges' ratings for the *first* statement on my list have been transcribed from the usual A to K scale and are listed below. Compute a scale value for this statement.   (ans: 3.07)

Judge	Favorability category	Judge	Favorability category	Judge	Favorability category
1	C	11	A	21	C
2	B	12	C	22	D
3	B	13	B	23	D
4	C	14	C	24	C
5	D	15	C	25	C
6	C	16	B	26	B
7	C	17	D	27	C
8	E	18	C	28	D
9	D	19	B	29	D
10	C	20	D	30	C

SUMMARY

Interests and attitudes are closely related, but they are not identical constructs. An attitude is a predisposition to accept or reject a psychological object; an interest is a tendency to participate in activities. For example, I may have a positive attitude toward women's rights, but what activities am I likely to participate in to evidence this attitude? I could write letters to politicians, march in a parade, run for office, write a book, or reinforce the desired behaviors of other people. The activity which I select reflects my interest.

Interest inventories are typically constructed under one of three procedures: homogeneous keying, empirical keying, or logical keying. Interest-scale interpretation is complicated by several problems. The scales are fakable, some of them are ipsative, identifying the motivations that lead to choosing a scale area is difficult, the breadth of the student's experience may influence his responses, and interest scores are often mistaken to mean aptitude. The careful user of interest inventories will note these problems to avoid misinterpreting inventory results.

Interest assessment of students has not played a large role in planning curriculum and instructional methodology. Educators may wish to investigate this source of information as a means of adapting programs more closely to their students, hence capitalizing on the intrinsic motivation involved.

Attitudes are continually being developed and modified by school experience, but we know little about the direction or magnitude of the change. Two procedures for assessing attitudes are the Likert, or summated rating, approach and the Thurstone, or equal appearing intervals, method. Using these two procedures, schools can go far in assessing attitudes of students and the support of the community so that programs may be appropriately responsive to prevailing attitudes.

REFERENCES

Berdie, R. F. "Prediction of college achievement and satisfaction," *Journal of Applied Psychology*, **28** (1944): 239–245.

Bridge, L. and M. Marson. "Item validity of the Lee-Thorpe *Occupational Interest Inventory*," *Journal of Applied Psychology*, **37** (1953): 380–383.

Canning, Leslie, Katherine Taylor, and Harold Carter. "Permanence of vocational interests of high school boys," *Journal of Educational Psychology*, **32** (1941): 381–494.

Clemens, William V. "An analytical and empirical examination of some properties of ipsative measures," *Psychometric Monographs*, 1966, No. 14.

———. "Interest measurement and the concept of ipsativity," *Measurement and Evaluation in Guidance*, **1** (1968): 50–55.

Corey, Stephen M. "Professed attitudes and actual behavior," *Journal of Educational Psychology*, **38** (1957): 271–280.

Edwards, Allen. *Techniques of Attitude Scale Construction*, New York: Appleton-Century-Crofts, 1957, 256 pp.

Edwards, Allen L., and Katherine C. Kenny. "A comparison of Likert and Thurstone techniques of attitude scale construction," *Journal of Applied Psychology*, **30** (1946): 72–83.

Jacobson, C. F. "Interest patterns and achievement in medical school," *Journal of Association of American Medical Colleges*, **17** (1942): 153–163.

Jurgensen, D. E. "A nomograph for rapid determination of medians," *Psychometrika*, **8** (1943): 265–269.

Kelly, E. L. and D. W. Fiske. *The Prediction of Performance in Clinical Psychology*, Ann Arbor: University of Michigan Press, 1951.

Krathwohl, D. R., B. S. Bloom, and B. B. Masia. *Taxonomy of Educational Objectives, Handbook II: Affective Outcomes*. New York: David McKay, 1964.

Krech, David, *et al. Individual in Society*, New York: McGraw-Hill, 1962, p. 177.

Likert, R. A. "A technique for measurement of attitudes," *Archives of Psychology*, No. 140, 1932.

Longstaff, H. P. "Fakability of the *Strong Interest Blank* and the *Kuder Preference Record*," *Journal of Applied Psychology*, **32** (1948): 360–369.

Melville, S. B. and N. Frederickson. "Achievement of freshman engineering students and the *Strong Vocational Interest Blank*," *Journal of Applied Psychology*, **36** (1952): 169–173.

Robinson, J. B. and R. M. Bellows. "Characteristics of successful dental students," *Association of College Registrars*, **16** (1941): 109–122.

Rosander, A. C. "The Spearman-Brown formula in attitude-scale construction," *Journal of Experimental Psychology*, **19** (1936): 486–495.

Strong, Edward K., Jr. *Vocational Interests 18 Years after College*, Minneapolis: University of Minnesota Press, 1955.

Strong, Edward K., Jr. and David P. Campbell. *SVIB Strong Vocational Interest Blanks, Manual*, Stanford, California: Stanford University Press, 1966.

Super, Donald and John O. Criter. *Appraising Vocational Fitness by Means of Psychological Tests*, New York: Harper & Row, 1962.

Thurstone, L. L. and E. J. Chave. *The Measurement of Attitude*, Chicago: University of Chicago Press, 1929.

Tyler, Leona E. "Antecedents of two varieties of vocational interests," *Genetic Psychology Monograph*, **70** (1964): 177–277.

Wesman, Alexander G. "Faking personality-test scores in a simulated employment situation," *Journal of Applied Psychology*, **36** (1952): 112–113.

CHAPTER 12

THE TEST TAKER
AND HIS ENVIRONMENT

To this point we have concentrated on the nature of various types of tests and on ways of judging the quality of tests. It is now time to look at the test taker himself as a dynamic element in an environment that imposes an array of stimuli on him. Some of these stimuli influence the test taker's responses to the test. Also, various internal characteristics, some rather transient, influence his test responses. In part, these characteristics decrease the likelihood that a student will be able to reproduce tomorrow the score that he got on our test today.

It is these characteristics of test takers in the test-taking environment that we shall view in this chapter. The topics discussed here are by no means exhaustive, but they are designed to allow test users to assess the importance of personal and environmental conditions in evaluating test results. In this regard we shall consider the following topics: the characteristics of the test administrator, motivation, test anxiety, physical elements of the test-taking environment, special instructions given to the examinee, test-wiseness, physical condition of the test taker, and response biases.

THE TEST ADMINISTRATOR

Presumably, the important characteristic of a test administrator is that he convey to the examinees what they are to do and under what conditions they are to do it. His job is essentially one of communicating the standard conditions prescribed for the test. Traits that are not part of his communicating activity would logically appear to be irrelevant.

But test takers come to the testing situation with a complex system of attitudes and ready-made systems for reacting to persons who can be fitted into given general categories. For example, we may have a stereotype for tall, thin women with short-cut hair, or for fat, rosy-cheeked men. For this reason the test taker's readiness to attend to and respond to persons in one class of test administrators may be quite different from his readiness to do so with another class. The fact that the test administrator is male or female, is black or white, or is older or younger provides the child with a disposition to respond before the first word of instruction has been given by the test administrator.

Several studies bear out the contention that people may indeed respond to seemingly irrelevant qualities of the test administrator. For example, Benny, Riesman, and Star (1956) suggested that age of an interviewer, relative to that of the interviewee, may be an important factor in eliciting certain types of responses. Ehrlich and Riesman (1961) noted that younger interviewers received more "peer-oriented" and slightly fewer "adult-oriented" answers than did older (over 53) interviewers.

Benny, et al. also found that the sex of their interviewers was an influential factor. Males were more critical of other males than females were of females. Although both sexes "felt most at home" when the examiner or interviewer was female, sex of the examiner did not produce the impact on client responses that age did. Pederson, Shinedling, and Johnson (1968) also studied the effect of examiner sex, but younger (third grade) subjects were used. Female examiners elicited better performance on the WISC than did male examiners. The results were most striking for female examinees. These findings were corroborated by Cieutat (1965), using the Stanford-Binet.

The personality of the test administrator is also an important factor at least in getting results from individually administered tests. Sacks (1952), studying preschool children, noted that positive social relationships established between the examiner and the subjects before testing resulted in higher scores on the Stanford-Binet than when less positive social relations had been developed. These results may or may not generalize to older children.

Further data on the role of the examiner's personality were provided by Young (1959). He found that the extent to which students were successful with digit span (repeating a series of digits immediately after an examiner has presented them) varied with the personality characteristics of the examiner. Surprisingly, subjects with "poorly adjusted" examiners did better than subjects with "well-adjusted" examiners.

The examiner's personal traits have also been seen to affect the results of individually administered personality assessments. Sanders and Cleveland (1953) noted differences among examiners in the number and kind of responses elicited from Rorschach cards. These researchers tied at least some of these differences to "anxiety" and "hostility" in the examiner. Possibly, the tension introduced into the setting by the examiner elicited higher motivation. Similarly, Turner and Coleman (1962) noted differences among examiners in the type of material elicited in response to *Thematics Apperception Test* (TAT) pictures, but their attempts to relate these differences to measured personality traits produced equivocal results. Aside from particular personality traits, Bernstein (1956) found that the mere presence of an examiner could be inhibiting to the test taker. In the absence of the examiner, the material developed by subjects was more emotionally toned than that produced by subjects in the presence of the examiner.

The impact of the race of the examiner on scores of individually administered tests has also been studied. Katz, Roberts, and Robinson (1965) found that if the task was described as a coordination skill, black southern male college students produced significantly higher scores on digit-symbol tasks when the examiner was white. However, when the task was described as an intelligence test, the subjects elevated their performance for black examiners, but lowered it for white examiners. As a result, the previously observed examiner differences disappeared.

Slightly different results were obtained by Abramson (1969), who used both black and white examiners in testing the intelligence of both black and white kindergartners and first graders. Across both grade levels, white examiners tended to get higher performance from both races of children than did black examiners. However, black examiners elicited about equal performances for black and white first graders, whereas white examiners elicited a higher level of achievement from white children than they did from black children. The performance of black children with white examiners was about equal to their performance with black examiners. That is, the white children appeared to perform better with white examiners, but black children performed equally well with either black or white examiners. No significant differences appeared for kindergarten children. Abramson speculated that race awareness may not emerge until children are in the first grade. However, Pasamanick and Knobloch (1955) believed that assessment of intelligence of preschool black children could be affected by their lack of responsiveness to white examiners. Apparently, children in their study did have some racial awareness.

What can we conclude from all of these studies? We may hypothesize that at least in individual interviews in school settings, "younger," and possibly female, examiners would be preferred. We can also state that the examiner's personality traits probably are important variables, at least in individual testing sessions. Examiner characteristics that may be relevant are those that introduce sufficient tension into the situation to stimulate the client to work diligently. The race of the examiner also affects children's responses, but again, the direction of the influence appears to be tied to the nature of the task involved and the age of the children being tested.

The common thread that appears to be running through these studies of examiner influences on performance of subjects seems to be associated with Rosenthal's (1966) idea about teacher expectancies. Although Rosenthal's findings have been contested, he believed that children tend to conform to the high or low expectations of their teacher. Could it be that children respond to an examiner in relationship to their perception of the examiner's expectations of them? If so, we can rationalize the effects of age differences among examiners and the equivocal findings on the effects of personality and race differences. The association of the examiner's "hostility" and "anxiety" with the test-taker's Rorschach responses may mean that examiners who evidenced these traits projected to their clients a sense of urgency or demand. Similarly, white examiners may have projected greater expectancies to white than to black children.

We must be quick to note, however, that as an explanation for the seemingly discordant findings in the studies cited, the expectancy hypothesis is not founded on an extensive data base. However, Jacobs and DeGraaf (1973) have provided some evidence that expectancy is indeed a relevant factor in test situations. In their study both black and white examiners were used, and both black and white children were tested. Prior to testing, the examiners were given either "high" or "low" expectancies for each child. The results showed that while race of the examiner or of the child was an insignificant variable, the expectancy of the examiner was clearly significant.

We have looked at the effects of the examiner on subject behavior, but at least one study (Masling 1959) has shown that the behavior of examiners is also influenced in an important way by the persons being tested. Accomplices were trained in providing "warm" and "cold" responses to the administrator of the Wechsler test. Their test responses were memorized by the subjects and were preselected to be difficult to score. Each of 11 administrators gave one test to a "warm" client and one to a "cold" client. The results indicated a significant score advantage in favor of the "warm" clients. We can probably conclude that both test takers and administrators mutually influence each other in interesting ways within the test-taking environment. However, research at this point does not clearly indicate the directions of the influence.

MOTIVATION FOR TEST-TAKING

Flanagan (1955) has shown that students must be motivated to put forth a serious effort on tests if the scores are to be maximally reliable. Flanagan has also shown that for best results, students need to see how test results are relevant to them personally. Naughton (1968) confirmed this finding. Before his tenth graders took the DAT, a third of the class received a pretest orientation in which they were advised how each of their test scores was to be used, and the importance of maximum effort was explained. The results showed that the scores of the orientation group exceeded those of the rest of the class on all scales of the DAT, up to 10.3 standard-score points (on the spelling test).

The nature of the test as perceived by the students may also be a motivating factor. Yamamoto and Dizney (1965) found that children did better on the average if a test was called an "intelligence" rather than an "achievement" or "routine" test. The researchers suggested that the concept of IQ held a higher prestige value for children and hence elicited better performance. These findings may be offered as a possible explanation for Naughton's results cited above. Could it be that his orientation indeed raised the prestige value of the test and hence increased student motivation?

The opposite side of the motivation coin also deserves recognition. Students' motivation may indeed be depressed by the test administrator. Gorden and Durea (1948) showed that for a group that was discouraged, scores were significantly depressed, i.e., up to one-third of a standard deviation on the average, compared to scores of a group that was not discouraged. It appears, therefore, that examiners should maintain a positive attitude toward testing and that students need to see a useful purpose in taking the test. However, as we shall soon see, the test taker's personality characteristics must be considered before we make too much of this generalization.

TEST ANXIETY

Students have long known the feelings of anxiety that are associated with having to take a test. However, it was not until measures were devised (Sarason 1958) to assess this trait that investigators could concentrate their attention on test anxiety. Here, we shall note only a few studies that have looked at test anxiety in terms of its relationship to test-taking behavior.

Mandler and Sarason (1952) looked at the effects of test anxiety on performance on an intelligence test. Midway in the testing, the investigators advised the subjects that they had done well or that they had done poorly. High-anxious subjects performed less well than low-anxious ones before being advised of their progress. However, knowledge of progress depressed the scores on the last half of the study for the high-anxious examinees, but increased scores for low-anxious subjects. What were the optimal conditions for test-taking? Making no reference to the progress of the group appeared best for high-anxious subjects, and reporting that they were not doing well appeared best to motivate low-anxious subjects. Consistent with this outcome, Sarason and Harmatz (1965) found that high-anxious students did their best work under neutral appeal for achievement.

A speculation here may help us rationalize these findings. At least in part, test anxiety is associated with the threat of failure. A very optimistic approach on the part of the examiner could suggest to the test taker that a low score is probably an unacceptable expectation. If this is so, a very positive approach by the examiner could actually raise the student's anxiety level, whereas a neutral approach, leaving open lower expectations, would not.

These conclusions are interesting in that test administrators are often advised to encourage test takers to do their very best work. This appears to be an unfavorable approach for high test-anxious students. Also, we attempt to put anxious clients at ease with expressions of approval. The findings above suggest that no advice to test takers at all should elicit the best performance from the anxious student.

We noted earlier that students generally achieve higher scores if they have a particular purpose in taking the test and are encouraged to do well. However, the test-anxious student does not appear to operate this way. Sarason, Mandler, and Craighill (1952) separated a group of college freshmen into high- and low-test-anxious subsamples. The test comprised five trials through a stylus maze. Half of the students were given ego-involving instructions which emphasized that the maze was an intelligence test designed to assist in interpreting the student's entrance test scores. The other half of the students, the nonego-involved, were told merely that data were being collected to standardize the maze. The low-anxious students performed slightly better under ego-involving instructions, whereas the high-anxious students did clearly less well under ego-involving instructions. Ego involvement in test outcomes, generally believed to produce good motivation and performance, may well have a detrimental effect on persons who are typically anxious in test settings. Again, the unacceptability of failure appears to be a relevant point in explaining behavior.

PROBLEMS

1. You have a group of 250 seniors in high school who will be taking an intelligence test. You are to plan the testing session. What characteristics do you want in your test administrator? What advice, if any, should we give students in an effort to motivate them to do well? As a motivation, shall we tell students that their placement in next semester's courses is tied to these test scores? What is your rationale for your statements?

2. In what way might examiner influences on students' test performances affect test reliability? Test validity?

THE TESTING ROOM

The administrator's manual that accompanies a test usually advises us that a well-lighted, well-ventilated room, shielded against outside noise, is optimal. Although these conditions seem highly desirable, the research on testing environments indicates that some latitude in these conditions can be tolerated without grave consequences.

Presumably, poor ventilation in a room seriously reduces the oxygen content of the air and consequently reduces the availability of this vital element for the test takers. However, Terman and Almack (1929, p. 396) found that the increase in carbon dioxide in a typical classroom without intentional ventilation is actually slight and far below the critical point needed for efficient mental work.

The ventilation problem appears to arise from changes in room temperature and humidity rather than from changes in the chemical composition of the air. For example, when students were enclosed in a cabinet in which the carbon dioxide content of the air was several times higher than it is in most classrooms, they suffered no ill effects. However, when the temperature inside the cabinet was elevated only slightly (to 72°), students very soon reported dizziness, faintness, headaches, and mental dullness. However, students outside the cabinet who were breathing the air from inside the cabinet through a tube did not report any of these symptoms. Further, subjects inside the cabinet who breathed the outside air through a tube did not gain relief from their discomforts (Kingsley 1946, pp. 198–199). It appears that the cooling effect of circulating air is an important consideration for test administrators, but that "fresh air" is less important, if not irrelevant, in the typical classroom setting.

Test manuals also advise the use of well-lighted rooms and desks or tables that allow the students comfort and freedom of operation. These seem like reasonable conditions under which children can show their best ability. However, once more, the adaptable human organism may not be impaired by less suitable environments. Ingle and De Amico (1969), for example, found that children who took tests in a "poorly lighted" auditorium in which lap boards were used as a writing surface did no worse on a standardized achievement test than did the children who worked in well-lighted classrooms with "adequate" writing surfaces.

The effects of distractions on test results have also been investigated. Super, Braasch, and Shay (1947) used two groups of college students, one to be distracted, the other to be a control. Distraction included a trumpeter playing periodically in an adjoining room, intrusions into the room by outsiders, audible comments and walking around the room by "planted" test takers, loud conversation in the hallway, and mistiming of the test with instructions for the test taker to proceed after the time clock bell rang.

The typical test administrator would no doubt be quite upset if all of these distractions occurred during a normal testing session. However, the results of the study suggest little cause for alarm. There were no statistically significant differences between test scores of the distracted and control groups. In fact, on two of the three tests taken during the study, the distracted group actually produced mean scores higher (but not significantly so) than those of the control group, which had no distractions.

The extent to which this study can be generalized is a matter of speculation. The subjects were young adults, committed to the kind of academic work that demands a resistance to distraction. A similar study done with younger students (sixth graders), who presumably have shorter attention spans, showed that distraction may indeed have an impact on scores (Trentham 1972). Further, personality variables, such as anxiety, may cause some students to suffer more from distraction than do others. If this is true, distractions could invalidate a test for such a student, while having little impact on the scores of the total group being tested. In any case, Super *et al.* have opened the door to some interesting speculations as to just how carefully we must control the noise element during testing sessions with students whose daily study periods are often fraught with uncontrollable noises.

Although we try to provide the most ideal circumstances possible for children taking tests, some latitude in varying the physical environment appears to be acceptable. However, it should be pointed out that research studies deal with average performances for the group, but test results are often applied to questions about individuals. It is entirely possible that some individuals are quite sensitive to poor test environments. For these people, we may be grossly in error in making judgments based on scores from tests taken under poor conditions. Therefore, we should continue to strive for optimal working environments for test administration.

INSTRUCTIONS

Tests are constructed and normed on the basis of a standard set of instructions. Will variations in these instructions have an impact on student responses? They very well may have an effect, and they should therefore be avoided. For example, Bloxom (1968) found that instructions designed to evoke mild anger in his subjects resulted in greater negative self-reports on a personality inventory, i.e., the subjects appeared to abase themselves more than was true when the additional instructions designed to annoy were not used.

Many test instructions advise students whether or not they should guess. Will students heed these instructions? Swineford and Muller (1953) found that students will guess more often when told to do so and less often if told not to guess. The question, of course, is: Does it make any difference in a student's scores if he guesses or does not guess? Michael *et al.* (1963) concluded that it does make a difference. They found that higher scores resulted when guessing was encouraged and that scores decreased when guessing was discouraged.

This finding has clear implication for both test norming and test administration. If tests are normed on the basis of "don't guess" instructions, one may expect lower scores than if guessing were advised. Nonetheless, if norms tables are to hold any meaning for test interpretation, it is imperative that tests be administered with the same guessing instructions as those given to the norming sample.

Other types of instructions for test takers have also been studied. Should test takers attend to accuracy or to speed? Lamb (1967) found that when the administrator directed the group to attend to speed or to accuracy, it made little difference for boys in the number of items attempted or in the number of errors. Girls, by contrast, did show some change in the number of items attempted. Could it be that test takers' work styles are sufficiently predominant to make instructions about speed and accuracy of limited effect?

Borreson (1967), using a personality-rating device, obtained results similar to Lamb's. Borreson gave subjects three different sets of instructions involving purpose of the rating, amount of subjectivity to employ, and whether results of the ratings would be reported. None of these three types of instructions was associated with score patterns different from any other instructions or from the control. Similarly, Trentham's (1972) anxiety-producing instructions for a test of creativity produced no difference in performance from nonanxiety-producing instructions. Again, test takers appear to have a work style that they bring to an inventory or test, and this work style is sufficiently predominant over variations in instructions to negate suggestions concerning mode of attack.

However, administrators' efforts to motivate test takers do have an effect on test scores. For example, Hall, Tocco, and Schwartz (1973) found that "stress" instructions produced scores that correlated with their final test more highly than did scores made under "relax" instructions. Naughton (1968) found that "motivated" subjects made significantly higher scores on the *Differential Aptitude Tests* than did "nonmotivated" subjects. Conversely, as noted above, Gordon and Durea (1948) found that discouragement by the administrator was associated with clear reduction in IQs for the experimental group, compared to a nondiscouraged control group.

These findings are consistent with the body of research on praise and reproof as an incentive for performance in academic achievement. However, as we noted earlier with test anxiety, personality differences among children may render some children more sensitive to motivating attempts than is true for other children.

FATIGUE

The effects of fatigue are presumed to reduce both mental and physical efficiency; however, we must distinguish between the psychological effects (which impair motivation) and physiological effects (which impair motor functions). In the typical testing situation, impairments resulting from psychological effects are far greater than those caused by physiological effects.

We are apparently capable of operating under considerable fatigue with little evidence of a decrease in mental functioning. Edwards (1941) found that avoidance of sleep for up to 48 hours had little effect on his subjects' ability to take a psychological examination. Conspicuous impairment did appear, however, after subjects had gone 72 hours without sleep. Nonetheless, five of the 17 persons in the study continued to perform with almost no noticeable loss of ability up to the end of the 100-hour experiment, but it appeared that great effort was required for mental work as time wore on.

In almost no typical testing session will we find subjects who have gone as much as 24 hours without sleep. Physiologically, fatigue should not be a great problem for most test takers, provided they can maintain their motivation. If the examinee believes his sleep loss affects his ability to achieve and therefore causes him not to try as hard, the sleep loss will have a detrimental effect on his score. But if motivation can be maintained, fatigue is probably not a problem in normal testing situations.

No doubt individual differences in the ability to tolerate fatigue are also important. Some persons have a lower threshold for feeling fatigue than do others, and these examinees will first become motivational problems. Considerable loss of sleep may have little effect on mean scores for the group, but for any one person, fatigue can produce scores that are misleading. For example, John has had only three hours' sleep in the last 24 hours. His score on an intelligence test he just finished its lower than expected. Is this low score tied to John's low threshold for sensing fatigue and consequent loss of motivation? We simply cannot say. If there is a question, retesting with an alternate form of the test is recommended. Although many people can perform mental tasks well after considerable loss of sleep, it seems safe to administer tests only when the chance for any examinee to be fatigued is most unlikely. Otherwise, scores must be regarded with greater caution than they usually deserve.

RESPONSE BIAS

A large number of studies have shown that some test takers have a tendency to select a given response category (e.g., "true") more times than a simple chance probability would predict. For example, if a set of 50 true-false items (half true, half false) is written on a level of difficulty at which guessing may have at least a partial role in the student's marking of the test, some test takers will show proportionately more "trues" than "falses," while others may have clearly more "falses" than "trues." A general term for all such response tendencies is "response bias."

Two types of response biases have been proposed to account for disproportionate selection of a given type of response: response style and response set. Some test takers appear to be responding to a response category itself. For example, persons who prefer the "true" category in a true-false format are of this type. This tendency to select a response category will be referred to as "response style." Response styles are contentless in that the marking bias is determined by a response category, not by the content of the items.

The second type of bias, response set, is evident when the student has a desire to answer in such a way as to produce a certain picture of himself. For example, a subject may wish to make himself appear "liberal" on an attitude inventory, or appear "sick" on a military questionnaire, or appear to have a high mechanical interest on an inventory tied to an application for a machinist's job. The more explicit the test content is, the greater the likelihood that response sets will appear, whereas less explicit content opens the door to response styles.

Do response styles and sets actually exist? Some evidence suggests that they do. Cronbach (1950) has reviewed a wide variety of studies illustrating the extent to which response types seem to be favored by test takers. Some of these studies also show that the reliability (split-half or test-retest) of choosing a given response category is reasonably high (.75 or more). Cronbach concluded that:

1. Any test in which examinees select one of several categories (like true-false; a, b, c) allows individual differences in response styles to operate. However, the influence of response styles on multiple-choice examinations appears to be of minor importance.

2. Response styles are likely to appear most conspicuously when tests are difficult or when the subject is uncertain of the response.

3. If response styles are present, an item is measuring more than one trait —its keyed trait and a trait associated with preference for a response position.

4. Slight changes in either test direction or practice in test-taking can change the extent to which response style appears in a test.

5. Response styles have been shown to correlate (modestly) with personality characteristics. To this end, response styles could be considered valid test variance for measuring these characteristics.

6. Test items are typically written so that their content is tied to the trait being assessed. If true scores for two examinees are equal, but response style influences one examinee's response selection more than it does another's, response styles most likely will dilute test validity.

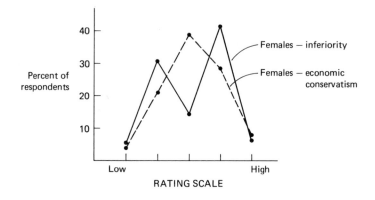

FIG. 12.1 Distributions produced by personal-reference items and sociopolitical items. (Data adapted from Rundquist and Sletto 1936, p. 257.)

These conclusions from Cronbach's review suggest that students' responses on tests may be determined by more than the trait supposedly being assessed. We can partially avoid the problems of response bias by clearly defining to the test taker what his job is, by adjusting the difficulty level of the test appropriate to the examinee, and by eliminating ambiguities in test content.

But test topics themselves may have an interesting biasing effect on students. Response sets often create patterns of responses not predicted by random-sampling techniques. For example, Rundquist and Sletto (1936) provided students with an attitude scale in which favorability was expressed on a scale of 1 to 5. Neutral feeling got a rating of 3. A typical sample of opinion should show most people piling up around 3, with fewer people at the extremes of opinion. However, the shape of the response distribution in Rundquist's study depended on the variable being assessed. Items in scales with direct personal reference (such as inferiority, or morale) produced a bimodal distribution of responses, but items in scales referring to sociopolitical conditions (law, education, politics) produced a unimodal, symmetrical distribution (Fig. 12.1).

This figure shows clearly that the test takers reported neutral feelings less often when the scale items made reference to personal behavior than when the content dealt with extrapersonal events. The data seem to indicate that the examinees were more concerned with making themselves appear to be more definite about their stance on some topics than they were on others.

It has also been shown that response styles, at least, can be altered during the course of the examination by manipulating the test form or content (Chase 1964, Pugh and Chase 1969). If the test gives the student an opportunity to practice a given response style, successive items are more likely to evidence that style than if it had not been practiced. For example, if Mary responds "true" to one group of items, she is more likely to respond "true" to a successive group of items than if she had not practiced marking "true." The fact that changes in one's response biases can occur within the act of test-taking must have a deleterious effect on item validity, because item content may have less of an influence on the test taker's responses in one section of a test than in another.

It should be reiterated, however, that some response biases are probably associated with personality characteristics (Lewis and Taylor 1955). To this end, they may be valid inventory responses and should not be eliminated from scoring keys.

PROBLEMS

Below is a list of student comments. How would you respond to each of these?

1. "That testing room was stuffy! You can't do your best work in a room like that!"

2. "Did you hear those students talking in the hall during the test? How can they expect us to work with all that noise?"

3. "They told us to guess on the test if we didn't know the answer, so I guessed. I'll bet my score is miserable because of it!"

4. "I was up until 2 A.M. last night working on my history. With only five hours' sleep, I'll bet I bombed my SAT today."

TEST-WISENESS

In most areas of academic work there are some standard work-attack skills that students employ to maximize success in dealing with problematic situations. Test-taking also has a set of work-attack skills that can be applied to the student's benefit. These skills should help a student achieve higher scores on ability tests, regardless of his skill in the content being assessed. The test taker can sometimes exploit characteristics of the test format or of the test situation to improve his score. Millman, Bishop, and Ebel (1965) have described how this exploitation may indeed be carried off, i.e., they tell us how to become "testwise." Here are the operations involved.

Elements independent of either test construction or test purpose

1. Make opportunistic use of time. Begin to work rapidly, setting a time schedule for progress through the test. Do not waste time on "hard" items, but skip over them (or guess). Then return to these items after all others have been completed.

2. Utilize error-avoiding strategies. Pay careful attention to instructions so that you are sure what is to be done and in what manner. Also, carefully attend to each item to avoid "foolish" errors. Ask questions if uncertainties arise.

3. Employ guessing strategies. Always guess if only right answers are to be counted. If a "correction for guessing" formula is to be used, you can improve your guessing chances over the penalty provided in the formula. How can you do this? One common way in multiple-choice tests is to eliminate one option as clearly wrong, then guess among the remaining. For example:

George Washington was born in the year

a) 1490
b) 1673
c) 1732
d) 1750

Since the (a) response is before Columbus came to America, many students would see this option as obviously wrong. The usual scoring formula for a four-choice item gives us on the average a 25 percent chance for guessing. If I eliminate option (a) and guess among the other three, average chances now are 33 percent, so I will guess.

4. Use deduction to eliminate probably wrong responses. If one of two options implies that the other is correct (and only one answer is correct for a given item), then avoid both of these options. For example:

Which of the following modes of transportation traveled the *fewest* passenger miles in the United States in 1972?

a) automobiles
b) railroad trains
c) river boats
d) cars

Since only one answer can be correct and answers (a) and (d) are synonymous, we should probably avoid both of these choices.

Sometimes the content of one option is included in a second option. If so, the most expansive option should always be selected if both options appear correct. Here is an example.

Which of the following are in the category of "stringed instruments"?

a) banjo
b) guitar
c) lute
d) all of the above

If you know that a guitar and a banjo are stringed instruments, the broader category is "all of the above," and a test-wise student would choose this option.

Elements tied to either test construction or test purpose

1. Think about the test maker's style. Attend to previously noted idiosyncracies of the test writer. What does he look for in test results? Adopt the level and style of sophistication that the test writer has previously shown he prefers.

2. Utilize cues in test construction. Does the test writer make the correct option longer (or shorter) than others? Does he make more false items than true (or vice-versa)? Does he usually place the correct option at position (a) or (e), or in between? Does he employ textbook language? Does he use "specific determiners" in true-false items (see Chapter 6)? These and similar questions can be used to sift out test writers' styles and, consequently, can be applied to achieving better scores on teacher-made tests.

Can children be taught test-wiseness, and does it improve their scores on tests? Slakter, Koehler, and Hampton (1970) showed that test-wiseness did indeed increase as children moved through the grades, and Moore, Shutz, and Baker (1966) and Wahlstrom and Boersma (1968) demonstrated that test-wiseness, as described by Ebel *et al.*, can be easily taught. Further, test-taking strategies appeared to improve scores on poorly constructed tests, but were rather ineffective in changing scores on well-constructed instruments.

But many teachers are rather unskilled test makers. To this end, the child with the test-taking strategies will have an edge over a peer who does not have this skill. It therefore behooves every student to acquire a good deal of test-wiseness. It further behooves every teacher to become a skilled test writer so that scores on his test will be minimally influenced by test-taking skills.

SUMMARY

In any test situation, many stimuli are acting on the examinee in addition to the examination itself. The examination is only one element in a complex of conditions impinging on the test taken.

There is some evidence that in individually administered tests, characteristics such as the age, sex, and race of the test administrator have an impact on test results. Also, certain types of motivating instructions produce better results than when no attention to motivation is given. However, instructions that attempt to alter the examinee's work styles may not be effective.

Although test literature often emphasizes careful regulation of the light, ventilation, and distractions in a testing room, it appears that test takers tolerate some latitude in these conditions without changes in performance. Similarly, students appear to be able to work satisfactorily under conditions of at least mild fatigue.

Response bias is a condition that often infuses errors into test scores. Response biases may be reduced by carefully defining the test taker's job, by adjusting the difficulty of the test appropriate to the student's talent, and by eliminating ambiguity. Some response biases may be correlated with personality traits, and on scales assessing personality, response bias could be a source of valid scale variance.

Individuals are expected to respond differently from one another in the extent to which they are sensitive to various environmental presses. Therefore, although various conditions in a test situation may not affect group scores, they may affect the score of a particular member of the group. To the extent that tests are used for counseling individuals, the environment in which tests are administered should be guarded.

REFERENCES

Abramson, Theodore. "The influence of examiner role on first grade and kindergarten subjects' *Peabody Picture Vocabulary Tests Scores,*" *Journal of Educational Measurement,* **6** (1969): 241–246.

Benny, Mark, David Riesman, and Shirley Star. "Age and sex in the interview," *American Journal of Sociology,* **62** (1956): 143–152.

Bernstein, Lewis. "The examiner as an inhibiting factor in clinical testing," *Journal of Consulting Psychology,* **20** (1956): 287–290.

Bloxom, Bruce. "Effect of anger-arousing instructions on personality questionnaire performance," *Educational and Psychological Measurement,* **28** (1968): 735–745.

Borreson, Hugo A. "Effects of instruction and item content on three types of ratings," *Educational and Psychological Measurement,* **27** (1967): 855–862.

Chase, Clinton I. "Relative length of option and response set in multiple-choice items," *Educational and Psychological Measurement,* **24** (1964): 861–866.

Cieutat, V. J. "Examiner differences with the Stanford-Binet I.Q., *Perceptual Motor Skills,* **20** (1965): 317–318.

Cronbach, Lee J. "Further evidence on response sets and test design," *Educational and Psychological Measurement,* **10** (1950): 3–31.

Edward, Allen S. "Effects of the loss of one hundred hours of sleep," *American Journal of Psychology,* **54** (1941): 80–91.

Ehrlich, June Sachan and David Riesman. "Age and authority in the interview," *Public Opinion Quarterly,* **25** (1961): 35–56.

Flanagan, J. C. "The development of an index of examinee motivation," *Educational and Psychological Measurement,* **15** (1955): 144–151.

Gorden, L. V. and M. A. Durea. "The effect of discouragement on the *Revised Stanford-Binet Scale,*" *Journal of Genetic Psychology,* **73** (1948): 201–207.

Hall, Bruce W., S. Salvatore Tocco, and Larry Schwartz. "Effect of differentially motivating instructions on the predictive validity of a test device," a paper read at the annual meeting of the American Educational Research Association, New Orleans, 1973.

Ingle, B. and G. De Amico. "Effect of physical conditions of the test room on standardized achievement-test scores," *Journal of Educational Measurement,* **6** (1969): 237–240.

Jacobs, John F. and Carl A. DeGraaf. "Expectancy and Race: Their Influences Upon the Scoring of Individual Intelligence Tests," a paper presented at the annual meeting of the American Educational Research Association, New Orleans, 1973.

Katz, Irwin, S. Oliver Roberts, and James M. Robinson. "Effect of task difficulty, race of administrator, and instructions of digit-symbol performance of Negroes," *Journal of Personal and Social Psychology,* **2** (1965): 53–59.

Kingsley, Howard L. *The Nature and Conditions of Learning,* New York: Prentice-Hall, 1946.

Lamb, George S. "Teacher verbal cues and pupils performance on a group reading test," *Journal of Educational Psychology,* **58** (1967): 332–336.

Lewis, Nan A. and Janet A. Taylor. "Anxiety and extreme response preferences," *Educational and Psychological Measurement,* **15** (1955): 111–116.

Mandler, George and Seymour Sarason. "A study of anxiety and learning," *Journal of Abnormal and Social Psychology,* **47** (1952): 166–173.

Masling, Joseph. "The effects of warm and cold interactions on the administration and scoring of an intelligence test," *Journal of Consulting Psychology,* **23** (1959): 336–341.

Michael, William B. "An experimental determination of the optimal scoring formula for a high-speeded test under different instructions regarding scoring penalties," *Educational and Psychological Measurement,* **23** (1963): 83–99.

Millman, J., C. H. Bishop, and R. Ebel. "An analysis of testwiseness," *Educational and Psychological Measurement,* **25** (1965): 707–726.

Moore, J. C., R. E. Shutz, and R. L. Baker. "The application of a self-instructional technique to develop test-taking strategy," *American Educational Research Journal* **3** (1966): 13–17.

Naughton, Jack. "A modest experiment on test motivation," *Personnel and Guidance Journal,* **46** (1968): 606.

Pasamanck, B. and H. Knobloch. "Early language behavior in Negro children and testing of intelligence," *Journal of Abnormal and Social Psychology,* **50** (1955): 401–403.

Pederson, Darhl, Martin M. Shinedling, and Dee L. Johnson. "Effect of sex of examiner and subject on children's quantitative test performance," *Journal of Personnel and Social Psychology,* **10** (1968): 251–254.

Pugh, R. and C. I. Chase. "Test content as a determiner of response habits," *Journal of Clinical Psychology,* **26** (1970): 32–34.

Rosenthal, R. *Experimenter Effects in Behavioral Research,* New York: Appleton-Century-Crofts, 1966.

Rundquist, Edward A. "Item and response characteristics in attitude and personality measurement, a reaction to L. G. Rorer's 'The great response style myth,'" *Psychological Bulletin,* **66** (1966): 166–177.

Rundquist, Edward A. and R. F. Sletto. *Personality in the Depression,* Minneapolis: University of Minnesota Institute of Child Welfare, Monograph series No. XII, 1936.

Sacks, Elmor. "Intelligence as a function of experimentally established social relationships between child and examiner," *Journal of Abnormal Psychology,* **47** (1952): 354–358.

Sanders, Richard and Sidney Cleveland. "The relationship between certain personality variables and subjects' Rorshach scores," *Journal of Projective Techniques,* **17** (1953): 34–50.

Sarason, Seymour, *et al.* "A test-anxiety scale for children," *Child Development,* **29** (1958): 105–113.

Sarason, Seymour and Morton G. Hermatz, "Test anxiety and experimental conditions," *Journal of Personality and Social Psychology,* **1** (1965): 499–505.

Sarason, Seymour, George Mandler, and Peyton Craighill. "The effect of differential instructions on anxiety and learning," *Journal Abnormal and Social Psychology,* **47** (1952): 561–565.

Slakter, M. J., R. A. Koehler, and S. H. Hampton. "Grade level, sex, and selected aspects of test-wiseness," *Journal of Educational Measurement,* **7** (1970): 119–122.

Super, Donald E., William F. Braasch, and Joseph E. Shay. "The effects of distractions on test results," *Journal of Educational Psychology,* **38** (1947): 313–377.

Swineford, Frances and Peter Muller. "Effects of directions regarding guessing on item statistics of a multiple-choice vocabulary test," *Journal of Educational Psychology,* **44** (1953): 129–139.

Terman, Lewis M. and John C. Almack. *The Hygiene of the School Child,* Boston: Houghton Mifflin, 1929.

Trentham, Landa L. "Anxiety level, distraction conditions, and instruction types in a creativity testing situation," Ed.D. diss., Bloomington: School of Education, Indiana University, 1972.

Turner, George and James Coleman. "Examiner influences on Thematic Apperception Test responses," *Journal of Projective Techniques,* **26** (1962): 478–486.

Wahlstrom, M. and F. J. Boersma. "The influence of test-wiseness upon achievement," *Educational and Psychological Measurement,* **28** (1968): 413–420.

Yamamoto, Kaoru and Henry F. Dizney. "Effects of three sets of test instructions on scores on an intelligence scale," *Educational and Psychological Measurement,* **25** (1965): 87–94.

Young, Robert. "Digit span as a function of personality of the experimenter," *American Psychologist,* **14** (1959): 375.

CHAPTER 13

ASSESSING AND REPORTING ON SCHOOL PROGRAMS

Daily, school people must make decisions about a wide variety of events. Teachers face questions such as: "How effective is my instruction in the topic we took up last week in fractions?" Curriculum supervisors ask, "Shall we introduce a nongraded reading program?" "Is science program A better than program B for our students?" Administrators ask, "Is the cost-benefit ratio of program X satisfactory?" "What type of athletic programs can the system afford?" "What physical facilities will be necessary to accommodate program Y?"

At all levels of school operation, we are asking questions that need answers. To provide the answers, we must have hard data; impressions are not good enough. Tests can provide some, but by no means all, of these data. It is the purpose of this chapter to comment on the school testing program and on reports to parents. However, the broader question of evaluation in the school will be surveyed so that we may see test data in the perspective of the total school needs for data.

THE TESTING PROGRAM

School testing programs characteristically call for broad administration of standardized tests at specified intervals in the school program, e.g., in the spring of each year. But the decisions school people must make are not timed that way. Decisions are made daily, so information for decision-making is a perpetual requirement of teachers, supervisors, and administrators. The nature and timing of data collection should be determined in reference to particular decisions that must be made.

This brings us to the essential distinction between evaluation and measurement. Measurement refers to quantifying an entity according to a standard scale, whereas evaluation refers to making a judgment about the quality of an entity in reference to a purpose. Measurement is the process of providing data; evaluation is the process of holding data up to prescribed criteria. So far in this book, we have dealt largely with measurement; this chapter will bridge the gap between measurement and evaluation.

TABLE 13.1 Typical functions and purposes of a school testing program

Function	Purpose
To identify levels of ability, achievement, and affective development for various groups of students (typically grade levels).	To see if typical growth, relative to the norms group, has occurred; to provide an estimate of the effectiveness of the institution, and to validate the hypotheses upon which schools are established.
To diagnose strengths and weaknesses in group performances.	To evaluate curricular programing and expenditure.
To group students on common performance levels.	To adapt new instruction to current achievement levels.
To assess group gains in achievement and/or affective development.	To evaluate a particular instructional program or module on a cost-benefit basis.
To identify conspicuous discrepancies in a given child's achievement profile or between his achievement and aptitude.	To help the child and his parents understand the child's strengths and weaknesses; to locate students for special diagnostic testing and possible remedial work.
To assess special aptitudes and interests for students.	To help students make appropriate career, and hence curricular, choices; to indicate levels and varieties of programs to be offered.

Table 13.1 lays out the common functions and purposes of the school testing program. This table shows that standardized tests tell us nothing about the social and physical context into which we have imposed instruction. Tests tell us nothing about the fidelity with which we have followed a curriculum plan. They tell us nothing about the quality of the instructional materials used. They do, however, tell us something about what children can do, but they do not point to the variables which led to, or failed to lead to, this achievement.

Test scores have real meaning for our school only in reference to a variety of other types of information. But teachers are likely to give tests more status than this. For example, three out of ten secondary teachers from a large public school sample reported that achievement tests were the *single* most accurate measure of a student's intellectual ability, whereas four out of ten secondary school teachers (and almost half of the elementary school teachers) said intelligence tests were the best indicators of ability (Goslin 1967, p. 52). This means that about seven out of ten secondary school teachers report considerable faith in test results as indicators of a child's potential, aside from other information. In view of this faith in test results, we must again emphasize that complex human behavior should be observed from a variety of viewpoints. Standardized tests are only one of these viewpoints, and test scores get their most effective use when interpreted in terms of other kinds of observations.

Schoolwide testing programs typically involve only two types of tests: aptitude and achievement. Therefore, we shall look primarily at these two items in the school program.

Aptitude

A group test of academic aptitude has its greatest usefulness in the early years of a child's educational program. There are two main reasons for this. First, as the child gets older, successive test scores tend to have less variability among them than do early scores. Since the IQ becomes more stable as the child get older, additional tests are less likely to tell us something new about the child. Second, as children get older, such indicators as teachers' marks and achievement tests become increasingly good predictors of the child's future performance. Hence, the need for aptitude scores becomes less acute with the child's successive years of school.

A good group test of intelligence can serve as one source of advisory information to the teacher in organizing children for instruction, can assist teachers and curriculum supervisors in creating programs and selecting materials, and can help school personnel in scheduling topics within the program. These tests, however, should not be administered too early in a child's school career. Pupils need to be adapted to their classroom routine and to be acquainted with classmates and the teacher. The first test, therefore, may well be placed at the end of the first grade or the beginning of the second grade, if major instructional grouping is to take place.

In addition to the rapport value of delaying testing, we gain some score reliability by postponing the administration of the test. Reliability of scores tends to increase with the child's age and familiarity with pencils, papers, and the following of directions. The second aptitude testing should follow the first by about two years. After this, longer intervals between tests are satisfactory.

Individual tests such as the Binet or Wechsler are capable of more precise measures of aptitude than are group tests; however, their use is limited primarily by the expense of administering them. Therefore, these tests are reserved for children with special learning problems. They are also widely used where utmost accuracy of assessment is desired, such as in the assigning of a child to a special class for slow learners. The interpretation of the results of these individual tests of intelligence is left to persons, e.g., school psychologists, who have greater psychometric knowledge than classroom teachers typically have.

In the secondary school or late junior high school, a multifactor test is likely to take the place of the general group test of academic aptitude. These tests—with subscores in a variety of ability areas such as number, verbal, spatial relations, clerical speed and accuracy—help a student to identify his areas of strength and weakness and consequently help him and his advisors make realistic academic and career choices. Such tests produce a profile of the student's talents, but as in the use of all profiles, we must exercise care in the interpretation of subtest score differences.

Achievement testing

Probably the single most useful group test in any school system is the achievement battery. It is a valuable aid in determining where we are doing well in the instructional program and where we need to improve; it helps us identify children who need special diagnostic work; it becomes a fair predictor of achievement in successive grades; it can be a tool in the school's public relations program; and it can be a source of affirmation for teachers who seldom get answers to the question, "How am I doing?"

The possible uses of achievement tests are wider than any other test the school may employ. However, few schools exploit this source of data as well as they might. Oftentimes, test results are not readily available to teachers who might use them. Schmalgemeier and Watson (1970) showed that the school's test data were typically deposited in the principal's office or with the counselor or pupil personnel specialist. It is not always handy for teachers to get at test results in these offices. When they can get to the files, work space is seldom available. Furthermore, in 13 percent of the Schmalgemeier and Watson cases, classroom teachers were not even *allowed* to see test data!

If teachers are to use test results more extensively, these data must be readily available to them. Teachers feel the need for this information that is on hand but inaccessible. In the Schmalgemeier and Watson study, 25 percent of the teachers said that improved methods of reporting test results were of necessity in their schools, while another 20 percent said improvements in reporting were in the planning stage. Obviously, school people believe that tests can give more information than is now being provided. Greater availability of scores should aid teachers in getting and using that information.

Also, additional statistical analysis of scores must be done if we are going to capitalize on achievement-test data in curriculum planning. For example, we need to know the mean performances of all third graders in reading, arithmetic, study skills, and science if we want to see which skills we are promoting effectively and which ones we are not. Before we can make data-based decisions about curricular changes, we must have class profiles, based on average performance of our children in each subject area.

So far, we have spoken only about general-achievement tests. However, there are also achievement tests for special program areas, such as reading and arithmetic. Such tests are not typically part of the schoolwide testing program, but they may be of considerable value in special situations. Suppose we are trying out a new approach to teaching reading. We may well wish a more detailed assessment of the reading progress made by our students than is provided by a general-achievement test. A specialized test of reading ability would then be appropriate.

One area in which a specialized test is of great use is reading readiness. When children enter the first grade, they bring with them a variety of preparations for the big job in this grade—learning to read. Optimally effective instruction will be adapted for each pupil; clumsy handling can make a child a reading cripple for the rest of his life. At this crucial point we need all the help we can get in making plans appropriate for each child. Readiness tests can provide some of this help, and they should therefore be widely exploited in developing individual programs for preprimer students.

Other measures

Although interest and personality inventories have a role in the academic scene, they do not fit well in the schoolwide testing program. Interest inventories typically are reserved for career guidance courses or for the use of counselors in vocational guidance. They may also be used for curricular planning and for devising approaches to the content of a variety of courses. Personality inventories should be used sparingly in school programs. They are easily misinterpreted, and the kinds of questions often included in them are found objectionable by some school patrons. Also, if these instruments are to be used at all, they must be carefully selected so that subtest titles cannot be misconstrued to provide objectionable labels for the test taker who may have a deviant score on one or more of these subscales.

Of all the tests mentioned above, personality inventories have the most limited function in school programs. They are clearly not for teacher use, and they must be closely guarded by pupil personnel specialists who are trained to decide when the prescription of a personality inventory is of optimal value, who know how to interpret the results, and who are keenly sensitive to the ethical problems involved in personality assessments.

Priorities

What about priorities in the testing program? The answer to this question, of course, varies with school objectives, but to the extent that some communality of objectives exists across many schools, the following suggestions are offered.

In the elementary school, high priority must be given to measures of all the basic academic skills, especially reading ability. Since so much of a child's total environment, not just his school work, involves reading, his skill in this area must be promoted as best we know how. Reading, at this point, should be interpreted in its broad, service role: reading for pleasure, reading technical material such as charts and graphs, scanning in information searches, etc. The extent to which reading test scores predict success in other skill areas makes the reading test doubly useful (Nettleton 1972).

If you have a good achievement test, you may find the reading subtests therein are sufficient to do the job for most children, but specialized tests of reading should be available for each child whose scores on the reading scales in the general-achievement battery are notably below his total achievement score. It should also be noted that useful diagnostic information can be gained from well-constructed classroom tests. This source of data should not be ignored.

At the secondary school level, a multiple-aptitude battery should probably have first priority. Career choices are of painful concern to many students in high schools. Also, more instructional program options are available than in elementary grades. How shall we advise John in selecting his course pattern? A set of test scores indicating his aptitude in several performance areas would be very helpful at this point, (but only if we know how these test scores correlate with success in our programs). What shall we say to Suzanne who wants to go to college but is undecided as to which of several possible major subject areas she should pursue? Again, a set of scores on a multiple-aptitude test could be of real assistance. An added advantage of multiple-aptitude batteries is that general academic aptitude scores can often be derived from the data in the profile. For example, a combination of the verbal and numerical reasoning subtests in the DAT correlates quite well with group measures of general intelligence.

Managing the program

Who organizes the testing program? Effective testing programs must have two basic characteristics: (1) an official (with authority to make school-wide administrative decisions) to be in charge of, and provide leadership in, the program; and (2) a committee of teachers, counselors, and curriculum supervisors to establish broad guidelines, to choose instruments, and to establish timing for the program.

Many decisions must be made in getting the tests to the children, eliciting their best efforts on the tests, and getting the results into the hands of the people who will use them. The bulk of these decisions are administrative in nature, but they affect the activities of many, if not all, of the school staff. Therefore, the person who makes these decisions must have authority to make plans that cannot be casually vetoed by various staff members.

However, tests are employed to provide data to users. It is therefore the users who should say what data they need and what tests will best get it for them. Also, the users should say when they need to receive the data and in what form they need it. For this reason, general policy for the program should be set by a representative committee of users. This committee should also select the tests that will be administered. However, the extensive use of expert advice should characterize the test-selection committee's work.

The user-committee approach to organizing a testing program, however, is probably not found in many schools. One study (Schmalgemeier and Watson 1970) reported that teachers were members of the testing committee in only 44 percent of the schools surveyed, whereas principals were represented in 81 percent of the schools and counselors, in 75 percent of the schools surveyed. Certainly, principals and counselors are test users, but the important front-line delivery of instruction is the teacher's job. Therefore, if we are to deliver test data best suited to teachers' needs, teachers must help plan the testing program. Yes, teachers should also be in on the selection of tests. Only they know in detail what they have tried to teach, and therefore only they can locate tests that best reflect the curriculum.

The actual administration of tests can well be managed by the classroom teachers. Group tests are typically not difficult to administer if the instructions in the manual are carefully studied and rigorously followed. Also, teachers as a group typically have a rudimentary background in testing, which has already provided them with the essentials of test usage. Goslin (1967, p. 35) reported that four out of five public secondary school teachers had completed one or more courses in measurement and that three out of four elementary school teachers had had at least one course.

If there is a question about the qualification of teachers as test users, Cook (1958) has prepared a list of topics with which teachers should be familiar. The following items from Cook's list seem especially important for teachers to know about if they are to participate effectively in the administration and use of standardized tests. The following five items should be considered minimal qualifications.

1. Be able to analyze a standardized test as to the appropriateness of content and mental processes for the grade level or subject area being taught.

2. Be aware of the ethics and procedures of test administration and use of test results.

3. Know how to interpret basic data reported in test manuals, such as reliability coefficients, indicators of validity, and standard error of measurement.

4. Know how raw scores are converted to standard scores (*T*-scores, percentile ranks, grade norms, stanines) and be able to interpret each of these types of scores.

5. Know how profiles are constructed for individuals and for the total class and be able to interpret the profile.

Teachers should not, however, be responsible for the routine clerical chores of scoring tests, alphabetizing, etc. If the school system does not have its own machine-scoring service, commercial agencies are now available for scoring tests at a relatively low cost. These agencies also provide some statistical analyses necessary for broader uses of test results in curriculum planning, and therefore these sources should be investigated as an alternative to local scoring operations.

When should tests be administered? This question actually has two parts. First, when, during the course of the year, should tests be administered? Second, at what grade levels should various tests be scheduled? The basic rule is that *tests should be given as near to major decision points as possible*. Since different school systems have different major decision points, no blanket answer can be given to this question. A school system with six clearly defined elementary grades, three junior high school grades, and three senior high levels cannot follow the same test schedule as a system that has an ungraded elementary plan and a modular schedule program in the senior high school.

Each system, therefore, must plot its own program, identify principal decision points, and assign appropriate tests at those points. As we have seen, intelligence tests need not be given as often as achievement tests. We expect fluctuation in IQ throughout the school years, but an abrupt change in IQ is not expected to occur very often. For this reason, intelligence tests need not be given as near to the decision point as achievement tests should. For example, if achievement-test data are to be consulted as an aid to making promotion decisions, an achievement battery may be administered in the spring of each year. However, two or three administrations of an intelligence test during the elementary school years is probably quite sufficient.

Another point to keep in mind in planning the testing program is that once a test by a given publisher is administered to a group of children in a lower grade, this same test should be given to these children all through their elementary years. For example, if the first test I apply to my primary children is the *California Achievement Tests*, I should continue to use these tests throughout the elementary school career of these children. We want to compare performance of our children one year with their performance in successive years. We can do this best if we administer the same test from year to year. Test content from publisher to publisher varies, the nature of the standardization sample varies from company to company, and even the mode of reporting scores is not the same for all tests. Therefore, comparing scores on tests from one publisher with scores on tests put out by a second publisher is almost useless.

Does this mean that once I begin to use test X, I am forever stuck with it? No, of course not. The solution, as cited in Chapter 9, is to phase out test X by continuing it in the upper grades while introducing test Y with the primary grades. For example, suppose I have used test X with my children in all grades this year and want to switch to test Y. Next year I will continue to use test X with grades 3, 4, 5, and 6, while starting new test Y in grade 2. The following year, grades 4, 5, and 6 will get test X, while grades 2 and 3 will get new test Y. This gradual phasing out of test X and phasing in of test Y allows us to use the same test for any given age group straight through their elementary program, but at the same time it allows us to change test publishers if we wish.

This brings us to the problem of selecting a basic set of tests. How should we go about it? The first question is: What behavior, skills, etc., is our school program designed to develop in our children? This list will be long and will vary somewhat from school to school and certainly from region to region. Not all, or even most, of these objectives can be assessed by standardized tests. Our next problem, then, is sorting out the skills, etc., we hope to develop that can be assessed by published tests.

When we have selected the skills that can be measured objectively, we are ready to start looking at specimen tests. Our job now is to find the test, or tests, that require children to perform those tasks that best represent the behaviors we planned to develop. Test publishers will mail you samples of their tests, along with manuals and supporting data, for a very nominal charge. Before your school's testing committee chooses a test, specimen sets of all the major publishers' tests (see Appendix B) should be on hand.

Schools typically have on file much information about children. The role of the standardized test is to provide additional data beyond that which is already available, i.e., how our children compare to a national sample, and how we are doing in one subject area compared to another subject area. In selecting tests we should be careful to choose those that provide as much new information, and as little data redundant with information already on hand as possible.

In selecting achievement tests the importance of investigating test content can hardly be overemphasized. Some tests appear on the surface to have the qualities we are seeking. By format and style, they look like they will do the job for us. We say that such tests have *face* validity. There is no way of knowing how many tests are bought on the basis of their face validity, but the number must be large. The format and style of a test are important, but the tasks the test asks a child to perform are salient. We want tests that require our children to perform tasks that reflect the abilities we have been trying to develop and about which we will make decisions. If a test does this badly, no neatness of format or attractive administrative gimmick can compensate for this deficiency.

Once we have located tests whose content is satisfactory for our purposes, we begin to look for other characteristics. How reliable are the subtests and the total scale? Is the test relatively easy to administer? Are there several interchangeable forms of the test? What kind of norms are available, and how easy are these norms to interpret to professional school people, to parents, and to the children? Can the test be scored easily and economically?

The test committee may also wish to consult several very useful reference books on standardized tests. Probably the most useful will be the *Mental Measurements Yearbook*, edited by Oscar Buros (1965, 1972). The yearbook contains detailed information on many hundreds of tests, listing publishers, ages for which the tests are suitable, subtests, time necessary to administer the test, prices of materials, scoring, date of publication, bibliographical references, and reviews by prominent test specialists. Other references that may be consulted are textbooks, publishers' manuals, and professional journals such as *Educational and Psychological Measurement* and the *Journal of Educational Measurement*. However, the single most useful reference for most school testing committees will continue to be the *Mental Measurements Yearbook*.

TEST DATA IN THE BROADER CONTEXT OF EVALUATION

Now that we have measured some variables associated with the end products of our educational effort and have looked at the profile of achievement for selected grades in each school, is this the end of the assessment problem? Certainly not. It is only one facet of it. Before these data can be maximally useful, we need to collect considerable amounts of other information.*

What is the *context* in which our school operates? What needs exist in our constituency that are not met by the school? What objectives should be pursued in order to meet these needs? Are these objectives realistic in terms of our resources? Do they have a wide base of support in our com-

---

* The following guide for collecting information is extracted from Stufflebeam (1968). Other plans are available. The curious student may also wish to read Metfessel and Michael (1967) and Stake (1967).

munity? These questions are fundamental to our interpretation of test data. For example, if widespread unemployment exists in our community and our people desperately need saleable skills, a functional instructional program would place high on its list of objectives the promotion of work skills that fit the market demand. In this context, low scores on an achievement test emphasizing knowledge of English literature would have a different relevance from those made by a largely college-bound clientele.

A second set of questions emerges here. What kinds of *input* did we employ to manage the context problems? What strategies for reaching our objectives were available? How were these strategies implemented? Against what criteria were strategies tested before implementation? These questions deal with the procedures of instruction and the materials used in the composition of the instructional system. We clearly cannot expect to see children in School A with one set of basal readers, no library, and using only a look-and-say method to produce the same achievement-test scores as children in School B, who have readers at three levels of difficulty and interest, whose teachers use a combination of instructional methods tied to a running inventory of every child's progress. Our achievement scores, therefore, can have meaning only in terms of the input variables in the instructional setting.

But how well did we carry it all off? How well did we use the materials we provided? Were we on schedule? Did our staff have the skills they needed? These *process* conditions should have been under continual observation during the instructional period, modifications should have been made in materials, workshops should have been arranged for the staff, and administrative conferences should have been held to eliminate obstructions to the effective use of materials and methods.

After we have dealt with a collection of questions like these, we are then ready to make sense out of data presented in our achievement tests. Instruction is always in a context—what do we know for sure about the nature of that context? Hunches and folklore are not good enough data here. We need objective evidence—sample surveys, case studies, and reviews of literature. What instructional inputs should we impose on this context? Again, we need evidence—advice of experts, reviews, research in instructional methodology, consultation with persons who work in similar contexts, and comparison of pilot projects which use competing strategies. Do the data suggest that deficiencies in test performance are tied to ineffective input?

Achievement data can help us develop our curriculum, but first, we must know how well we have followed our instructional plan. When you look at a profile of your fourth-grade class and see that they are doing poorly in arithmetic, but better than the average of the national sample in reading, what does this mean? Does it say we should spend more time on arithmetic? Does it mean we need a new method for teaching arithmetic?

We cannot say without first knowing how diligently we followed the method we are now using. The best method available can achieve little if we have inefficient use of materials by teachers who bungle the method. Shall we change our method? Before we can say, we need data on how effectively the process of instruction was managed. This means classroom observations with the aid of prearranged check lists and schedules; it means interviews with teachers and children, again using prearranged checklists.

In summary, before we can effectively interpret the results of our testing program, we need to know quite a bit about the context into which we imposed instruction, the details of the instructional strategy, and how faithfully the strategy was executed. Only then can we say something about the outcomes of instruction as reflected by our test data.

It is interesting at this point to note how much of the total evaluation of a school program does not involve standardized tests. Much useful data can be collected by using questionnaires, checklists, and observation schedules. And only in the light of these data can we really exploit the results of standardized tests.

PROBLEMS

1. Suppose you have been asked to set up a testing program for your school.

   a) Make a list of questions you would want to ask before you began selecting tests. (Note the context of your program, the inputs, the instructional processes, and desired outcomes.)

   b) What questions would you ask about tests you were considering?

2. Suppose you could administer only one kind of test (intelligence, achievement, etc.) and could administer it no more than once every two years. (Make your own assumptions about the nature of the school context and program.)

   a) What kind of test would you choose and why?

   b) At what grade levels would you administer it and why?

3. Suppose you have given the *Iowa Test of Basic Skills* to your fourth-grade class. The class profile shown in Fig. 13.1 (p. 278) resulted. What questions do we need to ask about the context, input, and process of our instructional program in order to make this profile most meaningful?

GRADING AND REPORTING TO PARENTS

Grades

School people have traditionally summarized a student's performance in a given course of study by assigning him a single letter or numerical grade

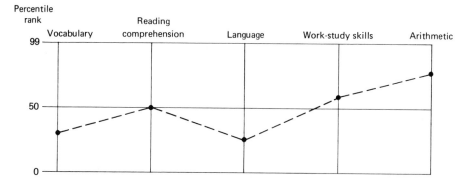

FIG. 13.1 Sample class profile.

that represents a position on a "defined" scale of quality. For years, percentages were used, presumably representing the portion of the content that had been mastered. Of course, any teacher can build a test on which no one could score over 50 percent. On the other hand, we can build tests on which everyone scores over 90 percent. Class achievement thus becomes a function of test difficulty.

An additional problem with percentage grades is that the precision of measurement required to assign a final mark of 91 percent to Myrtle and 90 percent to Sue seems unrealistic in terms of what we know about the accuracy of measurement. The difference in performance between two such people is likely to be undiscernible if they score that closely on tests.

The letter system, involving broader categories of quality, largely supplanted the percentage method of marking. Here, the highest-performing segment of the class was assigned "A"; the next highest "B"; "C" was the middle, or average, performance group; and "D," the low, barely satisfactory students. Students with below satisfactory performance received an "F." In most schools the definitions of performances that merit the various grades are broad and indefinite. As a result teachers have used their own definitions, earning for some instructors a reputation as a hard grader; for others, an easy grader. As a result of general definitions, grades across classes and among teachers have often been described as meaningless.

The problem involved in determining appropriate grades for students has led to appeals for abandoning school marks, or grades. Reasons range from the instructor's not knowing how to give marks, to the claim that grades are middle-class devices used to suppress the lower class. However, we must all agree that by any criterion, the impact of a course of study leaves a clear range in levels of achievement among the members of most classes. Further, the student, his parents, the school, and agents of the broader society, e.g., employers, need evidence of where the student stands on certain relevant criteria. Grades can provide some of this evidence.

The student needs to know how well he has achieved given levels of proficiency that are prerequisite to advanced work or to employment (gainful or otherwise) in the broader society. Parents want to know how their child is progressing with the academic skills important for children to acquire; they want to know how to plan ahead for their children. School administrators need evidence of student achievement in making a variety of decisions. Employers also want to know what level of achievement a potential employee is expected to possess. All of these people find that their requirements are fulfilled at least in part by a grade-marking system.

Grades are intended to reflect achievement. Granted, the assigning of grades is often done badly, and accurate interpretations are difficult, but these difficulties do not mean that grading should be abolished. Instead, let us see if we can do a better job of assigning marks so that they may be more useful to everyone.

Of course, we face serious difficulties in interpreting school marks. Two teachers who teach the same course may use different criteria for arriving at grades for their classes. Does John's "B," given by Ms. Tuff, mean the same as Joe's "B," given by Mr. Eazigo? If our answer is no, maybe we can improve our procedures to ease this difficulty. Can a "C" in chemistry be compared with a "C" in clothing construction? Clearly, the basis for grading is different from course to course. But do we have any business comparing across courses? Should we compare the skills in pole-vaulting with the skills in the 100-yard dash? In spite of problems posed by detractors, we have evidence that there is a sufficient common base for grades among teachers to make marks fairly useful data. For example, grade-point averages continue to be among the best predictors of future academic success available (Hills 1964). Also, the reliability of grade-point averages has been found to be as high as the reliability of many tests (Barrett 1964); however, reliability varies widely among teachers (Lesser, et al., 1962), suggesting that some of our problem lies in lack of measurement skill on the part of teachers. If grades continue to prove useful, it seems reasonable to see what we can do about improving our marking practices rather than abandoning them.

It probably should be pointed out now that most teachers lean too heavily on grading, often substituting a grade on a paper for insufficient diagnostic comments for the student. Because a teacher has noted errors in checking a paper, it does not necessarily follow that he should also place a grade on that paper. An exercise can be a fine learning device and can provide the student with knowledge of his progress, even without a grade marked on the paper. However, diagnostic aids must be written out for the student. Certainly in out-of-school life we are not given a grade on all acts we perform, although we may find them to be excellent learning experiences. For example, after reading a number of stock market reports, I buy some stock in Alphomega Company; the stock goes up $5 in a week; I sell.

My broker does not give me an "A" for my prudent investment. A home maker tries a new recipe with some penny-saving variations of her own. It turns out so-so. The family does not assemble and after deliberation say, "Mom, you get a 'B' for the new meatloaf." Teachers often believe a mark on a paper must finally be affixed or the job of instruction is not well done. For much class work, this is not so. What is more important than the mark are the teacher's comments that will point out ways of doing the exercise better the next time. Very often, instructional uses of tests are best served not by citing how many items the student missed, but rather how he can avoid missing these items in the future.

Are students motivated by marks? It probably depends on how rewarding the students see the mark as being. Hurlock's (1927) early study showed praise to be an effective motivator, while in the long run reproof actually produced a decrease in performance. More recently, Solomon (1964) described circumstances under which punishment may be an effective motivator, but the gross, extrinsic nature of grades does not appear to fit these circumstances. If grades provide praise for good work (not a meaningless gift), we may hypothesize some motivating effect for them. But for the students who find grades to be punishment, inconsistent with attainment, it is doubtful that grades are of much value as a motivator. Also, Goldberg (1965) found that "hard" grading (giving few high grades) does not appear to motivate students more than does "easy" grading (giving many high grades). Applying a low grade to a given child primarily as a reproof for lack of effort, uncooperativeness, or some similar behavior is unsound educational practice!

How should marks be assigned? This depends on the purpose for giving a grade in the first place. Remmers, Gage, and Rummel (1960, p. 267) listed 11 purposes for marking. The following are extracted from their list.

1. Grades provide information for parents and students on the student's progress;
2. Grades help establish a student's qualification for promotion and graduation;
3. Grades provide a data base for educational and vocational planning;
4. Grades allow us to identify and reward honor students;
5. Grades provide a base for recommendations to employers;
6. Grades provide data for curriculum studies;
7. Grades allow us to summarize a student's work when he transfers to another school.

These purposes are best served when the grading system effectively summarizes how well a child is doing in a class. This "how well" is typically tied to three conditions—how he is doing in relation to his peers in the class, how he compares with his peers in a national sample, and how well he is doing relative to a list of skills the children are learning to perform. In the first case we can rank the child among other children on his performance of class objectives. When we grade a child relative to his position in the class, we often call this procedure "grading on the curve," because the bell-shaped curve is typically used as a basis for grouping the class into achievement levels. But it is a rare class that fits a bell-shaped curve exactly. At best, the curve can provide a general guide for agreeing on the percentage of students who will receive each letter grade. However, forcing grades into exact percentages based on a normal curve is inadvisable for most classes. The requirements for use of the curve simply are not met in the typical classroom.

When we rank children among their peers and assess a child's status on the basis of his position among his peers, we are using "norm-referenced" evaluation. We are looking at a child's performance as compared to that of other children. Certainly this is useful information to both a child and his parents. A good deal of a child's concept of "what am I like" depends on how he is able to manipulate things and ideas, compared to the ability of other children to perform these acts. Parents, in getting a realistic image of their child and in making educational plans, can profit from knowing how Mary compares with her peers. This information should include not only Mary's local peers, but also her national age mates. In today's mobile population, Mary and her parents need a broader view of her achievement than local data provide.

The problem at this point becomes one of assigning letter grades to various levels of status in the class. How many levels can we delineate within a class? This depends on the accuracy of our measuring tools and the heterogeneity of the class. The use of letter grades A, B, C, D, and F establishes five levels, but if we add + and − to each grade, we have 15 levels. Having this many levels probably taxes the accuracy of classroom testing devices. The five-level procedure appears more realistic in terms of the error in teacher-made tests. Now, the job is to define the levels *and stick with the definition*. A teacher who defines "C" as "average performance" for his class and then gives a blanket "C" to all students who score below the class mean is not abiding by his own definition of a "C" grade. Such obvious deviations from the definition dilute the meaning of a symbol system already fraught with complex problems.

It should be pointed out, however, that no set of definitions can eliminate arbitrariness from the decision of placing the dividing lines between letter-grade levels. This decision rests with the professional judgment of the teacher. However, it is encouraging to note that there is notable agreement among instructors as to which students perform well and which perform poorly (Fricke 1965), suggesting that operationally there is some general understanding of the meaning of grades among instructors using a common grading scale.

As popular as norm-referenced grading is, instructional planning cannot be tied entirely to how other children perform. There are certain skills that schools intend to promote. A first-grade teacher may set as one of her goals for her instruction a basic sight vocabulary for all children. Her criterion of success is for the child to be able to recognize on sight 75 most frequently used words based on a popular word count of newspapers and magazines. A second-grade teacher may have as one of her instructional goals the ability for each child to add and subtract the 100 basic number combinations. Her criterion might be for each child to compute with 100 percent accuracy the sum and difference of all possible combinations of pairs of numbers 0 through 9. We prescribe the tasks, define proficiency, and inventory the tasks the child has mastered when we grade the child.

When we assess a child's achievement by looking at a set of success criteria, we are using "criterion-referenced" evaluation. This kind of information is most useful to parents and to children. Here, we are pointing to skills that have been mastered; we are setting a base for instructional planning designed to compensate for the deficiencies in performance and to capitalize on skills that have been mastered.

One of the advantages of criterion-referenced evaluation is that we must clearly structure instructional objectives in terms of observable behaviors* and then decide what level of finesse is necessary before mastery has occurred. This procedure clearly spells out to students and to their parents where instruction is intended to lead them. However, setting such objectives is not universally easy. Behavioral objectives are most easily devised for skills that can be measured on some absolute scale, e.g., running the 100-yard dash. In some subjects the nature of the content does not lend itself to the development of such objectives. For example, it is difficult, but not impossible, for social studies teachers to put hoped-for problem-solving skill on a scale where mastery criteria can be imposed. However, as Trow (1966) pointed out, almost any planned sequencing of instructional objectives would result in more meaningful marks than is true in many classrooms today.

Criterion-referenced evaluation provides a measure of achievement tied solely to one's ability to evidence specified skills rather than to one's position among his peers on a given measure. It also has other advantages.

---

* See Robert Mager, *Preparing Objectives for Programmed Instruction*, San Francisco: Fearon Publishers, 1962, for detailed instructions on how to write behavior-based objectives.

TABLE 13.2 Weighting measures to determine total student achievement

	Test 1	Test 2	Total	T-score (total)
Raw scores				
John	24	40	64	110
Marsha	20	55	75	110
Class data				
Mean	20	40		
S.D.	4	15		

It provides a basis for grouping students based on the level of skill achievement; it pits each student against a subject-matter hurdle rather than against his colleagues; it sets the scene for individualizing instruction; and it allows each student to progress at his own rate. These are pedigogical advantages on which educators should capitalize.

Regardless of whether we use criterion- or norm-referenced assessment, we typically will include several different measurements in a final course grade. This means that we must get a summation of scores from all measures for each student. With this procedure, the weight of each measure must be determined. Simply adding up raw scores on tests is usually not an appropriate means of arriving at a student's total achievement for the term. For example, suppose that we have given two tests which are to be weighted equally in arriving at a course grade for John and Marsha. The process by which we can determine their total achievement for the term is shown in Table 13.2.

John's score on Test 1 is one standard deviation above the mean (T-score of 60); his score on Test 2 is at the mean (T-score of 50). Marsha also has one test score at the mean (T-score of 50) and one at one standard deviation above the mean (T-score of 60)* If our summation is to represent the *average position in the class* for all tests, we must use some standard scoring technique, e.g., T-scores, to show this. Clearly, summing raw scores will not give us a fair picture of a student's class position across the semester. In the example above, Marsha got the larger raw-score sum because her highest mark was on the test with the larger, more widely distributed scores. But we are not trying to show who scores best on the tests that happen to have the greatest score range. Rather, we are trying to summarize a student's performance across several measures. To do this,

---

* If the reader does not see how these T-scores are found, he should go back and review Chapter 3.

we must put all measures on a common scale such as T-scores. On this basis, John and Marsha are equal; on a raw-score sum, they are not.

To give more weight to one exercise than to another also demands that we use standard scores, such as T-scores, in order to get valid results. Suppose (for simplicity) that we gave one test and required one term paper. The results were as follows:

Class	Paper	Test raw score
Mean	6	35
S.D.	2	10
Dave	6	45
Pauline	8	35

We decide to give the term paper a weight of 2 and the test a weight of 1. If we merely apply these weights to raw scores, we would have the following results for Dave:

$$2 \times 6 + 45 = 57.$$

The results for Pauline would be:

$$2 \times 8 + 35 = 51.$$

Dave is ahead of Pauline. However, if we first convert the two measures to standard scores (here, T-scores), Dave's score would be

$$2 \times 50 + 60 = 160,$$

and Pauline's score would be

$$2 \times 60 + 50 = 170.$$

Now, Pauline gets the higher rank. If we are going to combine scores on several measures, we first have to put the scores from all measures into a common scale. (We have used T-scores here because they are convenient.) Simply adding, or weighting and adding, raw test scores is not adequate to provide an indication of the student's typical performance among his peers across several measurements.

This brings us to another point. *The way we weight scores must be the same for all students.* This means that we cannot base 75 percent of John's grade on class tests and 25 percent on "work habits" while Marsha's grade is based 50 percent on test scores and 50 percent on "work habits." Why? If the grade is to have meaning, it must represent the same thing for everyone; we must apply the same yardstick to each child. If our criterion is speed, we would not give one child a blue ribbon in the 100-yard dash because he tried hard, but came in last. In this case, achievement is assessed by getting to the finish line before anyone else. If this is what the blue ribbon in the 100-yard dash means, we cannot alter the criterion for other runners, or the meaning of the blue ribbon becomes obscure. Similarly, if an "A" grade in an algebra class means skill in solving a series of selected types of problems, we must apply the success criterion to all students, or the meaning of the "A," already shaky, also becomes obscure. Of course, we can use multiple criteria for arriving at grades for students in a course (provided students understand what criteria are being used), but the same criteria, with the same weights, must be applied to all students.

This also means that the practice of giving, say, five tests, and allowing the student to drop the one with the lowest score is not satisfactory. Even if we weight each of the four remaining tests equally and have used T-scores for our summation, our assessment is not a sample of behavior common to all students. For example, suppose we have three tests in an English composition class. For simplicity, we will say that Test 1 is spelling, Test 2 is grammar, and Test 3 is punctuation. John's lowest score was on spelling; he drops this test from his semester total. Martin's lowest score was in grammar, and he drops this test. Suppose now that both students get a final grade of B—John's B represents punctuation and grammar, while Martin's represents spelling and punctuation. How do we interpret this grade under these circumstances?

PASS-FAIL GRADING

In recent years, pass-fail (P-F) grading has emerged as a means of encouraging students to explore topics they might otherwise avoid if regular grading were required. Also, the P-F system is designed to eliminate the pressure of tests and grading from students and to allow them more latitude in arranging their own time. How well does it work? Unfortunately, most of the research in pass-fail grading has been done with college students. However, these findings may provide interesting hypotheses for studies with younger adolescents in high schools.

In the typical P-F procedure, the instructor does not know who is in his course on a P-F basis and who is on a regular grading basis. He submits regular grades for all students; the registrar then converts all passing grades to P for pass-fail students. Stallings and Mock (1971) found that instructors reported grades almost one letter grade lower for P-F students than for regularly graded students. Karlin (1969) and Syan (1970) reported similar findings. Several hypotheses could be proposed to explain these grade deficits among P-F students. Possibly, they are not working as hard as regularly graded students, and evidence supports this suggestion. However, students may in fact be allocating greater amounts of time and effort to major courses, an option not open to them if the P-F course were more demanding.

Stallings also surveyed students and faculty for their attitudes about the P-F system. Among other things, students reported that they wanted the system continued, that they did not try as hard in P-F courses as in regular grading courses, that they felt less grade pressure, and that they expected an easier time of it in P-F electives than in regularly graded electives. These findings were in part supported by Pascal (1967) who found that students chose P-F marking because of course difficulty and to avoid test pressure. Further, Pascal's students reported less time spent in studying for P-F courses.

Stallings' and Smock's faculty reports showed that the faculty did not believe that students were using P-F options as planned (to explore new areas of academic work). They also believed that P-F students diluted the intellectual tone of the class, that P-F students did not do assigned reading, and that they did just enough work to get by. Also, instructors reported that they could identify most P-F students by the end of the term.

What can we make of these studies? Although there is some evidence that students use the P-F option to explore new academic areas (Stallings and Smock 1971), many use it for courses they probably would take anyway, but in which they wish to invest less effort than would typically be required. Student performance in courses with the P-F option is not as high as in courses they take under the regular grading plan. Students favor the P-F option, but faculty members have reservations about it and feel that it is not serving its intended purpose. It is these reasons that have led many schools to limit the P-F option to tangential efforts of the student.

Reporting to parents

Traditionally, reports to parents take one of three forms: report cards, letters, and parent-teacher conferences. Each has its advantages and its limitations.

In years past, report cards contained only course grades. Today, almost all cards not only report grades, but also contain a checklist of skills to help the parent interpret the grade. The addition of a checklist of skills has considerably improved the report card. However, checklists must necessarily be brief and consequently, they lose much of their potential as a diagnostic report. Also, many of the items on a checklist have not been formally assessed by teachers—they are subjective reports. Yes, parents want to know how teachers feel about Mary's work, but the teacher's impressionistic report often becomes fact for parents. Yet we are keenly aware of the error in subjective assessments. That is why the entire field of psychological testing has emerged. In developing report-card forms, we should concentrate on observable behaviors to be included in our checklist.

Report cards should not be modeled after any given form that might be presented in books like this one. Instead, teachers within a school (or high school department) should decide what their own report cards should contain. Programs vary, curriculum content and procedures vary, so report-card forms should vary. Probably the best report card, then, will be one developed cooperatively by a committee of parents and teachers—parents listing "what we want to know," and teachers deciding what information can best be observed and reported. Here is a list of things to note that will help us develop better report cards.

1. The card should provide for ratings on a variety of course objectives. For example, work habits are important, knowledge of the factual base of a subject is important, and skill in the application of factual matter to the solution of problems is relevant. Just as all courses are intended to affect a variety of behaviors, so must a report card give an account of a variety of topics.

Teachers must, however, resist the temptation to mark a child on behavior irrelevant to the achievement of course objectives. For example, in a history class we may wish to rate students on their ability to discuss with classmates topics of historical significance, but we must be careful not to rank our students on their extroversion rather than on a content-related operation important to achievement in history.

2. The methods by which achievement of course objectives is translated into data on the report card should be clear to parents and to students. A well-planned course begins with a set of objectives. Wrinkle (1947) pointed out that in ten years of work on reporting school progress, his most important finding was that teachers must plan specific objectives for their courses. Students and parents need to know not only what these objectives are, but also, how their attainment will be assessed. Will norm- or criterion-referencing be used? What behaviors will we require as evidence of progress toward the objectives? How will they be assessed? Finally, how will the assessments be translated into marks on the report form?

3. A space should be available on the card for brief comments by the teacher. Teachers are pressed for time, but a short comment about a student's strength or a point needing improvement may enlist the parents' aid in the instructional process, and in the long run this may well be worth the writing time.

4. Trying to establish grades relevant to talent does not generally improve objective reporting. This practice is risky, and teachers should be aware of the risks involved. We are all influenced by many irrelevant conditions in our estimate of other people's talents. The prim, well-behaved child gets the teacher's sympathy before his rowdy, unkempt peer. In addition, it is not clear how a teacher may objectively establish expectations for a child in a given curriculum area. Although intelligence tests correlate moderately well with total achievement, they do not correlate sufficiently

with attainment in many specific academic areas to place all children in categories of expected achievement. Further, Halliwell and Robitalle (1963) have shown that marking children in relationship to ability produced class rankings very much like those given when teachers marked on an achievement criterion alone. Marking relevant to "ability" appeared to make little difference in student grades. Therefore, risking the error of estimating an expected level of achievement does not seem to be worth the effort in altering grading systems.

5. Students themselves need to be involved in the assessment of their progress. They know much about their strengths and weaknesses in a given subject area, even in the primary grades. Children look at the work of their peers and compare their work to what they see around them. They know a great deal about how well they are doing on both an achievement-criterion and a normative basis.

There are some good reasons why we should involve students in preparing reports to parents. Students occasionally could profit from taking stock of their work in a guided fashion. What things do I do well that I want my parents to know about? Where could I use some help? How do I see myself among my peers? Parents seldom get this kind of information directly from the child himself.

Another reason children should be involved in reporting is that marking and reporting grades appear to be imposed on students. This imposition must be a source of irritation for many of our children. Indeed, Richardson (1955) found that young children wanted to be involved in the reporting process (in this case, teacher-parent conferences). The fact that adolescents declined to be involved may be a result of years of learning that they were denied a role in the assessment of their own achievement. Children must feel extremely impotent at grade-reporting time and feel that there is no recourse when they think they have been unfairly dealt with. This clearly weakens the possibility that marking and reporting will be a learning experience for the student. This condition might be altered if students could be involved in their own evaluation.

Older students could assist in preparing their own marking by checking a rating scale showing how they estimate their achievement of course objectives. Although this assessment might be only advisory to the teacher, it would undoubtedly provide not only a guide for marking, but also some interesting insights into the student himself. With young children, the job is harder; checklist data must be collected by private interview.

Letters to parents have also been used instead of the traditional report card. In this manner the teacher can candidly point out the child's strengths and weaknesses, can speculate about his potential, and can suggest ways in which the parent and teacher might work together to help the child. This procedure, if done well, is time-consuming. The time problem often leads teachers to use broad generalities or stereotypes, e.g., "doing well," or "needs improvement in study skills." These comments do not help parents or students do anything specifically. In this case the letter loses its value as a means of presenting detailed advice to parents. Letters also distract us from objective data and lead us into impressionistic reports in which a variety of irrelevant variables teases us into making statements about a child that are not directly relevant to the attainment of instructional objectives.

The parent-teacher conference has greater potential for effective communication than either the report card or the letter. However, it too has its problems. In conferences, parents can ask the questions about which they are concerned, and teachers can provide test data, samples of the child's work, and can discuss the child's strengths and weaknesses with examples right at hand. What more could be asked of a report to parents?

But it is not just that simple. Many parents find it difficult to arrange conferences. If both parents are working, or if travel of some distance is required, as may be the case when children are bused to school, we will have some "no show" parents. Even when parent and teacher meet, they often have communications problems. Parents may not know what questions to ask. They may be timid and hesitant in asking important questions. Teachers may be embarrassed to face a parent with a child's work if it is really bad. Social class and racial differences between parent and teacher complicate communications.

Conferences beyond the elementary school level are very difficult to arrange. In the secondary school where a student probably has five teachers in his program, it is almost impossible to schedule parents to visit all five teachers. At this level a carefully prepared report card is probably most practical for advising parents of student progress.

Will parents support a continuing schedule of conferences? Wrinkle (1947) noted that parents were unlikely to continue to meet conference schedules over an extended period of time. He found that many parents did schedule conferences on a voluntary basis during the first term in which conferences were used instead of report cards. However, the total number of parents who made appointments was less than half of the total number of students enrolled in school. Further, the number of parents who scheduled conferences was fewer with each successive term; one year following the institution of conferences, no appointments were made during the entire term. Parents either did not get what they wanted from conferences or found them unnecessary.

Clearly, the parent-teacher conference, like other techniques of reporting to parents, has its difficulties. However, its potential for transmitting useful information is considerable. The fact that it can be tailored for each child makes it especially attractive. The possibility of conferences merits exploration, but it cannot be worked out effectively in all schools.

PROBLEMS

1. Imagine that you are a member of a teacher committee responsible for establishing policy for reporting to parents.

    a) What objectives might you set up for reporting?

    b) What procedure might best meet these objectives and why?

    c) What variables in addition to tested achievement should be reported, and how should these variables be assessed? Should they be weighted in the grade or reported separately?

2. As a student, would you like to have been involved in preparing your own report to your parents? How could your involvement improve the report?

3. Write to a half-dozen schools for sample report cards. Form a group of your classmates and discuss how these report cards might be improved.

SUMMARY

The typical school testing program comprises aptitude and achievement tests, with tests in the affective domain reserved for special purposes. Priority in the elementary grades is given to tests of basic skills, especially reading skills. In the secondary school a multiple-aptitude battery gets top priority.

Testing programs should be managed by a school committee representing all users of test data. Teachers should be especially involved in setting up programs, since they know best what data they can use and what the instruction actually is supposed to achieve. The process of evaluation requires that much more information be collected than tests alone can provide. Test scores are interpretable only in light of various context, input, and process variables.

School programs tend to accentuate differences among people. Grading practices are intended to acknowledge these differences in reference to particular course objectives. To be descriptive, grading and reporting procedures should note a child's ranking among his classmates, among a national sample of peers, and in reference to a set of tasks (or criteria) the child is expected to be able to perform. A multiple grading system will be required to report performance when more than one type of information is to be used. Based on the accuracy of classroom tests, a five-point grading scheme is probably best. Definitions of grading levels should be developed and adhered to in operation.

Three procedures for reporting to students and to parents have typically been used: report cards, letters, and parent-teacher conferences. Each has its advantages and disadvantages. The parent-teacher conference probably has the greatest flexibility and potential for the greatest transmission of information.

School programs change students. How effectively have we obtained the changes we intended? School testing programs help us deal with this question, and grading and reporting devices are ways of announcing and recording selected changes associated with instruction. Without these operations, schools have great difficulty defending their activities and assessing their effectiveness.

REFERENCES

Barrett, Loren Spencer. "Note: The consistency of first semester college grade-point average," *Journal of Educational Measurement*, **3** (1966): 261–262.

Buros, Oscar K. *The Sixth Mental Measurements Yearbook*, Highland Park, N.J.: Gyphon Press, 1965.

Buros, Oscar K. *The Seventh Mental Measurements Yearbook*, Highland Park, N.J.: Gyphon Press, 1972.

Cook, Walter W. "What teachers should know about measurement," *Fifteenth Yearbook*, National Council on Measurements used in Education, 1958, pp. 16–19.

Fricke, Benno. "The evaluation of student achievement," *Memo to the Faculty*, Center for Research on Learning and Teaching, University of Michigan, April 1965.

Goldberg, Lewis. "Grades as motivants," *Psychology in the Schools*, **2** (1965): 17–24.

Goslin, David A. *Teachers and Testing*, New York: The Russell Sage Foundation, 1967, 201 pp.

Halliwell, J. W. and J. P. Rabitelle. "The relationship between theory and practice in a dual report program," *Journal of Educational Research*, **57** (1963): 137–141.

Hills, John. "Prediction of grades for all public colleges of a state," *Journal of Educational Measurement*, **1** (1964): 155–159.

Hurlock, Elizabeth B. "The use of group rivalry as an incentive," *Journal of Abnormal and Social Psychology*, **22** (1927): 278–290.

Karlins, M. "Academic attitudes and performances as a function of differential grading systems: an evaluation of Princeton's pass-fail system," *Journal of Experimental Education*, **37** (1969): 38–50.

Lesser, Gerald S., Frederick B. Davis, and Lucile Nahemar. "The identification of gifted elementary school children with exceptional scientific talent," *Educational and Psychological Measurement*, **22** (1962): 349–364.

Mager, Robert. *Preparing Objectives for Programmed Instruction*, San Francisco: Fearon Publishers, 1962.

Metfessel, N. S. and William B. Michael. "A paradigm involving multiple criterion measures for evaluation of effectiveness of school programs," *Educational and Psychological Measurement,* **27** (1967): 931–936.

Nettleton, Aileen. "Taming the standardized testing program." Paper presented at the Annual Meeting of the American Educational Research Association, Chicago, Illinois, April 1972.

Pascal, C. E. "Some preliminary data about the pass-fail option," *Memo to the Faculty, Center for Research on Learning and Teaching,* University of Michigan, April 1967.

Remmers, H. H., N. L. Gage, and J. Francis Rummel. *A Practical Introduction to Measurement and Evaluation,* New York: Harper & Brothers, 1960, 320 pp.

Richardson, Sybil. "How do children feel about reports to parents?" *California Journal of Elementary Education,* **24** (1955): 98–111.

Schmalgemeier, William L. and Richard P. Watson. *Michigan Schools: The Organization and Management of Their Testing Programs 1970,* Ann Arbor: University of Michigan, Bureau of School Services, 50 pp.

Solomon, Richard L. "Punishment," *American Psychologist,* **19** (1964): 239–253.

Stallings, William M. and H. Richard Smock. "The pass-fail grading option at a state university: a five-semester evaluation," *Journal of Educational Measurement,* **8** (1971): 153–160.

Stake, Robert E. "The countenance of educational evaluation," *Teacher's College Record,* **68** (1967): 523–540.

Stufflebeam, Daniel. *Evaluation as Enlightenment for Decision Making,* Columbus: Ohio State University, Evaluation Center, 1968.

Syan, M. R. "Letter grade achievement in pass-fail courses," *Journal of Higher Education,* **41** (1970): 638–644.

Trow, William C. "On marks, norms, and proficiency scores," *Phi Delta Kappan,* **47** (1966): 171–173.

Wrinkle, William L. *Improving Marking and Reporting Practices in Elementary and Secondary Schools,* New York: Rinehart, 1947.

APPENDIXES

STATISTICAL PROCEDURES

This appendix provides statistical procedures for students who may wish to have alternative or additional methods beyond those given in Chapter 3. We shall present computations of the mean and standard deviation with grouped data, and the product moment correlation. The computation procedures are provided without rationale. For a more detailed discussion of these topics, the student should consult a text on elementary statistics, e.g., J. P. Guilford, *Fundamental Statistics in Psychology and Education*, 4th ed., McGraw-Hill, 1965.

MEAN: GROUPED-DATA PROCEDURE

First we build a grouped-data frequency distribution as noted in Chapter 3. Two rules should be observed: use between 10 and 20 intervals; when possible, use an uneven range of scores as the interval width. Our computational steps labeled in the problem below are discussed in the paragraph that has the same number as the step in the example. In this manner you can associate the description of the computation in the following paragraphs with the actual computations in the example.

1. Guess at the interval that contains the mean (look for one near the middle of the score range, but any interval will do), and for the time being assume that its midpoint is the mean. (This midpoint probably will not be the actual mean, so the remainder of our job is to correct our guess). In the data that follow, the interval 17–19 has been selected; its midpoint is 18.0.

2. Next, we count off how far each of the other score intervals deviates from the selected interval. Score-interval deviations above the selected interval are given a plus (+) sign; below, a minus (−) sign.

3. Next, the interval deviation is multiplied by the frequency (i.e., the number of people in the interval), and the *algebraic* sum of these products is found (the algebraic sum is found by first adding all values with a plus sign, adding the values with a minus sign, and then subtracting the minus

sum from the plus sum). Note that the Greek letter sigma, Σ, means "sum of."

4. The data are now put into this formula:

$$\text{Mean} = \text{G.M.} + \left(\frac{\Sigma\, fd}{N}\right) i,$$

where G.M. is the midpoint of the interval in which we guessed the mean to be (Step 1);

Σfd is the algebraic sum (Σ) of the frequency-times-deviation products (Step 3);

i is the width of the interval; and

N is the number of cases we are working with.

A worked example follows.

	Score intervals	Frequency	(Step 2) Interval deviations	(Step 3) Frequency times deviation
	35–37	1	+6	6
	32–34	1	+5	5
	29–31	0	+4	0
	26–28	2	+3	6
	23–25	4	+2	8
	20–22	2	+1	2
(Step 1)	17–19	7		27
	14–16	5	−1	−5
	11–13	0	−2	−0
	8–10	3	−3	−9
	5–7	1	−4	−4
		26=N		−18

algebraic sum $+9 = \Sigma fd$

(Step 4) $\text{Mean} = \text{G.M.} + \left(\dfrac{\Sigma\, fd}{N}\right) i$

$$= 18.0 + \left(\frac{9}{26}\right) 3$$

$$= 18.0 + (.35)\, 3$$

$$= 18.0 + 1.05$$

$$= 19.05$$

STANDARD DEVIATION: GROUPED DATA

The standard deviation is computed from grouped data by beginning just as we did with the mean, adding one more step, and fitting the results into a formula. Here are the steps. Again, the number of the paragraph corresponds with the step number in the example below.

1. Begin with a frequency distribution and guess the interval that may contain the mean (as in computing the mean).

2. Mark off the deviations of other intervals above and below the selected interval (as in computing the mean).

3. For each interval, multiply the interval deviation times the frequency, and find the algebraic sum of these products (as in computing the mean).

4. For each interval, square the deviation and then multiply this squared deviation times the frequency (the number of people at that interval). Add all of these squared deviation-times-frequency products.

5. Fit the data into the formula:

$$\sigma = i \sqrt{\frac{\sum fd^2}{N} - \left(\frac{\sum fd}{N}\right)^2},$$

where i is the width of the score interval;
$\sum fd^2$ is the sum ($\sum$) of the interval frequency (f) times deviation squared (d^2) values;
$\sum fd$ is the algebraic sum of the frequency times deviation; and
N is the number of cases involved.

Here are the same data used to compute the mean above. Now, the standard deviation for the distribution will be found by following the steps above.

Score intervals	Frequency	(Step 2) Interval deviations	(Step 3) Frequency times deviation	(Step 4) Frequency times deviation^2
35–37	1	+6	6	$1(6 \times 6) = 36$
32–34	1	+5	5	$1(5 \times 5) = 25$
29–31	0	+4	0	$0(4 \times 4) = 0$
26–28	2	+3	6	$2(3 \times 3) = 18$
23–25	4	+2	8	$4(2 \times 2) = 16$
20–22	2	+1	2	$2(1 \times 1) = 2$
(Step 1) 17–19	7		27	
14–16	5	−1	−5	$5(-1 \times -1) = 5$
11–13	0	−2	0	$0(-2 \times -2) = 0$
8–10	3	−3	−9	$3(-3 \times -3) = 27$
5–7	1	−4	−4	$1(-4 \times -4) = 16$
	$26 = N$		-18	$145 = \Sigma fd^2$
			$+9 = \Sigma fd$	

(Step 5)

$$\sigma = i \sqrt{\frac{\Sigma fd^2}{N} - \left(\frac{\Sigma fd}{N}\right)^2}$$

$$= 3 \sqrt{\frac{145}{26} - \left(\frac{9}{26}\right)^2}$$

$$= 3\sqrt{5.58 - (.35)^2}$$

$$= 3\sqrt{5.58 - .12}$$

$$= 3\sqrt{5.46}$$

$$= 3 \times 2.34$$

$$= 7.02$$

PRODUCT MOMENT CORRELATION

Here, we will work with pairs of scores. To use the correlation, we must have *two scores on every person* being observed. Let us begin with an example and work it through.

Person	Score I (X)	Score II (Y)	(Step 1) X^2	Y^2	(Step 2) XY
Able	12	15	144	225	180
Bob	8	13	64	169	104
Cass	4	8	16	64	32
Don	10	14	100	196	140
Effy	6	10	36	100	60
Fred	11	16	121	256	176
Greg	3	7	9	49	21
Hal	1	5	1	25	5
Irv	7	17	49	289	119
Jill	5	9	25	81	45
Sums	67	114	565	1,454	882 (Step 3)

The steps in computing a correlation coefficient are listed below and correspondingly marked in the same problem above. We begin with two scores on everyone in our groups:

1. We first square each X score; we then square each Y score.

2. Then we multiply each person's X score by his Y score. This gives us XY.

3. We now add up the X values, the Y values, the X^2, the Y^2, and the XY values.

4. We will now put all of these sums into this formula:

(Step 4)
$$r_{XY} = \frac{\sum XY - \frac{(\sum X)(\sum Y)}{N}}{\sqrt{\sum X^2 - \frac{(\sum X)^2}{N}} \sqrt{\sum Y^2 - \frac{(\sum Y)^2}{N}}},$$

where ΣXY is the sum of the XY column;

ΣX is the sum of all X scores;

ΣY is the sum of all Y scores;

N is the number of *persons* observed;

ΣX^2 is the sum of the X^2 column; and

ΣY^2 is the sum of the Y^2 column.

These data fit into the formula like this:

$$r_{XY} = \frac{882 - \dfrac{(67)(114)}{10}}{\sqrt{565 - \dfrac{(67)^2}{10}} \sqrt{1454 - \dfrac{(114)^2}{10}}}$$

$$= \frac{882 - 763.8}{\sqrt{565 - 448.8} \sqrt{1454 - 1299.6}}$$

$$= \frac{118.2}{\sqrt{116.2} \sqrt{154.4}}$$

$$= \frac{118.2}{(10.8)(12.4)}$$

$$= \frac{118.2}{133.9}$$

$$= .88.$$

NAMES AND ADDRESSES OF TEST PUBLISHERS

The student may wish to correspond with various test publishers to avail himself of the services that publishers provide. Such services might include test catalogs and test specimen sets (available for a very small fee), which contain a copy of the desired test, the test manual, answer sheets, and very often additional technical material related to the construction of the test. Also, test companies frequently provide ancillary services such as general information pamphlets like Psychological Corporation's "Test Service Bulletin," and Educational Testing Services' "Evaluation and Advisory Service Series," a packet of pamphlets designed to aid school people select, construct, and use tests more effectively. Most of these ancillary publications by test companies are free. Companies providing free pamphlets are noted below by an asterisk.

Here are the names and addresses of several major test publishers. Addresses of other publishers may be found in Buros' *Mental Measurements Yearbook*.

1. *California Test Bureau/McGraw-Hill
    Del Monte Research Park
    Monterey, California 93940

2. Consulting Psychological Press, Inc.
    577 College Avenue
    Palo Alto, California 94306

3. *Cooperative Test Division
    Educational Testing Service
    Princeton, New Jersey 08540

4. *Educational Testing Service
    Princeton, New Jersey 08540

5. *Harcourt Brace Jovanovich, Inc.
    757 Third Avenue
    New York, New York 10017

6. *Houghton Mifflin Company
    110 Tremont Street
    Boston, Massachusetts 02107

7. Personnel Press
    20 Nassau Street
    Princeton, New Jersey 08540

8. *Psychological Corporation
    304 East 45th Street
    New York, New York 10017

9. Science Research Associates, Inc.
    259 East Erie Street
    Chicago, Illinois 60611

10. Stoelting Company
    424 N. Homan Avenue
    Chicago, Illinois 60603

AUTHOR INDEX

SUBJECT INDEX

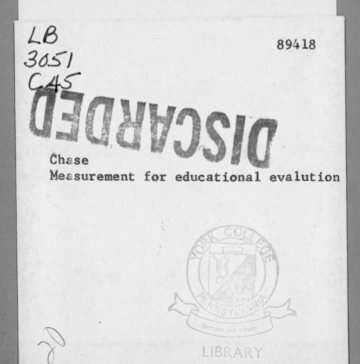